Labour Regimes and Liberalization
The Restructuring of State-Society Relations in Africa

Edited by
Björn Beckman and
Lloyd M. Sachikonye

UNIVERSITY OF ZIMBABWE Publications

First published in 2001 by
University of Zimbabwe Publications
P. O. Box MP 203
Mount Pleasant
Harare
Zimbabwe

ISBN 0-908307-88-8

Cover photograph courtesy of *The Worker Magazine* of the Zimbabwe Congress of Trade Unions (ZCTU)

Typeset by the University of Zimbabwe Publications

Printed by Mazongororo Paper Converters

Contents

Preface and Acknowledgements

This book is based on a workshop on "Labour Regimes and Liberalization: The Restructuring of State-Society Relations in Africa", hosted by the Institute of Development Studies, University of Zimbabwe, Harare, 16-18 May, 1996, and organized by the Department of Agrarian and Labour Studies of that Institute in co-operation with the Department of Political Science, Stockholm University. The conference looked at changing labour regimes, especially the impact of economic liberalization on the position of trade unions, and discussed the implications for the restructuring of state-civil society relations and processes of democratization. It received funding from SAREC — the Department for Research Cooperation, SIDA — the Swedish International Development Cooperation Agency, which we gratefully acknowledge. We also wish to express our appreciation of the hospitality and support offered by the University of Zimbabwe and the staff of the Institute of Development Studies.

This book is concerned with seven African countries, Egypt, Ghana, Nigeria, Senegal, South Africa, Zambia and Zimbabwe. For two countries, Nigeria and Zimbabwe, specific industrial unions are discussed in separate contributions, otherwise the focus is mainly on the national unions centres. All the case studies were presented to the conference except the contribution by Norbert Tengende, who was unable to attend as planned due to illness. Norbert, who held great promise as a scholar, tragically died later in 1996. As an homage, we have included a section from his excellent PhD thesis which he successfully defended at Roskilde University, Denmark, only a year before the workshop.

We wish to acknowledge the important contributions to the workshop by specially invited discussants, Dr Yusuf Bangura of the United Nations Research Institute for Social Development (UNRISD), Geneva, and Dr Inga Brandell, Department of Political Science, University of Uppsala, both accomplished scholars in the field of African and comparative labour studies.

We are sincerely grateful to the following participants who presented papers and made useful contributions during the workshop: Abdenasser Djabi, Ona Jirira and Ebrahim Patel. Maurice Mutowo of the University of Zimbabwe Publications Office was consistently helpful and encouraging during the stage of preparing the manuscript for publication and we express our thanks to him and his colleagues. Mrs. P. Kupamupindi assisted with the word-processing of the final draft of the manuscript . We are profoundly grateful to her.

Björn Beckman   Lloyd M. Sachikonye
Stockholm and Harare, November 1999

iv

Notes on Contributors

Emmanuel Akwetey taught in the Department of Political Science at Stockholm University, and is now with the Institute of Democratic Governance, Accra, Ghana.

Björn Beckman teaches in the Department of Political Science at Stockholm University, Sweden.

Omar El-Shafei studied in the Department of Political Science, American University in Cairo, Egypt.

Yahaya Hashim is Director of the Centre for Research and Documentation (CRD) in Kano, Nigeria.

Lloyd M. Sachikonye teaches and researches at the Institute of Development Studies at the University of Zimbabwe.

Norbert Tengende taught in the Department of Political and Administrative Studies at the University of Zimbabwe until he died in 1996. He is profoundly missed.

Eddie Webster and **Glenn Adler** teach at the Sociology of Work Unit and Department of Sociology at the University of Witwatersrand, Johannesburg, South Africa.

Bassirou Tidjani and **Alfred Inis Ndiaye** teach at the University of Cheikh Anta Diop in Dakar, Senegal.

CHAPTER ONE

Labour Regimes and Liberalization in Africa: An Introduction

BJÖRN BECKMAN AND LLOYD M. SACHIKONYE

AN OVERVIEW

How does economic liberalization affect the relations between state and society, and between organized labour and the state in particular? Our point of departure in initiating this study was that major changes in labour regimes (for this concept, see below) could be expected as a result of the shift in economic policy. We assumed that the social order existing before liberalisation would, in most cases, be characterized by modes of interest incorporation within state-dominated, monopolistic forms of organization. These could be expected to come under severe strain as a result of a fiscal and managerial crisis that made the state increasingly incapable of sustaining, not to speak of expanding, the formal wage sector, the basis of the union movement, either in terms of wages, working conditions or social services. The "social contract" that in many cases had tended to tie organized labour to a national development project of public sector expansion and industrialization was disintegrating. This tendency was reinforced in a more principled, ideological way by the changes at the level of economic policy, often pushed from outside by the international financial institutions as part of their "structural adjustment" programmes. Wage labour, as a social category, was under fire and so were the labour regimes which regulated the relations between labour, capital, and the state.

While the labour regime could be expected to be under severe strain, it was by no means obvious in what direction the resultant reordering would go. Much depended on the strategies chosen by the actors involved. How, in the first place, would organized labour respond to the new conjuncture? While it was likely to defend, more or less energetically and skilfully, its positions in society including the employment and welfare of the wage workers, the choice of method may vary. Would it disengage from the state and seek a more autonomous position from which it could bargain for members' interests and fend off the new anti-labour policies of the state? Or would it seek closer participation and representation in order to enhance its influence in the corridors of power? Much

1

depended as well on the strategies pursued by the state and the employers. Would they take advantage of the weak bargaining position of organized labour and disorganize the workers politically, suppress unions, and abolish union rights and privileges? Or would they intensify strategies of incorporation at the level of union leaders in order to ensure that they did not rock the boat? In the latter case, both state and employers may have an interest in preserving existing "corporatist" labour market institutions (for a discussion of the concept, see below), including state-supported monopoly unions, while exploiting their potential for control rather than representation.

Our concern in this study, however, is not just with the impact of economic crisis and liberalization. We also want to relate the changes in labour regime to the impact of political liberalization and democratization, including the advance towards multi-party politics. Did political liberalization facilitate or hasten the disintegration of previous, unitary or monopolistic modes of interest organization? How far were unions involved in the political restructuring of the state? Was labour able to confront and resist an authoritarian state? Could it use the democratic openings to strengthen its political influence? Our provisional hypothesis in this respect was that labour -- facing an increasingly hostile state pent on restricting or suppressing its rights -- would have a stake in political reform and broader democratic alliances that would enhance its own political bargaining power. Labour could be expected to act as a democratic force. This would be in line with the historical role played by wage workers in democratization elsewhere, being obliged by the centralization of production in large work places to seek collective forms of organization and thereby emerging as one of the most articulate and combative sections of civil society (Valenzuela, 1989; Rueschemeyer *et al.*, 1992).

Apart from such a direct role played by organized labour in democratic struggles, developments at the level of the labour regime could also be expected to have a more indirect and less obvious significance for democratization. The self-regulation and constitutionalization of conflict management within particular spheres of civil society, in this case, the sphere of wage labour relations, may contribute to a wider process of constitutionalization of state-civil society relations (Beckman, 1993; Beckman and Jega, 1995).

The notion of labour regime is used in this study to focus on the wider social arena within which these relations are regulated, including work places as well as communities, labour laws and legal practices as well as the institutions of civil society (Sachikonye, 1992; Andrae and Beckman, 1992). In this respect, the study contributes to current debates on the way in which processes of democratization are premised on the formation of social agents in civil society with sufficient autonomous social base to influence the management of state power in a responsible and accountable direction (Rueschemeyer, 1992; White, 1994).

The study is situated within the context of particular economic and political conjunctures characterized by a decline in state capacity to sustain corporatist modes of regulating state-interest group relations (Akwetey, 1994; Hashim, 1993; Sachikonye, 1993). The causes of decline include the deterioration of the fiscal resource base and political legitimacy as well as a policy shift in the direction of economic liberalization (Olukoshi, 1994). The politics of such policy shifts as well as the scope for political liberalization vary from country to country, depending on the balance of forces, local and international, that impinge on the exercise of state power. As governments confront increasingly assertive unions they may respond, as in the Nigerian case, by intensifying efforts of control and repression or as in Ghana, by shifting towards greater accommodation and concessions (Hashim and Akwetey, in this book). Attempts to promote multiple unions, may at one point be an effort by the state to undercut union resistance to its reform project as in Zimbabwe (Tengende, in this book), while in other instances, as in Senegal, be part and parcel of a process of political liberalization demanded by sections of the workers themselves (Tidjani and Ndiaye, in this book).

Unions may pursue different strategies of disassociation from or accommodation with the state. The Zimbabwe case is particularly volatile and unsettled in this respect (Sachikonye, in this book). They may engage themselves in broader movements to democratize governments, as in Zambia and South Africa, and/or demand political participation, with or without linkages to political parties (Akwetey, Webster and Adler, in this book). We also look at the responses of individual industrial unions to changes at the level of state and policy in the context of their organizational experiences, internal structure, and positions within changing political economies as in the chapters on the Nigerian textile workers and the Zimbabwean public sector employees (Beckman and Tengende, in this book).

THE INDIVIDUAL CONTRIBUTIONS

The argument on the relation between labour regime and economic and political liberalization outlined above is a general, ideal-type argument. It is elaborated below, theoretically and empirically. First, however, we wish to briefly summarize the individual contributions that provide our immediate points of empirical reference. The contributions were not prepared according to a set format and their choice of focus vary. The introduction is therefore an attempt to highlight some of their common concerns.

In his chapter, El-Shafei challenges the orthodoxy that suggests that economic liberalization facilitates democratization and shows how, in the Egyptian case, the widening of the market economy was accompanied by increased authoritarianism. The new labour laws of the mid-1990s conferred additional powers to capital when retrenching workers and unilaterally changing work contracts. The Nasserite "social contract", which once awarded important rights and benefits to the workers, was increasingly dismantled. Labour centres and unions ceased to have a representative role and trade union bureaucracies were further removed from workers' struggles. The balance of class forces shifted in favour of capital, and the liberalizing adjustment programme entailed intensified exploitation of both the urban and rural poor.

The Egyptian labour regime was the most authoritarian of those discussed in this book, confirming expectations of an heightened authoritarian, state corporatist response as one possible outcome of economic liberalization. It is less apparent, in this case, to what extent the ensuing alienation of the workers has generated new, more autonomous movements in the working class. In the Nigerian case, as showed by Hashim in an essay based on his doctoral dissertation (Hashim, 1994), the subordination of the labour movement to the state has been much less effective, despite an increasingly ruthless military dictatorship. Hashim's study, which primarily covers developments before the wave of state repression under the Abacha regime, is critical of dominant notions in the literature on African unions that exaggerate the element of state "incorporation" and control of the unions. He puts much of the blame on the uncritical application of the concept of "corporatism" and "state corporatism", which in his view, and most specifically in the Nigerian case, exaggerates centralization, bureaucratization and state imposition. The picture that emerges from his study is rather one of a weak national centre, strong independent industrial unions, and an urge towards a unitary organization rooted in the internal aspirations of the labour movement rather than in the logic of state control and bureaucratic imposition. Hashim shows how such unity and autonomy was used for the purpose of resisting central aspects of the structural adjustment programme. The autonomy of the labour movement made it a continuing obstacle to the consolidation of state authoritarianism.

Beckman's essay, based on a joint study with Gunilla Andrae on the Nigerian textile workers' union (Andrae and Beckman, 1998), takes the argument on union autonomy within a presumably "corporatist" national arrangement to the industrial union level. The impact of economic crisis and structural adjustment can in this case be studied in terms of the fortunes of a particular industrial sector. The study points to a surprisingly successful experience of union accommodation to far-reaching industrial restructuring and a tendency towards the consolidation of a contractual union-based labour regime, despite the declining fall in workers' market bargaining power. The constitutionalization of conflict regulation at the industrial level is seen as the development of institutional capacity from below with relevance for the prospects of both economic and political reform, including the strengthening of democratic forces, in a period otherwise marked by state authoritarianism, de-industrialization and policy failure. The roots of union power is seen in the autonomous militancy of the workers as effectively mediated by the union.

In many parts of Africa, monopolistic, state-corporatist labour regimes have been part and parcel of authoritarian, one-party political arrangements. Trade unions have been the subordinate affiliates of ruling parties. This was also the case in Senegal. As shown in the contribution by Tidjani and Ndiaye, some element of political liberalization, including a modest opening for more political parties, preceded the imposition of liberalizing adjustment policies. This element of political pluralism was also reflected at the level of the trade union movement. The dominant trade union centre, affiliated to the ruling party, was increasingly challenged by new unions, often in their turn affiliated to the fledgling opposition parties on the left. Increasingly autonomous unions, however, provided in the early 1990s a basis for the formation of a rival national labour centre. This element of union pluralism simultaneously placed pressure on the dominant established unions to distance themselves from the state in order to reduce members' defection to the new autonomous ones. This was reflected, for instance, in the broad based opposition to the adjustment policies of the state as demonstrated in the 1993 strike. Organized labour generally was weakened by the reform of labour legislation, privatization and the decentralization of collective bargaining. Tidjani and Ndiaye discuss current pressures for the development of a new labour regime with more scope for participatory structures in the work-place.

Issues of autonomy and participation are equally central to Akwetey's discussion of changes in the labour regime prompted by economic and political liberalization in Ghana and Zambia, a follow up on his doctoral dissertation on trade unions and democratization in the two countries (Akwetey, 1994). Unlike Senegal, Ghana experienced almost a decade of structural adjustment under a populist military dictatorship (Rawlings) before a modest opening was made in the early 1990s in a liberal democratic direction. Unions, which had once been enrolled as part of the one-party structures of the early post-colonial days, had since struggled to maintain their autonomy. They also sought to resist and moderate the impact of structural adjustment, although under heavy pressure from the regime to conform. While clearly supporting the demand for multi-party democracy, the unions carefully avoided being enlisted on the side of either government or opposition, seeking instead to enhance their influence through tripartite or other participatory and consultative institutions.

In the Zambian case, the trajectory was quite different. Having once been the backbone of Kaunda's one-party regime, and used to considerable political leverage, the union movement which was dominated by the powerful mine workers, became increasingly alienated and threw its weight behind the Movement for Multiparty Democracy (MMD). While succeeding in getting one of their kind elected as national president, the union leaders were soon to be bitterly divided among themselves, many feeling betrayed by the new government's commitment to structural adjustment. As in the case of Ghana, the new pro-adjustment government in Zambia could draw on heavy foreign financial and political support, thus being able to insulate itself from domestic anti-adjustment pressures, including those from the workers that suffered from the new policies. With part of the union movement tied up politically, the new regime succeeded in changing labour laws as to further weaken the scope for collective action. Having been brought to power on the shoulders of labour, the regime, once in power, shifted its search for allies to the business community. Irrespective of the radically different strategies chosen, union involvement in the transition to multi-partyism in Ghana or Zambia did not result in any significant changes in what Akwetey calls "a despotic labour regime". Movements in a more participatory direction were largely aborted.

Although South Africa finds herself in a different political conjuncture, the labour movement faces similar problems in deciding how to relate to a democratic regime which it has been instrumental in installing when this regime adopts liberal policies of "macro-economic stability" and world-market adjustment that workers widely see as a threat to employment and working conditions. Its political vision was largely a socialist one, as documented at successive Confederation of South African Trade Unions (COSATU) conferences. Webster and Adler highlight the growing tensions within the "Triple Alliance" between COSATU, the African National Congress (ANC) and the South African Communist Party (SACP). The suppression of the ANC and SACP during the apartheid regime, enhanced the role of organized labour in the liberation struggle. With political transition, the balance of forces in the alliance shifted in favour of the ANC and the parliamentary struggle. Leading unionists were absorbed by party politics and government duties. Webster and Adler review the development of the labour movement and its alliances and the attempts to arrive at a common position, the Reconstruction and Development Programme (RDP), which became a major focus of conflict between the allies. The transition generated new participatory institutions which seemed to give labour a platform, like the National Economic Development and Labour Council (NEDLAC). But what could they be used for? Should labour aim at a corporatist social pact, accepting wage constraints in exchange for expanded social security as part of a new welfarist social order? Or should it distance itself from the ruling party and its class compromises in order to pursue its own socialist visions and defend the workers against the liberal agenda? South Africa, according to Webster and Adler, is in a "process of transition from a despotic labour regime based on a racially segmented labour market, restrictions on union rights, and limited social welfare" but it is by no means clear what the new order will look like. Quoting a unionist, they speak of "an exodus without a map".

The South African labour movement has a unique position on the continent due to its long history and the intensity of its struggles in both political and industrial arenas in the pre-transition period. What was the experience of Zimbabwe which also had a late transition after a period of intensified racial oppression and civil war? At independence in 1980, widespread strikes undermined the colonial labour regime and pressured the state into designing a more accommodating legislative framework which spelt out and guaranteed basic rights and minimum wages for workers. The concessions were matched with a strategy of co-optation which drew the labour leadership into a corporatist framework. The pact survived until the mid-1980s. Liberal adjustment policies in the late 1980s led to retrenchments and reduced income. Rules governing employment security were undermined and management was awarded greater flexibility and power in enterprises. In the face of these changes in policy and labour regime, the labour movement has become more assertive, occasionally finding a common platform with local firms which had been hurt by liberalization. Significantly, a bilateral commitment to collective bargaining developed in an attempt to fend off state intervention. By the mid-1990s, the relations between state and labour had further deteriorated. Attempts at breaking the stalemate led to a search for a new tripartite framework for consultations, opening up at one point for a renegotiated social pact. However, continued confrontations between state and labour have contributed to the deepening political crisis.

The specific impact of adjustment on the Zimbabwean public sector workers and their responses are assessed in Tengende's contribution. He shows how the labour law was revised as to reverse the "one industry, one union" policy in an attempt to undermine the consolidated unions and their resistance to differential wage awards and retrenchment as part of the restructuring of public sector enterprises, especially in railways and telecommunications. In the case of the railways, the attempt to split the workers succeeded and the artisans broke away. However, a similar attempt to drive a wedge between the telecommunications workers floundered. Authoritarian managements in the public sector took unions to court in order to block wage increases. The unions, in their turn, sought court action to challenge employers over wages and mass dismissals. The public sector labour regime was under considerable pressure. Strikes flared up, demonstrating the undiminished strength of the unions. Tengende's case studies show that the strikes resulted in concessions although the de-regulation agenda was not changed.

THE CONTEXT OF ECONOMIC AND POLITICAL LIBERALIZATION

Most African countries have experienced some economic liberalization in the 1980s and 1990s involving market reforms centred on de-regulating fiscal and monetary policies, labour and social safety net policies and the introduction of trade reforms and investment incentives. Public enterprise reforms, including privatization, were another integral element of the liberalization process, so was the objective of reducing budget deficits, and more generally, state spending. In most instances, fiscal and monetary measures included currency devaluation and significant hikes in interest rates. The reduction of budget deficits often entailed massive cuts on state expenditure on the social service sector (mainly education and health), and the retrenchment of public sector workers. Similarly privatization usually resulted in a great number of jobs being lost. Trade liberalization undermined an ill-prepared domestic industrial sector.

By the mid-1990s, about 30 African states had implemented one form or another of economic liberalization measures, mostly as part and parcel of "structural adjustment" programmes (SAP) designed by the World Bank and the International Monetary Fund (IMF) and dependent on their financing. Although the depth and consistency of implementation of SAPs varied, economic and social policies were affected to a significant extent. In this book, we focus on the impact of SAP on labour regimes.

Economic liberalization preceded and was, in most of the cases discussed here, followed by a movement in the direction of political liberalization, the latter taking a broader momentum in the late 1980s and early 1990s. The sources of pressure behind this process were mainly domestic, aiming at the replacement of one-party state systems and military regimes. Movements for democratic change grew and mobilized on a national basis for multi-party systems and "free and fair" elections, from Benin to Zambia, from Niger to Tanzania, from Togo to Kenya. Political liberalization became associated with conceptions of liberal democracy, "good governance" and "the rule of law". International financial institutions and development agencies engaged themselves in intense discussions over the nature of the links between economic and political liberalization. While some emphasized the need to get the economy on a sound footing before attempting any democratic opening, others argued that political reforms in the direction of "good governance" should be a condition for the funding of national SAPs.

By the late 1990s, the initial euphoria which greeted the adoption of certain forms of political liberalization (such as multi-party elections) had subsided and turned into disappointment. In instances where changes of parties in government have actually taken place, as in Zambia, the authoritarian habits associated with the past have tended to reassert themselves. Some one-party state regimes had succeeded in adjusting to the multi-party system and held onto power as in Senegal. Military regimes have had a second coming in civilian dress, as in Ghana; others dug themselves in, like in Nigeria (until 1999), despite their mounting unpopularity, domestically and externally. In other cases, as in Egypt, a military-bureaucratic establishment had entrenched itself so thoroughly, in alliance with a thriving business elite, enjoying both liberalization and state protection, that it did not need to worry about a weak, subdued parliament.

The limited achievements so far are, of course, no reason to write off the continued struggles for a constitutional, liberal democratic order. However, it may give added emphasis to attempts, as in this study, to address problems of political reform from the perspective of what happens in state-civil society relations and within the civil society itself, between the groups whose diverging interests and aspirations lead them to organize themselves collectively and to take an interest in the rules that govern the regulation of conflict at that level. This is where we see a much neglected but critical link between the rights of groups to organize, meet, and publish in defence of their perceived interests and their involvement in the advancement of wider political rights. The rules regulating the role of labour, both in production and in the wider society, constitute a vital arena for the struggle over such interconnected rights. We use the concept of labour regime to indicate the way in which this arena is regulated.

LABOUR REGIME

By labour regime we refer to the complex of institutions, rules and practices through which relations between labour and capital are regulated both at the work-place as well as in society at large. It also denotes the ways and means in which state and organized interests intervene and mediate in those relations (Andrae and Beckman, 1992). In discussing what constitutes a labour regime one may also be concerned with the way in which the reproduction of labour is regulated, including the way labour is trained, and supported by family, community and state outside the work-place. Labour regimes can, therefore, be specified with reference to different interlocking "arenas" such as the individual work-place, the industry or sector, the locality, region or national economy.

Central to labour regimes is the need to ensure that labour performs in accordance with the requirements of production. They are therefore relations of domination as well as of contestation and resistance. Labour regimes can be characterised by the way in which they ensure compliance with the directives of management. They are more or less repressive, more or less consensual. Domination may be exercised through despotism or through hegemony, that is, the acceptance of subordination by the subordinated (Burawoy, 1985). The mechanisms for securing labour's compliance may be situated at the technical level of the labour process (for instance in the conveyor belt) or in the modes of supervision and work-place regulation. The organization of a "division of labour" based on the segmentation of the work-force may be an important element of labour control, drawing support from ideologies of gender, ethnicity and race. Labour regimes may be sanctioned or contested at the level of interest mediation (for example, by unions and the collective bargaining system) and regulated by the state through factory rules, labour laws and *ad hoc* interventions. Labour regimes are also concerned with making labour available in quantities and with characteristics that are functional from the point of view of the requirements of production. The process which determines the price of labour is a particular focus of regulation.

The terms under which labour is ready to make itself available and willing to comply are determined by its bargaining power in the work-place as well as in the labour market. It reflects skills, availability, options and ability to inflict costs on capital and management through non-cooperation or disruption of production (the latter euphemistically termed "industrial action"). It may also reflect differences in aspirations and ideology related to the segmentation of the labour market. Organization is critical in enhancing the potential bargaining power of labour. It makes the regulation and control of trade unions a central feature of any labour regime. The granting or withholding of "recognition" of unions by the state or management, by legislation or in practice, generates sources of union power independently of membership support. We speak of the process of "incorporation" signifying the subordination of unions, reducing their autonomy vis-a-vis the state and management. High autonomy, in this respect, does not by itself signify that unions express the interests of their members. They may also have secured autonomy from pressures from below, and may be more concerned with reproducing their role as intermediaries in the capital-labour relation to their own advantage than with accurately representing the interests of their members.

The duality of unions as more or less representative agencies of the workers and as mediators or "managers" of capital-labour relations is also reflected in state-union relations. In "corporatist" labour regimes, unions are granted more or less monopolistic rights by the state to represent the workers in exchange for accepting constraints on industrial action. There is a distinction between more "state-centred" and more "societal" forms of corporatism, reflecting the extent to which unions enter into a deal with the state from the strength of its own societal base, or whether the arrangement is imposed from above. The former is illustrated by the "social democratic" labour pacts of welfare capitalism, the latter by authoritarian labour regimes under fascism, and in the third world. The co-optation of union leaders by the state allows for intermediary forms (for references to the corporatism literature, see Cawson, 1986 and Hashim's essay in this book).

Labour regimes are formed in the interaction of discrete but mutually determined processes whereby capital, wage-labour as well as the state itself are being formed. The development of the capacity of capital to subordinate labour is central to its very constitution as capital. The formation of capital in this sense develops dialectically with the formation of wage labour, including the wider societal processes that make labour available for subordination, and influence its qualification and reproduction as wage labour. The state, in its capacity as a regulator of the capital-labour relation and its reproduction, develops within the logic of that dialectics. The development of state capacity in this respect is central to the process of capitalist state formation but also to the processes of capital and wage-labour formation. The state assists capital to become capital by helping in subordinating labour. It helps labour to become wage-labour by contributing to the processes that make it available and qualified.

Trade unions are part of the process of wage-labour formation, regulating the terms under which labour makes itself available. As such they may be part of the self-organization of wage-labour, protecting its interests vis-a-vis capital and state. But they are also part of what Burawoy called the "political apparatuses of production", seeking to channel such processes of self-organization into lines conducive to capital accumulation as well as exercising functions in the disciplining and qualification of labour.

The labour regime is constituted at different levels from the work-place, via the industry-sectoral level to the national one, each depending on the other but each with their own characteristics. The *work-place labour regime* is an intrinsic part of the framework of the national level regime to the degree that structures, regulations and practices inscribed in labour legislation are reflected at the work-place. The provisions of national labour laws may vary but they commonly include rules relating to supervision and consultative structures, grievance handling procedures and industrial action. In some instances, as in the Zimbabwean case, workers' committees or work councils have been inscribed into labour law as a mechanism of consultation between management and workers at the shop-floor. In others, as in South Africa, committees of shopstewards play a critical role. In addition to what is stipulated in the labour law, some firms or establishments have worked out their own codes of conduct or company rules by which workers are expected to abide. Such codes may be dictated "despotically" by management or negotiated with the representatives of the workers. They form part of the work-place labour regime to the degree that they regulate the conduct of workers and production conditions. It may cover reproduction aspects relating to health care, skills training and protective clothing as well as housing. Such conditions may have been negotiated or simply introduced on the initiative of the management in a more or less paternalistic manner. When certain aspects of the work-place labour regime are challenged, the dispute may result in industrial action, often entailing external mediation, drawing on the institutions that make up the higher levels of the labour regime.

At the *industrial-sectoral* level the labour regime is likely to be more formally structured and regulated than at the work-place level. In all the countries discussed here, each industrial sector periodically negotiates a collective agreement that becomes binding on the unions and employers' organization in that sector. Such collective agreements would concern wage levels and certain centrally negotiated benefits. They may also lay down disciplinary and other procedures for managing grievances. Negotiations at this level may provide for skills training, medical aid, occupational health and safety, leave, pensions and gratuities and other retirement conditions. As the agreements are supposed to be binding, there are often legal sanctions to ensure compliance. In some countries, the agreements need to be registered with the Ministry of Labour in order to be enforceable. In most, they are a key feature of the labour regime.

At the national level, finally, labour legislation would typically spell out provisions relating to procedures to follow to avert or resolve industrial action, and to arbitration and conciliation and provisions relating to maternity leave, and against discrimination based on race or gender. Supportive structures such as industrial tribunals or courts would play a role in arbitration and conciliation. The legislation may or may not provide for social security provisions, skills training and pension contributions, and other features relating to the reproduction aspects of labour. Legislation may also provide for tripartite bodies consisting of the representatives of the state, the employers and the workers which may address general issues of income and pricing and other policy issues.

Most important for our study is the legislation which regulate the structure of the union system itself, including procedures for the establishment, registration and de-registration of unions, rights of recognition and representation, membership requirements, modes of public accounting, monitoring by the state, etc. These, as we shall see from our case studies, were the aspects of labour legislation which were particularly challenged in the struggles over labour regimes that were precipitated by either economic or political liberalization. A key area of contest concerned the legal backing for the "one industry, one union" arrangement, involving for instance the legal obligation of employers to deduct union fees and pay into the account of the only legally recognized union. These were rules that were challenged both from below (e.g. in Senegal) and from above (in Zimbabwe) under the banner of union pluralism and which were defended in the name of unity against the forces which were seen as being out to destroy or divide the movement.

The labour regime, however, cannot be understood only from the formal rules that are supposed to operate in the work-place and at the industrial and national levels, but from the way these are followed in practice. This requires an understanding of the balance of forces underpinning such practices and how it changed over time as a result of shifts in bargaining power due to favourable or hostile economic and political conjunctures as well as the organizing efforts and competencies of the actors involved. Most labour legislation in the countries covered by this study lays down cumbersome procedures, for instance, for the consultations and conciliation which have to be followed before a strike can be embarked upon. In practice, however, strikes come about, not when such procedures have been exhausted but when unions or groups of workers feel that their case is strong enough and that they have enough on their feet in terms of membership support to confront management or the state.

THE RESTRUCTURING OF LABOUR REGIMES

Labour regimes have been profoundly affected by the policies and politics of economic restructuring. In part, this has been a side-effect of the massive cuts in employment which have undermined labour's market bargaining power. But the impact has also come about as a result of a deliberate move on the side of the state and employers to change the rules, especially concerning rights to hire and fire and to set wages but more specifically rights of unionization. Although the implementation of structural adjustment programmes have in many instances been partial and half-hearted, such attempts at revising the labour regime have belonged to the more common features of actual adjustment policies, as the case studies in this volume demonstrate. The reason for this is not difficult to find. The dramatic cuts in employment and real wage levels have been one of the more persistent outcomes of the adjustment programmes, even the more half-hearted ones, including large-scale retrenchments in the formal wage sector and in the public sector in particular, motivated by efforts to curb state spending and budget deficit. While the magnitude of retrenchments have varied, depending on the depth of the crisis and the choice of adjustment policies, the effect, however, has been to set governments and workers on a collision course. The capacity of unions and workers to resist retrenchment has been a decisive factor influencing policy options. The ability of governments to overcome such resistance, politically, has similarly been important when their "adjustment performance" has been assessed by donors and finance institutions. Governments have therefore sought to revise the rules in an attempt to undercut uncooperative unions and labour leaders and to boost the cooperative ones. Direct intervention in union affairs has increased, with recourse to intimidation as well as co-optation.

The revision of labour laws was also pursued in order to provide an attractive environment for investment, especially foreign investment, on which much hope was placed in the adjustment programmes. Rules governing employment security and minimum wages, for instance, were de-regulated, withdrawing protective safeguards and rights achieved by the workers under pre-adjustment labour regimes. In several of the countries covered by this study, economic liberalization has proceeded to the extent that national labour legislation has been suspended in export processing zones, in an attempt to copy the presumed success stories of rapidly industrializing Asia. Although the interest of foreign capital has so far been lukewarm, the move has provided state legitimation for the revival of a despotic work-place labour regime, and opened up new frontiers in the confrontation between the state and the labour movement. The actual reach of national labour legislation was of course confined to certain work-places, types of wage-labour and sectors of the economy also before the coming of the new, union-free zones. However, the struggle to extend and deepen that reach has met with new obstacles.

As our case studies report, resistance to the liberalization measures that undermine erstwhile gains and the current position of labour has continued. Unions have been joined by other social groups including communities and consumers in coalitions against the policies of adjustment. The existing networks and cadres of the unions have often been able to provide leadership and cohesion to such anti-SAP forces. Yet, as the case-studies show, the capacity of the unions to take on this role varied. In some countries, as in Zimbabwe, labour militancy was accentuated by the growing experience of confrontation with the state, while in others, as in Zambia, the movement was divided and largely neutralized as a result of the partial incorporation of the labour leadership within institutions of the state.

While the effects of adjustment on the labour regimes were primarily retrogressive, those of political liberalization were more ambiguous. Labour's successful participation in the struggle for political reform against an authoritarian state, as most notably in South Africa, was partly rewarded by an enhanced position in society in general, allowing it greater influence on the post-liberation development of the labour regime. Some of the legislative reforms and institutions of concertation that were introduced in post-apartheid South Africa were a recognition of the special status of the labour movement in this respect. An early history of political liberalization in Senegal may have facilitated the development of a more autonomous labour movement. Similar modest openings in a multi-party direction in Egypt have not, however, been accompanied by any such openings. On the contrary, as El-Shafei argues, state control of the unions has been reinforced. In the Nigerian case, labour's participation in party politics backfired, inviting fresh state repression, without advancing the union agenda. The Zambian experience is equally ambiguous. Although the union's decisive involvement in the Movement for Multi-party Democracy may be seen to be confirming their political standing in society, labour was not able to reap any rewards in terms of a stronger position in the labour regime as a result of "its" victory at the polls.

At a more general and diffuse level it is probable that the pressures for political liberalization, globally and locally, may have given some encouragement to the labour movement in keeping an increasingly critical distance to the state as well as to its resistance to state impositions. In certain instances, political liberalization has facilitated mobilization against the structural adjustment policies of the state. Such greater autonomy and resistance may not have been sufficient to prevent a shift in the labour regime to the disadvantage of the workers, reflecting the decline in workers' bargaining power caused by crisis and adjustment. It is possible, though, that without the modest gains in political liberty the shift at the level of the labour regime may have been even more disadvantageous. On the whole, liberal political reforms have contributed to greater space and freedoms for both opposition parties and civil society groups, including labour unions.

SOME COMMON THEMES

While the individual contributions to this book were not designed in accordance with a joint comparative framework, there are some recurring common themes. A central one relates to the impact of crisis and adjustment that radically undermined the bargaining power of the workers. The essays highlight the retrenchments, the fall in real income, and the general deterioration in the conditions of reproduction. They discuss the implications of this shift in bargaining power for the labour regime. The developments were not passively accepted by the workers and another recurrent theme relates to the experience of resistance. Much of the struggle at the national level focused on the labour laws which governments sought to change to suit the new liberal order, taking advantage of the decline in workers' bargaining power. What was at stake in all the cases was a changing relationship between state and labour but also the relations with management were up for revision. In some instances, new forms of cooperation and consultation were developed to defend production and employment and there is evidence of unions that succeeded in strengthening their positions in the process of industrial restructuring. Let us elaborate on these common themes.

The essays report a *dramatic decline in workers' bargaining power* as related to mass retrenchments and the collapse of earnings. The retrenchments were particularly extensive in the public sector, where they had become a key conditionality linked to foreign funded adjustment programmes. In all the national experiences reported in this volume, such mass retrenchments were a central feature of adjustment. The policy of retrenchment contributed to a keen sense of job insecurity among the workers and provided managements with new leverage even in sectors not directly affected. A consequence was the tightening of the work-place labour regime, including the intensification of the pace of work, longer working hours, and more authoritarian forms of work-place discipline. The vulnerability of labour to further revisions of the work-place labour regime increased as reflected, for instance, in the greater recruitment of casual or contract labour employed on a temporary basis. As already mentioned, the establishment of export processing zones went even further by exempting firms from national labour legislation, including basic rights of unionisation.

The developments at the labour regime were part and parcel of a process of economic decline that had caused a *crisis in the reproduction of wage labour*. This crisis predated the introduction of adjustment policies but was further accentuated by the nature of the reforms. The real earnings of the workers collapsed under the impact of repeated devaluations and inflationary spirals.

Material gains achieved by the workers in an earlier period, as, for instance, in Egypt under Nasser, were wiped out. Inflation undermined the process of collective bargaining as a means of protecting workers' income. In addition, the element of a "social wage" that at one point had been provided through public-sector spending on social services, especially health and education, was similarly badly hit by cuts in government expenditure and a decline in public management. Poverty increased sharply with the proportion of those classified as poor, for instance, rising to 62 percent of the population in the case of Zimbabwe. In all the cases discussed in this book, the struggle over the direction of the labour regime thus took place at a point in time when the working-class was experiencing a profound crisis of reproduction. In most instances, workers were unable to subsist on their wages and the supplementation of incomes from other sources, informal sector activities, food production, and remittances, had become a precondition for survival. The material basis of the working class was eroded and so was its bargaining power.

Workers, however, did not passively accept this deterioration in their material conditions. All the countries covered in this book experienced *strikes and demonstrations and other forms of protest against adjustment* related measures, both localized in individual work-places and communities or involving mobilization at the national level, successful as well as unsuccessful ones. In Senegal, for example, there was a successful national strike against the "Austerity Plan" in 1993. There were organized massive stay-aways in South Africa in 1993 and 1994 against the introduction of value-added tax (VAT). Protests against heavy state-sponsored taxes were the immediate background to national strikes in Zimbabwe in 1997 and early 1998. However, these strikes were also aimed at adjustment-related effects such as inflationary food prices and retrenchments. Public sector strikes in the railway and telecommunications sectors in Zimbabwe were directed against the changes in the labour regime which threatened workers' job and income security, as Tengende outlines in his chapter. In Zambia, several industrial sectors were hit by industrial action as labour sought relief from adjustment measures. The Nigerian workers were no less militant.

A central theme of all the essays relate to changes in the *relations between the trade unions and the state* which in the pre-adjustment phase had been dominated by a variety of corporatist arrangements, although Hashim, as mentioned above, warns in his contribution that such epithet may be misleading, especially as it tends to exaggerate the element of state control. Certainly, the degree of autonomy and state incorporation of the unions varied from case to case and so did the level of authoritarianism and interventionism of the state. In Ghana, unions had succeeded in maintaining their autonomy from political parties and the state. The collapse of state corporatist arrangements in Zimbabwe in the early 1990s, similarly, paved the way for the growth of a more assertively autonomous labour movement. The hardships stemming from the implementation of adjustment programmes hastened the schism between the state and unions despite attempts in the mid-1990s to patch together a social contract. A process of alienation in relations between unions and the state also occurred in Zambia and Senegal. The growing assertiveness of unions — as they sought to respond to the interests of their membership — created conditions of conflict. In Senegal relations between unions and political parties took a nose-dive — state-sponsored national centres collapsed while new ones negotiated different relationships with political parties and the state. In Zambia, unions and the Chiluba regime found themselves increasingly at loggerheads as the terms of adjustment (and especially the effects of privatization) became more onerous. The erstwhile cordial relations between the Zambian Congress of Trade Unions (ZCTU) and the MMD government therefore froze. State attempts to fragment the labour centre were much resented. In Egypt, important elements of the state corporatist order remained and the state continued to offer legal backing for a highly hierarchical union structure, in which the dependence of the leadership on the state was enhanced while it was simultaneously alienated from the workers. There is evidence of a growing resentment by members against this collaborationist role. At the opposite end of the spectrum, unions in South Africa have sought a more advantageous relationship with the state, a relationship that recognizes their power and representative functions at the shop-floor and in the broader society. The implementation of liberal economic reforms in 1996 have created a rift between the labour movement and the state. The outcome of the developing rift is uncertain but it has had a weakening effect on the efforts to negotiate a social contract, both at the level of union-party relations and within tripartite institutions.

Much of the new conflict between the state and the unions was a *struggle over labour legislation* and its centrality in the reform process. The struggles were precipitated by amendments and revisions of the labour laws. In most cases, we found an established body of labour law which tended to regulate in great detail the parameters of collective bargaining, unions, and workers' rights, and the position of national labour centres and their relations to government or the ruling party. Much of this labour law had been adopted at an early time in the post-independence period and contained an explicit commitment to protect workers' interests. To the liberal reformers, such laws were seen as part of a defunct national developmentalist social order with its excessive statist and welfarist features that were strangulating the free development of wealth-generating market forces.

Labour law reform was therefore an obvious arena for political contestation and changes were introduced to facilitate economic liberalization. Typically, such changes aimed at raising labour market flexibility in wage determination and job security. They also invariably sought to reduce the power of unions. Egypt's "Unified Labour Law", for instance, restricted the right to strike and facilitated the procedures for laying off workers. With the purpose of weakening industrial unions and the national centre, the Zambian state introduced amendments to the "Labour and Industrial Relations Act" in 1993 under which mandatory union membership and the check-off system were abolished. Similarly, amendments to Zimbabwe's "Labour Relations Act" introduced the principle of a multiplicity of unions where one industrial union had previously existed. Furthermore, the provisions relating to employment security were expunged from the Act. In Senegal, article 47 of the "Labour Code" transferred more powers to employers to "hire and fire". In general, such revisions and amendments tended to remove or water down the protective provisions relating to workers' welfare which previously had legal backing. Even if the protection granted by such clauses were more symbolic than real, especially after long periods of uninterrupted economic decline, their removal reflected a significant political shift.

However, not only labour but also other groups were badly hit by adjustment, including sections of the business community, especially industry, which were negatively affected by trade liberalization, currency devaluation and cut-backs on state expenditure on infrastructure. Another common theme of the essays relates to the attempts of both unions and employers' organizations, with or without state participation, to seek *mutual accommodation* in a way as to allow for *the restructuring of enterprises* and prevent further decline in production and employment. Agreement between the parties on the terms of such restructuring was not easy in view of the antagonism created by retrenchments and the collapse of real income. In the Nigerian textile industry, for example, the restructuring necessitated technological upgrading, higher labour productivity, backward integration and the re-organization of management and finance. In Senegal, unions and employer organizations negotiated a "Social Pact", although short-lived, paving the way for increased worker participation in the running of enterprises. National Employment Councils (NECs) in Zimbabwe became an important joint union-employer negotiating forum on production conditions as well as collective bargaining. In South Africa, although the economy was less battered, the liberalization of the economy was also here seen as a precondition for its survival and unions were drawn into consultations over restructuring at all levels. In Ghana, similar tripartite institutions had been promoted by both unions and employers but they became increasingly ineffective as the state tended to disregard their decisions. The attempt to institutionalize tripartism in Zambia seems also to have been a failure.

Most of the experiences recounted in this book point to major setbacks for the workers and their organizations as a consequence of the crisis and the policies of adjustment. However, many also point to *remarkable achievements* in the face of such adversities. It is possible to document advances in strengthening the autonomy of unions and growing union pressures for union-based labour regimes as opposed to the authoritarian solutions mostly favoured by capital and state. The pre-requisites for such union-based regimes would include, amongst other aspects, the development of factory-level leadership directly elected by rank and file workers and directly accountable to them. Like in the South African experience, as explained by Adler and Webster, a strong shop-floor presence in which shop stewards play a central role would be imperative. Just as importantly, unions would need to construct contractual labour regimes with capital at the various levels which we identified in an earlier section of this chapter. Evidence from the Nigerian textile industry suggests the development of such a contractual, union-based labour regime, a process of deepening constitutionalism, premised on the evolution of a social contract, involving state, employers and unions, as Beckman explains in his chapter. The upgrading of competence and work discipline went hand in hand with the generalization of collective bargaining. In such a labour regime, the union assisted management in disciplining labour but simultaneously achieved the extension of workers' rights in the work-place. The ability of the unions to intervene in the "political apparatuses of production" at work-place level, supervising and challenging managerial practices of labour control was enhanced.

IMPLICATIONS FOR THE POLITICS OF ECONOMIC AND POLITICAL REFORM

This book is about labour regimes and the way they have been affected by economic and political liberalization. We have primarily commented on the impact on capital-labour relations at the work-place and the industrial sector level and, in particular, on the relations between state and unions. We also observed, however, how labour movements got involved with other groups in society, demonstrating their capacity to contribute to wider struggles, both in support of political liberalization and in opposition to the policies of adjustment. These experiences point to broader questions about the preconditions for political and economic reforms to which we now turn, in concluding this introduction.

The failure of adjustment programmes has been attributed by the World Bank to the absence of "a strong government commitment and widespread public backing":

> When an adjustment programme is launched, there must be a solid consensus on the need for change and an increase in the power of interest groups that will benefit from reforms in the course of the adjustment. If government commitment is weak, opposition strong or short-run costs high, the likelihood of stalls or reversals in policy reform is high (World Bank, 1994).

In the national cases presented in this book, such widespread public backing of adjustment was conspicuously absent. In some countries, a clearly "neo-colonial" pattern had emerged, characterized by the dominance of a foreign-trade-oriented or financial elite (Ghai and de Alcantara, 1991). In others, already fragile political pacts were further weakened, threatening the disintegration of national societies as regional and ethnic conflict were spurred by declining standards of living and the strains caused by adjustment policies. In general, such policies have tended to accentuate tensions in state-society relations without generating the conditions necessary for some social contract or pact between major social groups that are capable of sustaining the reforms politically. In addition, they have weakened the capacity of the state with far-reaching consequences for its ability to offer leadership in society. The ability of ruling groups to sustain existing patronage relations and to respond to sectional claims has also been reduced. Attempts to target "alleviation" measures on "vulnerable groups" have been too limited in scope to accommodate aggrieved populations, nor have they removed the conflict between a neo-liberal strategy and popular conceptions of what the state is for (Beckman, 1992). The logic of adjustment has been to further weaken the motivation of the state to respond to the popular demands that have been built into the process of post-colonial state formation. It has accelerated the erosion of the political coalitions and alliances which were constructed in the course of that process. This is not primarily a question of urban-based or biased coalitions losing out in favour of rural or agrarian ones. While adjustment in some cases shifted the balance of benefits and costs in favour of the latter, all popular expectations of the state, urban and rural, were frustrated. Although the purchasing power of some urban groups may have fallen more rapidly than that of some rural ones, both were upset by the declining ability of the state to deliver what was expected of it.

The problem was compounded by the disintegration of the more or less "corporatist" methods for securing domination and compliance that had been developed by the post-colonial state in relation to organized interest groups in society. Labour unions and professional associations caused particular problems to SAP in this respect (Beckman, 1992; Bangura and Beckman, 1991). They had "vested interests" in the public sector economy, both as producers and consumers, while simultaneously having an organized base from which to challenge SAP. African governments had in the past shown varying degrees of success in their efforts to subdue and control such organized interests by restrictive legislation and by co-opting, buying off or imposing leaders. Such statist-corporatist arrangements came under severe strain under SAP. The capacity of co-opted leaders to mediate the relation between the state and their member constituencies deteriorated with the impact of crisis and adjustment. They faced a dilemma of either distancing themselves from SAP or risk losing whatever remained of their credibility in the eyes of their members. They were increasingly unable to constrain the rising forces of unrest from below.

Professional groups like lawyers, doctors and lecturers had traditionally steered cautiously close to state power. They, too, faced a combination of external and internal pressures pushing them into resisting SAP. The crises in their domains of operation, for instance the disintegration of hospitals and schools, combined with the impoverishment and declassing of their members (cf. Nigeria's "lumpen lawyers') in precipitating confrontation with the state. Interest group opposition was often regarded as particularly illegitimate by the advocates of adjustment, being viewed as coming from a small, privileged minority, pursuing narrow self-interests at the expense of the mass of the people, the poor, the underprivileged, the unorganized, the "silent majority". Governments often therefore felt justified in applying repressive policies against such organizations.

The labour movement may indeed be "self-seeking" in its opposition to the adjustment policies of the state and its international backer, but in defending its interests it has actually tended to see itself as guardian of the public institutions and the national developmental and welfarist aspirations of the post-colonial state. In that sense, it has often become a mouth-piece not just for its own corporate interests but for broad popular concerns about the state and the future of social services and public development projets. Governments and their backers often underestimate the capacity of interest groups to offer both leadership and backbone to wider popular movements against the state. It is because of this capacity, not merely because they defend the interests of an entrenched and privileged minority, that interest groups are in a position to obstruct adjustment.

Can a social contract be worked between the state and organized labour opposed to adjustment? Attempts by governments to over-ride, sideline, or ignore labour opposition have been largely self-defeating. The failure of the state to recognize the limits of its own power is a major reason for the stalemate that characterises so much crisis management in Africa. Foreign intervention tends to reinforce the impasse by propping up and shielding regimes from domestic political pressures. While succeeding temporarily in shifting the balance of forces in favour of ruling coalitions, such interventions simultaneously undermine the process of accommodations that may be required for more lasting solutions. The national experiences discussed in this book underscore the need to take the labour movement seriously in the effort to create the institutional preconditions at the level of civil society for economic and political reform.

REFERENCES

AKWETEY, E. O. (1994) *Trade Unions and Democratisation: A Comparative Study of Zambia and Ghana* (Stockholm, Department of Political Science).

ANDRAE, G. and B. BECKMAN (1992) "Labour Regimes and Adjustment in the Nigerian Textile Industry", Paper presented at a Workshop on *The State, Structural Adjustment and Changing Social and Political Relations in Africa* organized by the Nordic Africa Institute, Uppsala, May 1992.

— (1998) *Union Power in the Nigerian Textile Industry: Labour Regime and Adjustment* (Uppsala, Nordiska Afrikainstitutet; New Jersey, Somerset; Transaction Publishers, Kano).

BANGURA, Y. and B. BECKMAN (1991) "African Workers and Structural Adjustment: A Nigerian Case Study", in Dharam Ghai (ed), *The IMF and the South: The Social Impact of Crisis and Adjustment* (London, Zed Books). Also in A. O. Olukoshi (ed) (1993) *The Politics of Structural Adjustment in Nigeria* (London, James Currey).

BECKMAN, B. (1992) "Empowerment or Repression? The World Bank and the Politics of Adjustment", in P. Gibbon, Y. Bangura and A. Ofstad (eds), *Authoritarianism, Democracy and Adjustment: The Politics of Economic Reform in Africa* (Uppsala, Scandinavian Institute of African Studies). Also in *Africa Development* (1991), XVI, 1.

— (1993) "The Liberation of Civil Society: Neo-Liberal Ideology and Political Theory", *Review of African Political Economy*, 58.

BECKMAN, B. and A. JEGA (1995) "Scholars and Democratic Politics in Nigeria", in *Review of African Political Economy*, 64.

BURAWOY, M. (1985) *The Politics of Production: Factory Regimes and Capitalism and Socialism* (London, Verso).

CAWSON, A. (1986) *Corporatism and Political Theory* (Oxford, Basil Blackwell).

GHAI, D. and C. HEWITT DE ALCANTARA (1991) "The Crisis of the 1980s in Africa, Latin America and the Caribbean: An Overview", in D. Ghai (ed.) *The IMF and the South : The Social Impact of Crisis and Adjustment* (London, Zed Books).

HASHIM, Y. (1994) 'The State and Trade Unions in Africa. A Study of Macro-Corporatism" (PhD Dissertation, The Hague, Institute of Social Studies).

OLUKOSHI, A. O. (ed) (1994) *Structural Adjustment in West Africa* (Lagos, Pumark/NIIA).

RUESCHEMEYER, D., E. H. STEPHENS and J. D. STEPHENS (1992) *Capitalist Development and Democracy* (Cambridge, Polity Press of Chicago, Chicago University Press).

SACHIKONYE, L. M. (1992) "The New Labour Regime under SAP in Zimbabwe", in *Southern Africa Political and Economic Monthly*, 5 (vii).

— (1993) "Structural Adjustment, State and Organised Labour in Zimbabwe", in P. Gibbon (ed), *Social Change and Economic Reform in Africa* (Uppsala, Scandinavian Institute of African Studies).

— (1995) *Democracy, Civil Society and the State: Social Movements in Southern Africa* (Harare, SAPES Books).

TENGENDE, N. (1994) "Workers, Students and the Struggles for Democracy: State-Civil Society Relations in Zimbabwe" (PhD Dissertation, Roskilde University, International Development Studies).

VALENZUELA, S. J. (1989) "Labour Movements in Transitions to Democracy: A Framework for Analysis", in *Comparative Politics*, 21 (iv).

WHITE, G. (1994) "Civil Society, Democratization and Development (I): Clearing the Analytical Ground", in *Democratization*, 1 (iii).

WORLD BANK (1994) *Adjustment in Africa: Reforms and the Road Ahead* (Washington, World Bank).

CHAPTER TWO

Democratic Transition and Post-colonial Labour Regimes in Zambia and Ghana

E. AKWETEY

INTRODUCTION: ZCTU AND THE TUC AFTER THE TRANSITION TO DEMOCRACY

In December 1989, the Zambia Congress of Trade Unions (ZCTU) initiated a public campaign for the reform of Zambia's one-party state system and the establishment of pluralist political democracy. In pursuit of that goal, the ZCTU joined other social groups to form the Movement for Multiparty Democracy (MMD) which was elected as the first government of Zambia's Third Republic in October 1991. While its role in the founding of the MMD as well as the mobilization of its members in support of the campaign made the ZCTU a major agent of transition to democracy, the purpose of that involvement was to reform the post-colonial labour regime. In that regard, and especially from the trade union organizational perspective, democratization was also the means to reform despotic labour regimes.

Zambian workers' support for multiparty democracy was rooted in grievances over living conditions including insecurity of employment and wages, and shaped by the perception of aggrieved workers that one party-state authoritarian rule was also a cause of their economic hardships. Since the late 1970s, when Kaunda's government systematically expanded and intensified its implementation of economic stabilization measures, Zambian workers had been at the receiving end of austere measures. Public sector workers suffered wage losses as a result of escalating inflation and drastic cuts in employment and public expenditures (e.g. food subsidies). As living conditions of the large majority of formal sector workers further deteriorated, tension and conflict at workplaces spread and the breakdown of the existing labour regime for ensuring peaceful and stable industrial relations looked inevitable. Continuing decline in living standards led to the adoption of a variety of "survivalist" response strategies that enabled workers and their families to cope with the persistent severity of economic hardships but gave them no influence over the decisions that so negatively affected them.

Elsewhere, we have argued that the frustration of central trade union organizations, like the ZCTU and the Trades Union Congress of Ghana (TUC), over how to influence structural adjustment decision-making informed the general mobilization of workers' support for the transition to formal political democracy (Akwetey, 1994). There was an understanding that democratic political reform generates political conditions that could facilitate the solution of persistent economic problems that had undermined livelihood. Yet, by 1997, that is five years after the formal inauguration of Zambia's Third Republic as a multiparty democracy, the much heralded transition had neither led to visible and substantial improvements in the living standards nor secured for the ZCTU a place in high-level decision-making. On the contrary, decline in both living standards and organizational capacity and influence had accelerated. Such an outcome of the ZCTU's involvement in the MMD in Zambia has major implications for transition theory and its practice.

It questions the role of unions in shaping democratization beyond the formal transition processes. Political mobilization and constitutional reform do not necessarily translate into an ability to reform labour regimes. The Ghanaian experience suggests that mobilization strategies based on political alliance formation may not be sufficient for influencing a major reform of authoritarian labour regimes. Like the ZCTU, the TUC of Ghana has also had a history of struggle and opposition against the post-colonial labour regime (Akwetey, 1994). That struggle largely shaped the role which the TUC played in Ghana's transition to a multiparty democracy in 1992, ten years after military rule was imposed in January 1982. However, since 1993, that is the period after the formal inauguration of the Fourth Republic, the TUC was able to maintain the cohesion of its organization and deepened its autonomy from political actors including the ruling government of the National Democratic Congress (NDC). Despite its enhanced strength, the TUC, like the ZCTU, did not succeed in securing an institutionalized position in high level decision-making.

So, what actually changed about the despotic post-colonial regimes after the transition to democracy in the early 1990s? The chapter seeks to answer this question through a comparative study of Zambia and Ghana. The nature of post-colonial labour regimes and the impact of the changing economic and political contexts within which they operate are examined. The comparison of the two cases leads to the conclusion that unionized workers' organizational power may well be important to the initial mobilization of popular support for launching the transition to formal political democracy. But that power resource alone is not sufficient to reform despotic labour regimes, especially 'after the transition'.

THE CONCEPT OF LABOUR REGIME

A regime can be defined as a framework or arrangement that is consciously created to facilitate the rational management, if not effective resolution, of social conflicts arising from the interaction of two or more actors over a defined area of interest like production. The underlying idea of regime construction is that, outside a framework within which the actions of actors in interaction can be constrained or shaped, individual actors may tend to make decisions independently, in disregard of the interests of other actors. In such a situation, conflicts are more likely to be resolved by any means possible, including the use of force or violence. Since the growth of an anarchic condition can lead to an unpredictable and unrestrained resort to force, regimes are created to provide a 'political order' within which the scope of independent decision-making can be circumscribed and peace and stability sustained. Regimes differ in form and function and are shaped by the peculiarities of the historical contexts within which they arise. Labour regimes are shaped by the interplay of domestic and international structural conditions. Within the interface of the factors, the state acts in constraining the capacity of unionized workers to effectively influence labour regime reform.

Labour regimes, as Burawoy (1985) suggests, are political structures or mechanisms for regulating production relations and guaranteeing their reproduction (Burawoy, 1979, 15-16). The process of production, as he explains, consists of two inter-connected moments, that is the organization of work and the corresponding or distinctive political and ideological framework or mechanism for regulating production relations (Burawoy, 1985, 7). Defining the organization of work simply as the set of practical activities by which men and women transform raw materials into useful things, Burawoy argues that the activities are not purely economic but also explicitly political. The organization of work, as he suggests, "has political and ideological effects", just as the latter also has effects on the former. He therefore suggests that the notion of a labour regime or *"production regimes"*, or more specifically factory regime, must be understood to embrace economic, ideological and political dimensions (Burawoy, 1985, 8).

By describing labour regimes as the embodiment of the inter-connection between domestic and international regimes, attention is drawn in this chapter, to the interplay of micro and macro factors that shape their character and define the conditions within which reforms may be constrained or facilitated. However, because labour regimes are also situated within, and form part of the domestic political system, it is necessary to highlight those attributes that analytically separate them from international regimes. Domestic regimes are structures of unequal power between dominant and subordinate social actors. Unlike international regimes, domestic regimes arise not because of the need to overcome structural anarchy but rather to overcome political challenges that constrain the autonomy of dominant actors to make decisions independently of subordinate ones. Governments may seek to implement their decisions through coercive means of enforcement. But political and actual resistance to the implementation of such decisions can be so significantly constraining that they may consider it more rational to also seek direct support among subordinate actors. Hence, despite being characterized as structures of unequal power, labour regimes may also function in practice as a framework for 'manufacturing consent' through the mobilization of support.

Ideologically, the process might require the obfuscation of historical and structural inequalities momentarily through the use of concepts like "partnership" that is then practised at the level of decision-making and implementation. Where such practices occur, labour regimes may function not only as political arrangements but also as ideological constructs enabling the joint application of coercion and consent in social interactions. If this is the case, then under what conditions does the reform of the regime become necessary? Who demands reform and in what dimension and direction? According to Stein (1993, 41) where social actors perceive "common interests", regimes will be established to enable co-operation, but where a "conflict of interest" is recognized, regimes will be needed not only to facilitate conflict resolution but also the coordination of agreements under implementation. It is the regulation of relations of co-operation and/or co-ordination for which regimes are needed. The effective performance of these functions may require the institutionalization of a regime. Burawoy corroborates this view in his description of the functions and effects of factory regimes. According to him,

> collective bargaining concretely *co-ordinated* the interests of workers and management, the grievance machinery constituted workers as industrial citizens with rights and obligations, and the internal labour market produced a possessive individualism right there on the shop floor. These institutions materialized a balance of power, which first and foremost set limits on workers' struggles but also restrained management from its authoritarian impulses. The regulating institutions afforded an area of self-activity, free from managerial deprivations, that gave workers the opportunity to construct effective working relations and drew them into the pursuit of capitalist profit. *Co-operation* revolved around 'making out' a 'game' in which the goal was to make a certain quota, and whose rules were recognized and defended by workers and management alike. This making out had the effect of generating *consent* to its rule and of obscuring the conditions that framed them. Coercion was applied only when the rules were violated, and even then within bounds that were themselves part of a larger game (Burawoy, 1985, 10-11).

Burawoy's statement makes it clear that the organization of work, together with the arrangements made to regulate social relations of production, can generate consent while obscuring the coercive conditions that framed it.

Under what conditions is reform perceived as necessary and by who? Regime reform can be said to arise when prevailing political and ideological *conditions* either frustrate co-operation or co-ordination or effectively prevent the construction of consent to such an extent that dominant actors increasingly resort to making decisions independently and also rely increasingly on coercion, rather than persuasion, to implement its decisions. For Burawoy, the relationship between coercion and consent is the critical criterion by which regime-types are classified. He describes regimes in which 'coercion prevails over consent' as despotic and, subsequently, categorises despotism according to structural and/or actor characteristics. Regimes which are constituted by the administrative hierarchy of the state he calls *bureaucratic despotism*, while those constituted by the economic whim of the market are classified as *market despotism* (Burawoy, 1985, 12-13). In either of these regimes, the state plays a direct or indirect role both in the organization of work and in the regulation of attendant social relations.

Stein (1993, 48-50) also suggests that "the same factors that explain regime formation also explain regime maintenance, change, and dissolution. Regimes are maintained as long as the patterns of interest that gave rise to them remain. When these shift, the character of a regime may change; a regime may even dissolve entirely". This means that unless actors desire a total change of an existing pattern of interests, regimes may be reformed only partially rather than entirely. Aspects of regimes may persist, despite changes in economic and political power, because of reasons of ideology or tradition which sustain the legitimacy of seemingly outdated authority relations. This means that changes in economic and political conditions may not necessarily lead to the reform of all regimes functional at different layers of state, society and production relations. Under what conditions will a given actor prefer reform as opposed to persistence of a given regime? To bring this discussion to bear directly on the examination of the nature of labour regime reform in Zambia and Ghana, in the post-transition era, a general overview of the specific character of post-colonial labour regimes will be instructive.

RISE OF POST-COLONIAL LABOUR REGIMES

In their general and specific forms, post-colonial labour regimes can be described as authoritarian and despotic across the sub-regions of Africa as elsewhere in the developing world (Burawoy, 1985). For, in addition to the 'coercion prevails over consent' characteristic, the authoritarian attribute was also expressed by the ideological and practical fusion between the triangular spheres of the state, the market and civil society that significantly characterized the post-colonial era (Akwetey, 1994). State domination of the market and civil society was made rather conspicuous by both the absence or weakness of the formal market economy and the proscription of pluralist organizational politics. It resulted in an arrangement whereby state agencies or officials comprising of single-party politicians, bureaucrats, army officers as well as foreign capital and few private businessmen and women joined the ruling parties to form the principal actors of post-colonial labour regimes. Although centralized trade union organizations had earlier formed part of this "post-colonial arrangement", they were later marginalized as the strategies of economic crisis management adopted by the nationalist governments of the early years of independence led to their repression and exclusion from high-level decision-making.

Due to the dominant position of the state in the post-colonial arrangement, the labour regimes of the time were generally referred to as state-corporatist regimes (Akwetey, 1994; Schmitter, 1974). In that regime, the state functioned not only as the sovereign actor in the domestic polity but also as major owner of the means of production. It owned industries and commercial houses and also controlled public service networks and access to its utilities such as hospitals and clinics, schools and colleges, jobs and housing, banks and credits. Extensive public ownership made it virtually impossible for other social forces to establish and maintain economic distance from the state (Rothchild and Chazan, 1988). Thereby a relationship of dependency evolved shaping a culture of consent to state authority that was more authoritarian than democratic. Consent became rooted essentially in cost-benefit calculations that reflected the fear of individuals and groups of citizens that they risked being impoverished and repressed should they be perceived to be disobeying the party-state or the militarized state.

Nationalist ideology also played a significant role in the shaping of post-colonial labour regimes. The ideology of state and nation-building and rapid economic development or modernization, as Shivji (1986) persuasively argues, upheld the view that 'democratic politics', in whatever fora is allowed, was bound to impede development. Therefore, it had to be proscribed in order to facilitate the attainment of the defined objectives of nationalist ideology. Eventually, according to Shivji, this ideology of "developmentalism" led to the creation of an authoritarian state that, in practice, functioned as the predominant social, economic and ideological actor in society. The ideology also shaped different strategies of development which informed attempts to create either a "despotic socialism" as in Zambia, Tanzania and Ghana or "despotic capitalism" in Kenya, Cote d'Ivore, and Nigeria (Martin, 1989). Indeed, it can be argued that the construction of post-colonial labour regimes was much more influenced by the general development interests defined by the state than by the interests or self-determined preferences of subordinate actors such as trade unions and private employers.

The nationalist parties that formed the first governments of the then emergent independent states had difficulties managing industrial relations effectively in peaceful and stable conditions. Decolonization and independence had undermined colonial factory regimes and caused their eventual breakdown. Post-colonial labour regimes rose in response to this breakdown. Burawoy (1979; 1985) illustrates this point with an instructive reference to Zambia where the racist inspired colonial labour regime that had been operative on the copper mines, collapsed soon after independence. The impact was felt specifically at the level of 'shop-floor discipline' where productivity and production declined because workers refused to obey the orders of the expatriate supervisors who had hitherto abused and repressed them. The break-down of law and order on the shopfloor escalated to the national level as wild-cat strikes spread across sectors. The nationalist party government initially responded with offers of wage increases but the failure of the strikes or wage demands to abate led the government to advocate a regime that could facilitate control over workers' demands and activities and also restore or recreate order and discipline (Akwetey, 1994; Meebelo, 1986). In the final analysis, the government was able to reform the labour regime because sections of the trade union movement also believed that the proposal to 'Zambianize' management would benefit the workers (Bates, 1971).

The breakdown of colonial 'order and discipline' was hardly peculiar to Zambia since it occurred invariably in all the emergent independent states where both unionized and non-unionized workers had joined the anti-colonial struggle (Davies, 1965). While control over strikes was a major reason for the creation of centralized trade unions, the re-direction of workers' activities in support of government development objectives was the strategic consideration that shaped the despotic character of labour regimes. Both the state and foreign investors were concerned that the anarchy of wild-cat strikes and growing wage demands rendered the peaceful regulation of industrial relations ineffective, unreliable and unstable. It was argued that control over workers' demands and activities was essential if production were to be increased and private foreign investment attracted. Reforms were, consequently, considered necessary if labour regimes were to be rendered more effective and relevant to the challenges of the post-colonial era.

Initially, the organizational re-structuring was patterned on the model of the one-party state, giving rise to a corporatist structure in which industrial unionism, mandatory membership and monopoly representation was legislated. Similarly, employers' federations were restructured into central organizations that were also empowered and monopoly representation was legislated. Similarly, employers' federations were restructured into central organizations that were also empowered to represent all employers in an arrangement that was parallel to that of trade unions. Both the employers' and workers' organizations were subordinated to the party-state in a manner that rendered them economically and politically dependent on the state (Akwetey, 1994; Martin, 1989). Peak employers' and workers' organizations were expected to monitor and control the activities of their respective affiliate associations.

The effective performance of the co-ordination and co-operation functions subsequently became the basis upon which the state allowed the involvement of peak organizations in high-level decision-making. If their performance was deemed unsatisfactory, leaders of the peak organizations were held accountable and sometimes punished. When judged satisfactory, reward took the form of enhanced political status for identified individuals rather than the organizations themselves. Such co-optation did not necessarily make the individual leaders involved more respected within the organizations they led. As a number of studies have indicated, rank-and file members were rather alienated from such leaders as the position they took on government policies was seen as unrepresentative of the members (Akwetey, 1994; Bates, 1971). Despite the evidence that political co-optation undermined the legitimacy of the leaders involved, workers' and employers' consent to government policy was believed to have been generated also by other means. Reference has often been made to a so-called 'post-colonial social contract' according to which civil society groups were assumed to have traded off their right of organizational autonomy and democratic participation in government for state sponsored improvements in their material conditions of living.

For unionized workers in the urban areas, the concrete terms of the 'social contract' covered items like secure and abundant jobs, relatively high wages, access to heavily subsidized utility services in education, health, housing, transport and electricity as well as subventions that kept food prices low (Bangura, 1989; Jamal and Weeks, 1988). The package for employers comprised access to state credit facilities to local industrialists and the protection of the local market for their 'home-made' products against competition from foreign imports. In expecting the state to provide this broad range of welfare and developmental facilities, the social actors involved also perceived a relationship in which the state was expected to create socio-economic conditions conducive to the pursuit, if not attainment, of organizational interests or objectives.

For most of the post-colonial era, nationalist ideology and the state-led development strategy were generally hostile to the growth and development of indigenous private capital. Initially, official policies towards private indigenous industrialists were punitive and discriminatory. Those who were associated with opposition political parties were discriminated and disqualified from receiving credit facilities from the state-owned banks. Eventually, their businesses collapsed. This punitive policy later encouraged both established and potential private businessmen to join ruling parties with the view to promoting their interests. However, even pro-government businessmen and women were not particularly well treated. Constant threat of nationalization and official ideological rejection of private ownership of means of production made them feel unwelcome to the party-state. State attitude towards private investors can also be explained in terms of the vested economic interests of the state itself. The post-colonial state was indeed the major owner and employer in the industrial and service sectors of the economy. In that role, its repressive treatment of private business interests came across as an extension, to the economic sphere, of the state's political intolerance of opposition or challenge from all organizations which were relatively autonomous and could not be politically controlled directly.

Competition by private indigenous capitalists, as Tangri (1993) shows in his study of Ghana, was not only ideologically unacceptable but also perceived to be practically threatening to state economic power (also Killick, 1980; Loxley, 1989). Due largely to the unfriendly atmosphere for private business, the organizational development of indigenous private capital and the institutionalization of its relations with the state was impaired. This rendered such organizations too weak and marginal to have any significant influence over government economic policies. Until the mid-1980s, it was the widely held view that central trade unions were powerful and influential in the decision-making processes of the authoritarian state. This view does not appear to be substantiated by the record of relations between the central trade unions and the state in Zambia and Ghana. Indeed, prior to the mid-1980s, trade unions had lost most, if not all, of the direct political influence which they possibly exercised in the early years of independence when their leaders were recruited into top positions of government. The underlying factors were linked to the conditions that also undermined the effectiveness of the labour regimes.

DECLINE OF POST-COLONIAL LABOUR REGIMES

In the period in reference, the ability of the state to sustain the scope of effective management of industrial conflicts was further constricted by changes in other structural factors upon which it had earlier founded its economic and ideological hegemony in post-colonial society. For, in addition to the adverse impact of the oil price hikes in 1973-75 and 1979-80, the primary commodity export dependent economies also suffered revenue losses as earnings from leading exports like Zambia's copper and Ghana's cocoa and gold declined following recurrent drops in their global market prices. Persistent reduction of export revenues meant that the government would not be able to sustain the subsidies on local consumption of imported fuel and food products, imported or locally produced, and fund schools and hospitals. Faced with the progressive contraction of its revenue base, it might seem logical for the government to also respond by cutting the level of public expenditure and, thereby, restore some balance in revenue and expenditures. However, such a response did not appear practical as many governments perceived high political risks with such an approach and, consequently, decided to manage the crisis ensuing partly from its dwindling resource base through deficit financing.

By the late 1970s, the ineffectual management of the growing domestic economic crisis had created conditions which made extensive intervention virtually inevitable. Initial stone-walling by the affected governments eventually gave way to conditional multilateral and bilateral funding in an internationally solicited or induced effort to rescue the crisis-ridden economies. External intervention had major operative implications for the post-colonial labour regime. First of all, its ideological foundation was systematically undermined by the forceful argument that the state-led development strategy had not been particularly effective in promoting sustainable economic development and even less successful in building strong national societies. Secondly, the critics have argued that the social basis of the 'post-colonial social contract' was restrictive since it discriminated against rural communities while devoting enormous resources to the development of urban areas where workers and employers led lives of relative comfort (Beinen and Waterbury, 1989). Thirdly, the replacement of the hitherto predominant state-led strategy with an alternative neo-liberal and market-friendly strategy was not only strongly advocated but also rigorously imposed as an extensive package of political conditionalities was subsequently attached to both bilateral development aid and multilateral institutional lending (Havnevik, 1987).

During the first phase of implementation of the neo-liberal programmes, conditionalities were tied to strong-handed conflict management strategies that were simultaneously state-despotic as well as market-despotic. In practice, this meant that state agencies and market forces could unilaterally make crisis-management decisions which they attempted to implement by relying more on coercion and less on consent manufactured through dialogue and negotiated agreement. This was evident in the common adoption of a set of political measures in the two countries. The first was the tactic of 'insulating' decision-making processes from supposedly obstructive political pressures (Herbst, 1993). In practice, insulation translated into an effective exclusion of representatives of unionized workers and broad sections of affected civil society groups including the indigenous business organizations from public policy decision-making processes (Akwetey, 1994). Insulation facilitated the making of unilateral decisions to drastically reduce public expenditures through outright or phased withdrawal of subsidies on food and service utilities, the retrenchment of workers without adequate notice of lay-off and negotiated redundancy packages. Increases in taxation and a freeze on wages in combination with trade liberalization and the abolition of price controls escalated inflation.

The perception that groups affected by the cuts would oppose through protests and demonstrations in public led to the recommendation by some World Bank technocrats that the mobilization of opposition should be deterred through repressive measures (Toye, 1992; Hutchful, 1989). Repression, it was suggested, will facilitate the swift implementation of the decisions made unilaterally by removing the impediments associated with social protests and mobilized opposition. However, as the cases of Zambia and Ghana illustrate, neither exclusion/insulation nor repression succeeded in overcoming the resistance.

Zambia's one party-state government led by Kaunda and Ghana's military government led by Rawlings repressed both spontaneous and organized protests and people were detained over long periods without trial. Others were summarily dismissed from employment and systematic persecution through intimidation associated with surveillance by security agencies. In Zambia, violent street protests could only be controlled through army and police intervention that claimed human lives (Graham, 1989; Akwetey, 1994). This evident reliance on force to deal with protests was indicative of the collapse of the prevailing labour regime. Suppression of workers' protests did not necessarily translate into more support for indigenous private capital.

In both Zambia and Ghana, indigenous manufacturers and related business associations complained about the lack of consultation and neglect of their voices and concerns in the making of various decisions that affected them. During the second phase of structural adjustment, privatization of public economic enterprises and the adoption and implementation of 'new investment codes' intended to attract foreign private investors, led to the modification of the exclusionary strategy. Controlled representation was given to employers' and workers' organizations on national divestiture or privatization committees on which government agencies had a dominant representation. Both in Zambia and Ghana, the ZCTU and the TUC, as well as the employers' associations, accepted such representation and managed to use the allocated space to negotiate changes in privatization packages. Despite the apparent shift from coercion to limited consent-building, the major structural problems of labour regimes in decline was hardly addressed. Workers engaged in moonlighting and informal trading activities sometimes in stolen office or factory goods. Employers became engaged with cost-saving schemes involving tax evasion and paying bribes to circumvent excessively elaborate bureaucratic processes. Government officials, that is civil servants, military officers and politicians, also became more devoted to private rent-seeking than enforcing the law (Beckman, 1988a; Dutkiewicz and Williams, 1987).

Neither the state nor employers nor central trade union leaders could effectively control this informalization process. Not unexpectedly, therefore, the labour regimes in both Zambia and Ghana also declined as part of the decay of the state's institutional framework. The survival strategies adopted by unionized workers and associated employers, civil servants, professionals and politicians, were generally indicative of broad disengagement from, rather than inclusion in, the formal structures of decision-making and implementation of public policies (Azarya, 1988; Ninsin, 1991). Thus, it has been argued that this broad range of 'informal' and 'illegal' economic responses to the impact of economic liberalization, in combination with despotic crisis-management did not only perpetuate a crisis of production but also intensified the systematic decay of post-colonial institutions including the labour regime (Sandbrook, 1985;

Callaghy, 1988). Individual workers and employers, as well as government officials, took their own initiatives to minimize, if not cope with, the unremitting deterioration in living standards. Solutions based on collectively binding decisions were incrementally undermined, leaving existing institutional arrangements ineffectual.

DEMOCRATIZATION AND REFORM OF THE LABOUR REGIMES

Democratization can be considered as a response to the despotism that accompanied the institutional decay of the state and related labour regimes. Demands for democratic changes were primarily directed at the despotism which some social groups had experienced as hostile to the pursuit of interests in an open, peaceful and stable political order. In the mobilization of political opposition against despotism and support for democratic reforms, trade unions, business associations, and a broad range of interest organizations brought their specific experiences to bear on the definition of the nature of the democratic reforms required. Implicit in the terms of engagement in the post-colonial labour regimes was the assumption that the actors involved will neither be *autonomous* of the state nor its agencies including ruling political parties or groups. Furthermore, the vertical and unequal power relationship between the dominant state and the subordinate central trade unions and employers' associations was founded on the belief that they will be loyal to the latter by consenting to the authority of government and supporting its development policies. The unequal power relationship was weakened as subordinate actors opposed government policies, asserted their organizational autonomy and also demanded representation in high-level policy-making processes.

While opposition to government policies was itself a major source of conflict, linking politically autonomous organizations to high-level decision-making was even more challenging and threatening to the *status quo*. For, apart from the fact that the institutional framework of the state did not facilitate such a linkage, the government itself lacked the skill for managing the changes called for by the subordinate actors. It was difficult for post-colonial governments to relate to an alternative political relationship founded on the concept of social partnership between the state and autonomous social organizations because such a relationship would also imply power sharing between social actors rather than the institutionalized domination of a dominant actor over subordinate and dependent actors (Akwetey, 1994). The unpreparedness of governments to accept a restructuring of the terms of the relationship was evident in the general failure to institutionalize *tripartism* as a practical expression of such partnership in both Zambia and Ghana.

Although both countries made attempts in the 1970s and 1980s to establish tripartite fora, with the active encouragement of the International Labour Organization (ILO), the scope of such fora was never broadened beyond wage policy negotiations (Akwetey, 1994). Later in the 1980s and early 1990s, the simultaneous assertion of organizational autonomy and demand for representation in high-level decision-making was linked to the broader question of constitutional reform to facilitate pluralist democratic politics within formal structures of governance. Peak trade union organizations as well as employers' associations perceived the attainment of these outstanding demands to be more likely within the broader constitutional reforms which other domestic social groups were advocating. Bilateral donors and multilateral lending institutions later gave support by linking issues of transparency, accountability, the rule of law and multi-party politics, to the terms of development assistance to governments (Gibbon, 1992; Akwetey, 1994). Peak trade union organizations, workers and associated employers in Zambia and Ghana perceived an opportunity to shape the reform of labour regimes and proceeded as such, taking advantage of what seemed to be a withdrawal of international support for authoritarian regimes.

In Zambia, the ZCTU joined the MMD in a formal alliance aimed at building a common platform for mobilizing mass support for democratic reforms. Thereby, the ZCTU brought into that fold its considerable organizational and financial resources (Akwetey, 1996). Not only did it provide the MMD with a presidential candidate in the person of Frederick Chiluba, then Chairman-General of the ZCTU, but also put a nation-wide network of unionist activists loyal to Chiluba at the disposal of the MMD. This enabled the MMD to draw on organizational resources which it would not have been capable of building in the short span of political liberalization. The reasons why the leadership of the ZCTU put its full weight, at considerable political risk, behind the MMD have been variously explained. Some suggest that individual political ambitions of the two most influential leaders of the ZCTU, Frederick Chiluba and Newstead Zimba, then the Secretary-General of the ZCTU, were linked with similar ambitions of middle-ranking and influential unionists to transform the labour organization into a political machine. Elsewhere, we have argued that personal political ambitions may have influenced individuals in taking the risks involved. But the ultimate reason why the large majority of rank-and-file workers rallied 'religiously' to the call of Chiluba and Zimba lies in the widespread belief, among the majority of Zambian workers, that the election of Chiluba as the state president would enhance job security and improve their wages.

This belief was indeed, reinforced by the passage of a new labour law, the Labour and Industrial Relations Act of 1990 that sought to break-up the central organization and weaken its organizational coherence (Akwetey, 1994; 1996). The new legislation was enacted in infamous disregard of the criticisms and pleas of both the ZCTU and the employers association — the Zambian Federation of Labour (ZFL). Because it was enacted soon after the ZCTU had officially declared support and symbolically led the campaign for the restoration of multiparty democracy, it was perceived as a punitive relatiatory measure. Accordingly, the new legislation was perceived less in terms of the imperatives of neo-liberal market reform than as a political vendetta of an unpopular ruling party. The ZCTU's mobilization of unionized workers made a decisive contribution to the landslide defeat and exit of the Kaunda and UNIP government, after ruling Zambia for 27 years. The implications of union responses to the threats and challenges of prevailing economic conditions were largely unclear. The ZCTU leaders had made it quite clear that they would not accept direct political control by government and that the organization would also like to participate democratically in high-level economic and social policy decision-making. How it intended to protect its autonomy and simultaneously gain entry into high-level policy processes remained unclear.

In Ghana, the link-up between TUC support for democratization and reform of the labour regime took a somewhat different turn. Like the ZCTU, the Ghana TUC has also been defensive about its organizational autonomy and had raised the question of democratic representation and participation in high-level policy-making processes. But, whereas Kaunda's one party-state had responded to the ZCTU demand by attempting to reinforce UNIP's control, Rawlings' military-state attempted to create a parallel workers' organization to the TUC — the Workers' Defence Committees (WDC). Despite attempts to actively encourage a more pro-government organization of workers via the WDCs, unionized workers steadily dissociated themselves from the WDCs. This enabled the TUC to re-assert its leadership role in defence of workers' interests whilst the PNDC government increasingly repressed what it considered to be excessively radical interference in the productive management of enterprises by the WDCs. Beyond repression, however, government attempted to transform the WDCs into administrative structures for mobilizing support for government programmes (Akwetey, 1994; Hansen, 1986).

The repressive means of effecting this change alienated many workers from the WDCs causing their rapid decline in the workplace which in turn boosted the TUC as the more cohesive and credible representative of the workers. This position enabled it eventually to exact some policy concessions from the government while defending its own autonomy essentially within boundaries firmly defined by the state. Institutional openings occurred predominantly in the labour market sphere where a national tripartite wage negotiation committee as well as a national labour council were re-structured to broaden representation in public policy-making, although with little progress in terms of influence. Likewise, the defence of trade union autonomy proved quite fragile. For example, in 1988 when strong anti-PNDC opinion among workers appeared likely to sway the majority vote at the Sixth Quadrennial Congress of the TUC in favour of an outspoken critic of the government, the latter did not hesitate to politically intervene in the internal electoral campaign to ensure the re-election of the incumbent secretary-general (Akwetey, 1994). For most of the 1980s, the government disregarded the tripartite fora and its decisions. All this happened before Ghana's transition to democracy formally took off and led to the expectation that democratization might enhance the consolidation of the limited gains in labour regime reform while facilitating the resolution of outstanding issues.

Unlike the Zambian case, the Ghana TUC decided to pursue its specific interests within the broader democracy movement without entering into any formal alliance of pro-democracy forces. Declaring itself to be party-political neutral, the TUC advised its members to vote according to their political beliefs. The neutrality stance weakened the pro-democracy movement which was never able to organize itself sufficiently as a national force to challenge the political party which the PNDC formed and sponsored in 1992. Thus the earlier military-based government was able to effectively 'civilianise' itself through an electoral mandate that was further secured when the opposition political parties boycotted the parliamentary elections. So, in January 1993 when Ghana's transition to democracy was formally proclaimed, the question on many workers' minds was whether the unresolved issues in state-labour relations of the preceding era could be resolved under the civilianised government of President Rawlings. Would political neutrality assist the TUC in its reform of the post-colonial labour regime?

THE ZAMBIAN EXPERIENCE AFTER THE TRANSITION TO DEMOCRACY

UNIP's exit from government resolved a major aspect of the conflict over Zambia's labour regime. It ended the uncertainty that had hung over the ZCTU, for a very long time, as UNIP had persisted in its determination to control the organization and reduce it to the status of a branch of the party. What remained, however, was the equally significant demand for representation in high-level decision making. And the manner and extent to which the MMD responded to it was likely to shape its relations with the ZCTU in the long term. Prior to the 1991 elections, Chiluba and his ZCTU colleagues argued that raising workers' real incomes and ensuring the security of existing jobs, including the creation of many others, should be a major priority of national economic policy. The ZCTU Chairman-General, Chiluba, had emphasized that "economic restoration is restoration of our salaries and wages" (Chanda, 1993, 24-27). Later, as state president, Chiluba implored the ZCTU leaders to seek to represent the "true interests of workers within the broader national interest" (Chanda, 1993, 26). He urged workers, "like everybody else", to make a collective sacrifice to promote Zambia's economic recovery through growth, management efficiency and development. Accordingly, he entreated them to support the MMD's economic recovery programme aiming to "revive the economy" after several years of mismanagement.

From December 1991, the MMD government began to implement with great speed and enthusiasm its economic recovery programme. It removed subsidies on food and withdrew resources from health care, education and transportation. This was quickly followed by the devaluation of the national currency, the Kwacha, together with import and export trade liberalization as well as the abolition of price controls. The effects of these measures on workers were compounded by related measures of retrenchment, the freezing of public sector wages and the cancellation of all tax free allowances (Government of Zambia, 1993, 53; ZCTU File, "Speech" 18/1/96). ZCTU support for the measures initially took the form of silent acquiescence leading to a policy that can be described as "don't praise and don't criticize" the MMD government. As the workers began to feel the severity of the impact on incomes and job security, the ZCTU cautioned "their members to avoid going on strike as management may either send them on early retirement or dismiss them" (Simutanyi, 1995). The caution was later supplemented with official guidelines advising workers on how to conduct negotiations on labour redundancies and secure fair redundancy packages for those affected (ZCTU, 1993). Later, the ZCTU accepted a negotiated 'compromise' on the right of Zambian workers to strike in order to facilitate the resolution of industrial conflicts.

In negotiations to amend parts of the 1990 Labour Act that the ZCTU had strongly opposed, the scope of official restrictions on workers' right to strike was extended to cover areas that had hitherto not been classified as part of the essential services sector. As a result, strikes in the mines and banking sector were now prohibited as part of the restricted category that had hitherto comprised electricity, water and sewerage, fire brigade, medical services, the police, army and intelligence services. In addition to expanding the category of prohibitions, the amended legislation, i.e. the 1993 Labour and Industrial Relations Act (LIR, 1993), also made cross-sector solidarity strikes illegal. The 'compromise' had the practical effect of making the ZCTU more directly involved in seeking to control spontaneous strikes. For example, in early 1993, 500 bank employees went on strike over demands for improved wages and conditions of employment. The MMD government swiftly responded by dismissing all the involved workers. The Zambian Union of Financial Institutions and Allied Workers (ZUFIAW) , the financial sector union, tried in vain to persuade the ZCTU to lead in the mobilization of solidarity strikes so as to facilitate the reinstatement of those dismissed. ZUFIAW officials complained that the ZCTU had decided to "remain silent over the matter, instead of co-ordinating with other unions to save the sacked workers through solidarity action and international campaign" (ZCTU File, 1/96).

The failure of the ZCTU to come out in support of the bank workers left many Zambian workers confused and uncertain about the role of the ZCTU and the terms of its relations with the MMD government. As economic recovery programmes affected them and touched major industrial relations and collective bargaining issues, doubts about the efficacy of the new ZCTU leadership also grew. In the final analysis, support for government policies and restrictions on solidarity strikes combined to generate hostility towards the ZCTU leadership. Calls were made, not only for a more critical ZCTU voice against the economic policies of the MMD government but also for the amendment of section 78 of the 1993 labour legislation that bans solidarity strikes. Pushed by such internal pressures, the ZCTU leaders began to articulate a more critical position. Already, in October 1992, the organization had signalled a break with its tacit support for the MMD's economic recovery programme when it officially decided to function as a non-partisan actor, neither beholden to the MMD nor to any political party. The ZCTU claims that this critical-actor stand was a stand against orthodox SAP policies which had no apparent regard for issues of employment and labour income but rather focused on "the profit motive" to the neglect of "their effects particularly upon workers and other vulnerable groups".

The mode of retrenchment, from 1994, became despotic. Local unions and the ZCTU were not informed before-hand about retrenchments. The ZCTU leaders intensified their criticism of the programme of privatization, observing that "government seems to be in a hurry to privatize state-owned enterprises even in situations where the earmarked enterprises are not ready for privatization, leaving managers and workers uncertain about their future" (ZCTU QC/D No. 1, 26-29 October, 1994, 5-6). They claimed that the government was paying huge fees to city institutions for handling liquidation and sell-offs, and in some cases, massively undervaluing targeted enterprises to facilitate private acquisition. But then, there was no guarantee that privatized enterprises would either continue to remain in the hands of the new owners or succeed where the parastatal enterprises seem to have failed (ZCTU File, 18 January 1996). These arguments, according to the ZCTU leadership, did not mean a total rejection of the MMD's privatization programme but rather provided a basis for "consultation with social partners in an atmosphere of transparency" in search of practical solutions to economic and social problems (ZCTU File, 1/ 1996).

As ZCTU criticisms intensified, Chiluba and the MMD government interpreted them as a negative attitude, if not hostility, towards the president and his policies. Hence, relations between the MMD government and the ZCTU got badly strained and trust gradually gave way to mistrust which further undermined the basis for co-operation between the two actors. From 1994, the government began to block access to the presidency, a major sphere of high-level decision-making, to the ZCTU leadership. Later, the Minister of Labour also failed to convene the Tripartite Consultative Labour Council meetings regularly, hence interrupting the attempt to institutionalize policy dialogue (ZCTU File 1/1996; Interview ZCTU official, 1/1996). The closure of access to spheres of decision-making did not only affect unionized workers but also Zambian industrialists and entrepreneurs who, as employers, also depended on a viable labour regime to regulate relations with trade unions and the government. The transition to democracy had not led to a reform of Zambia's despotic labour regime. The ZCTU took a severe battering from worker retrenchments which progressively reduced the numerical and financial strength of the organization. Affected workers stopped paying their union membership dues. The loss of revenue was further aggravated by the amendment of the mandatory clauses that had hitherto facilitated the unionization of workers in Zambia.

Under the terms of the amended Act of 1993, mandatory membership of trade unions and compulsory dues check-off were abolished. Discontented workers who questioned the quality and effectiveness of the ZCTU leadership were thus encouraged to make a voluntary exit. In October 1994, four of the major industrial sector unions publicly announced their disaffiliation from the ZCTU. They were the Mineworkers Union of Zambia (MUZ), the Zambia Union of Financial Institutions and Allied Workers (ZUFIAW), the Zambia National Union of Teachers (ZNUT) and the National Union of Building, Engineering and General Workers (NUBEGW). The decision to disaffiliate was announced soon after the 9th Quadrennial Congress in October 1994, during which the involved unions had failed to get their candidates elected to powerful positions of ZCTU Chairman-General and Secretary-General. The defection was significant for a number of reasons. It indicated the intensification of power struggle within the central leadership of the ZCTU which had originated partly in the negotiated compromise on solidarity strike and partly in the ambition of members of the leadership to challenge the incumbent Secretary-General and Chairman-General of the ZCTU. The split accelerated the organizational decline of the ZCTU. Together, the defecting unions accounted for over 50 percent of total ZCTU membership and also the most militant and resourceful wing of the trade movement.

As a result, the break-away not only meant a decline in numerical strength but also the loss of a politically significant wing of the movement. The defecting unions withheld the remittance of affiliation dues to the central organization, thereby depriving the old centre of vital funding. While attributing the decline to the initial support of the ZCTU to the economic policies of the MMD government, it is also important to acknowledge the specific contribution of the amended Labour Act of 1993. The adoption of a more voluntary rather than a mandatory principle of unionization encouraged the belief among sections of the unionized workers that they can defect from the ZCTU and establish a rival trade union centre. Yet when the reality of the cleavage in the ZCTU evolved towards the formal registration of a new trade union centre, the ZCTU could count on the political considerations of the MMD government to uphold its monopoly representation of workers' interests in Zambia. Clause 8c of the Labour Act of 1993 stipulates that the registration of splinter trade union centres purporting to "represent a class or classes of employees already represented by an existing trade union", was prohibited. In practice, this clause was used as the legal basis for denying formal registration of a 'federation' of the defected unions. As a result, the defected unions have been compelled to register a co-ordinating organ under the Societies Act (Chapter 105, the Laws of Zambia) but without formal powers to represent its members in matters of industrial relations and collective bargaining.

The attendant frustration has promoted the defector unions to demand an amendment of both clauses 8a and 78 of the 1993 Act. None of these demands were acceptable to the MMD government because their retention served to effectively divide the trade union movement and impede the eventual mobilization of a unified workers' movement that could mount an effective opposition to the economic policies of the MMD government. The division within the ZCTU, together with the firm enforcement of anti-strike legislation, enabled the MMD government to pursue its structural adjustment policies despite trade union opposition. Five years after the ZCTU threw its powerful organizational weight behind the MMD alliance, in support of broader political and economic reforms, its specific goal to reform Zambia's despotic labour regime had not been attained. Not only had the organization failed to secure for itself an institutionalized representation in high-level decision-making, but also its political autonomy had become severely compromised as it now depended extremely on the political goodwill of the MMD government to protect its legal position as the representative of Zambian workers. However, the basis for that status no longer derived from the organizational coherence of the trade union movement in Zambia but rather the discrepant clauses of a labour law that sustained the despotism of the labour regime after the transition to democracy.

The ZCTU of 1999 looked merely a shadow of the ZCTU of 1990-91, divided without an effective unified leadership, drained of membership and financial resources and increasingly battered and irrelevant to Zambia's post-transition democratization politics. The labour regime in Zambia had been reformed in accordance with the interests of the MMD government, not those of the ZCTU. The Zambian experience draws attention to a familiar pattern where the political alliances formed to facilitate political transition processes do not necessarily guarantee that the labour organization will be any more influential in government, let alone succeed in reforming the labour regime, than it was prior to the transition. This was the post-colonial experience in many African countries and the recent experience of Zambia also seems to validate the point. Now, if the alliance strategy can be shown in this Zambian case to cause a decline in trade union power, is there evidence to suggest that non-alliance strategy will yield better results? Ghana is briefly discussed to illustrate and answer this point.

GHANA'S LABOUR REGIME IN THE POST-TRANSITION ERA

The Trade Union Congress (TUC')s policy of 'party political neutrality' officially put the labour organization outside the formal pro-democracy movement. This political neutrality was partly shaped by the history of the TUC's relations with past governments. Would it enable it to gain a more influential voice in high-level decision-making? In the 1980s, structural adjustment had been the focal point of conflict and crisis in Ghana's labour regime. The TUC maintained a consistently critical stance towards the economic recovery programme and the privatization policy of the government. It refused to acquiesce in the implementation of decisions which had been made outside of the existing institutional framework of the labour regime and accused government of acting arbitrarily in disregard of formal procedures and rules. The irritation caused by these criticisms eventually precipitated periodic confrontations as the government, determined to implement its economic recovery policies, simply ignored the TUC or dealt with its officials repressively.

In 1994, that is barely two years after the transition to democracy, 10,400 workers were retrenched. This time around, the democratically elected and civilianised Rawlings government decided to offer severance pay with a coverage for only six months (TUC 5th QC Report, 1996, 43-44). It took the decision without any consultation with the TUC which protested and eventually threatened a nation-wide solidarity strike in January 1995. The threat compelled the government to re-open negotiations that finally led to an award of 18 months severance pay to the affected workers. In other state enterprises, including those scheduled to be privatized, "tens of thousands of strong and able-bodied workers" were retrenched without any dialogue with the TUC. Because many of these unilateral decisions often violated existing collective agreements, it took a series of court actions, the threat of a solidarity strike, sometimes including the intervention of the ILO, to get the government to modify its decisions and to pay workers their redundancy entitlement (TUC 5th QC Report, 1996, 44). A despotic labour regime and structural adjustment of the economy combined to reduce TUC membership and financial subscriptions. In that regard, the experiences of Zambia and Ghana were rather identical. The similarity, however, did not extend to the relative ability of the central trade unions to control the impact on their organizational capacity.

Unlike the ZCTU, the TUC was able to defend the right to mobilize workers for general solidarity strikes and used it periodically as its most effective weapon to restrain government and contain the impact of the despotic labour regime. The threat of solidarity strikes had, indeed, pressed both the PNDC and the

NDC governments to withdraw unpopular decisions and engage in dialogue with the TUC. And dialogue bought the TUC time and space to develop an organizational capacity as a unified force on behalf of the unionized workers in Ghana. The building of organizational strength took a variety of forms. In response to the decline in membership, the TUC attempted to "organize the unorganized" that is mainly senior staff, in the industrial and commercial sectors. In the period between January 1993 and July 1996, 27,568 senior staff were unionized for the first time and integrated into the TUC organizational structure on the basis of industrial sector affiliation. It responded to the financial challenge of lost 'dues-revenue' by mobilizing its members to contribute to the establishment of Labour-Owned Enterprises (LOE) which were expected to "create some jobs within the economy as well as enable unionized labour to have a relatively high intervention in the management of the economy".

Relations with other labour associations in the country were managed effectively. The structure of labour organized in Ghana, compared to Zambia's, was more liberalized. Labour *associations* existed as professional bodies independently of the TUC. Relations with the separate associations − civil servants, teachers, nurses and judicial service staff − were managed within the framework of a national consultative forum and the Tripartite fora which included the Committee on Wages and the Labour Advisory Council. Within the labour organizational framework, the TUC functioned as the coordinator of workers' groups and the facilitator of joint collaborative efforts to defend workers' rights (Akwetey, 1994). Beyond the labour organizations, links to other civil society groups such as the Ghana Bar Association and the media were strengthened. The establishment and operations of 'labour desks' in the various press houses since 1993 is indicative of improved ties with the journalists. The TUC campaigned to encourage and institutionalize a policy dialogue between government and broad sections of organized civil society in a "non-partisan national forum on the economy". It argued that such a gathering was needed "to establish a consensus on the management of the economy to arrest further deterioration of the state of affairs" (TUC, 5TH QC-EB Report, 1996).

The idea of the national economic forum materialized in May 1996 when, under the auspices of the Tripartite Committee, labour, business and other civil society actors such as the Bar and Journalist Associations met the government and the political parties to dialogue over the economy. In Ghana, the post-transition era was a period of strengthening the TUC and consolidating its organizational coherence. It enhanced its strength both in terms of its autonomy from the government and the political parties as well as in its ability to network with the broader labour movement and other civil society actors over matters requiring policy dialogue among stakeholders. Business has also been affected in identical ways by the despotic traits that constrained the democratic reform of the labour regime. Its access to spheres of high-level decision-making has also not been institutionalized beyond the tripartite fora (Tangri, 1993; Addison interviewed May, 1996).

Despite their common exclusion from high-level decision-making, labour and business in Ghana did not agree on the nature of the democratic reform of the labour regime required. In the prevailing situation, the government was to retain a sufficient scope for independent decision-making and increasingly pulled business towards its preferred labour regime by means of a privatization and investment policy that appeared attractive to business but not to labour. Ghana's post-transition experience suggests that the 'no political-alliance' strategy had yielded a relatively strong labour organization but that TUC, like the ZCTU of Zambia, had failed to achieve institutionalized representation in high-level decision-making.

CONCLUSION: DIVERSIFIED OUTCOMES AND COMMON IMPLICATIONS

Ghana's transition to formal political democracy in 1992 occurred after nearly a decade of structural adjustment. The experience differed from that of Zambia with respect to the sequence of political and economic reform. Whereas structural adjustment in Zambia was largely possible only after the transition to democracy, Ghana's economic reforms preceded democratization. Irrespective of the differences in the phased implementation of the adjustment programme in the two countries, their impact on trade union organization and the institutionalization of democratic dialogue in labour regime management appear to be similar. In both cases, trade unions lost members and financial subscriptions and continued to be marginalised in high-level decision-making over public policy choices. The quest by both the ZCTU and the TUC for democratic representation in high-level decision-making did not yield the expected results. Aspects of the despotism of the post-colonial labour regime persisted despite the transition to formal political democracy. The factor of organizational autonomy has become all the more critical as a vital precondition for an eventual democratization of despotic regimes.

In Zambia, the ZCTU's quest for autonomy appears to have been fatally compromised when it forged a political alliance with the MMD without clearly defining the nature of mutual commitments and sanctions for defecting from existing agreements. After taking considerable political risks in challenging the domination of the one party-state and successfully campaigning for multiparty democracy and a change of government, the ZCTU failed to achieve specific reforms of the labour regime. Rather, its leaders made the fatal mistake of negotiating away its most prized asset, that is the right to organize solidarity strikes in support of workers' rights when they were violated. The ZCTU experience shows that without the retention and defence of that right, trade unions would not be able to effectively resist despotic rule by a relatively powerful and resourceful government. The Ghanaian case instructively substantiates this point as it clearly shows how a credible ability to mobilize unionized workers and threaten a solidarity strike can function as a check on despotic rule and compel a restoration of the institutional framework for democratic dialogue albeit limited. Whereas the TUC's ability to periodically restrain the despotic management of the labour regime has been attributed to its organizational power, it has also been noted that the political and organizational autonomy does not necessarily secure an institutionalized position of democratic participation in high-level decision-making.

We have also argued that factors such as distribution of power, as well as the nature of ideology and technology shape the interests upon which specific regimes such as labour regimes are founded. It is evident that the most obvious change that has occurred in the nature of these factors in relation to the two countries is that of ideology. Nationalist ideology and the state-led development strategy, together with the resultant authoritarian regimes, have been repudiated while neo-liberal inspired market reforms and liberal democracy have been accepted and vigorously promoted by powerful external actors. These changes have led to the demise of the so-called post-colonial development coalitions and undermined the basis of the imaginary social contract that has informed the interpretation of the authoritarian relationship between the state and a frail civil society. Governments implementing structural adjustment programmes no longer perceived trade unions as their indispensable allies in development as those who wanted to build state-led socialism once did in the 1960s and 1970s. The repudiation of nationalist ideologies had a direct bearing on the formation of political coalitions. The dominant role of international actors, however, has not changed. International funding of the state has remained substantial and contributed considerably to its ability to make decisions independently of the claims of domestic actors. Governments could draw on the support of aid and a reduction in annual interest payments on debts to insulate its decision-making processes from labour and business interests.

The growing availability of external funding, and the deepening dependence of governments on that facility, constitute a real constraint on the ability of unions to influence government economic decisions. The evidence suggests that both trade unions and employers associations remain relatively weak as subordinate actors of the labour regimes. While governments may now appear to be more inclined to forming coalitions with business rather than with labour, its relations with subordinate actors in general is still not informed and shaped by any strong notion of social partnerships. The state has been able to act independently of labour and business and to occasionally play them against each other. Both sets of actors have been marginalised in structural adjustment decision-making in the two countries. The democratic reform of the despotic labour regimes has been further impeded by the subordinate actors' lack of joint strategies for pursuing reforms that enhance their power and substantially alter their relations with the government. Transition theory emphasizes the strategic importance of the capacity of trade unions to mobilize support for campaigns for transitions to democracy. The experiences of Zambia and Ghana make evident the fact that while the ability to mobilize can facilitate the transition to democracy, that organizational resource might not be sufficient to shape the specific reform of labour regime. Whether the consolidation of democratization processes in the wider society might also lead to the practical elimination of the despotic elements of the labour regimes remains an empirical question for the future.

REFERENCES

AKWETEY, E. O., (1995) "Democratization and Labour Regime Reform in Post-transition Africa", Paper for the Joint Workshop on *Labour Regimes and Liberalization: Restructuring State-Society Relations in Africa* (Harare, Institute of Development Studies, University of Zimbabwe).

— (1994) *Trade Unions and Democratization: A Comparative Study of Zambia and Ghana* (Stockholm, Stockholm University).

ALEXANDER, David, (1993) *Workers' Education and Political Change* (Occasional Paper No. 42, Institute of African Studies).

ARTHUR, S., (1993) "Co-ordination and Collaboration: Regimes in an Anarchic World", in David Baldwin (ed.) *Neorealism and Neoliberalism: The Contemporary Debate* (New York, Columbia University Press), 29-59.

AZARYA, V., (1988) "Reordering State-Society Relations: Incorporation and Disengagement", in D. Rothchild and N. Chazan (eds.) *Precarious Balance: State Society in Africa* (Boulder, Westview Press).

BANGURA, Y., (1992) "Authoritarian Rule and Democracy in Africa: A Theoretical Discourse", in P. Gibbon *et al.* (eds.) *Authoritarianism, Democracy and Adjustment: The Politics of Economic Reforms in Africa* (Uppsala, Nordiska Afrikainstitutet).

BANGURA, Y and B. BECKMAN, (1991) "African Workers and Structural Adjustment with a Nigerian Case Study", in D. Ghai *et al* (eds) *The IMF and the South: Social Impact of Crisis and Adjustment* (London, Zed Press).

BATES, R. H., (1971) *Unions, Parties, and Political Development: A Study of Mineworkers in Zambia* (New Haven and London, Yale University Press).

BECKMAN, B., (1988a) "The Post-Colonial State: Crisis and Reconstruction", *IDS Bulletin*, 19, (iv).

BIENEN, H. and J. Waterbury, (1989) "The Political Economy of Privatization in Developing Countries", *World Development*, 17, (v).

BRATTON, Michael and VAN DE WALLE, N, (July 1992) "Popular Protest and Reform in Africa", *Comparative Politics*, 24, (iv).

BRATTON, M., (1994) "Economic Crisis and Political Realignment in Zambia", in Jennifer A. Widner (ed.) *Economic Change and Political Liberalization in Sub-Saharan Africa* (London and Baltimore, Johns Hopkins University Press).

BURAWOY, M., (1985) *Politics of Production* (London, Verso).

— (1979) *Manufacturing Consent: Changes in the Labour Process Under Monopoly Capitalism* (Chicago and London, University of Chicago Press).

CALLAGHY, T. M., (1989) "Lost Between State and Market — The Politics of Economic Adjustment in Ghana, Zambia and Nigeria", in Joan M. Nelson (ed.) *Economic Crisis and Policy Choice: The Politics of Structural Adjustment in the Third World* (Princeton, Princeton University Press).

DANSEREAU, Suzanne, (Sept., 1995) "Unions in Southern Africa: Structural Adjustment and Reorganization", *South African Labour Bulletin*, 19 (iv).

DAVIES, I., (1966) *African Trade Unions* (Harmondsworth, Penguin).

DUTKIEWICZ, P. and G. WILLIAMS, (1987) "All the Kings Horses and All the King's Men Couldn't Put Humpty Dumpty Together", *IDS Bulletin*, 18 (iii).

GERTZEL, C., (1984) "Dissent and Authority in the Zambian One-Party State", in C. Gertzel, C. Baylies, and M. Szefte (eds.) *The Dynamics of the One Party State in Zambia* (Manchester, Manchester University Press).

GUPTA, A., (1974) "Trade Unionism and Politics in the Copperbelt", in W. Tordoff (ed.) *Politics in Zambia* (Manchester, Manchester University Press).

HAVNEVIK, K. ed., (1987) *The IMF and the World Bank in Africa. Conditionality, Impact and Alternatives* (Uppsala, Nordiska Afrikainstitutet).

HUNTINGTON, S. P., (1991) *The Third Wave: Democratization in Late Twentieth Century* (Norman and London, University of Oklahoma Press).

HUTCHFUL, E., (1989) "From Revolution to Monetarism: The Economics and Politics of Structural Adjustment in Ghana" in B. K. Campbell and J. Loxley (eds.) *Structural Adjustment in Africa* (London, MacMillan Press).

JAMAL, V. and J. WEEKS, (1988) "The Vanishing Rural-Urban Gap in Sub-Saharan Africa" in *International Labour Review*, 127 (iii).

LOXLEY, John, 1994) "Rural Labour Markets in a Mineral Economy", in V. Jamal (ed.) *Structural Adjustment and Rural Labour Markets in Africa* (New York, St Martin's Press).

MAREE, Johann, (June 1982) "Democracy and Oligarchy in Trade Unions: The Independent Trade Unions in the Transvaal and the Western Province General Workers' Union in the 1970s", *Social Dynamics*, 8, (i), 41-52.

MARTIN, R. M., (1989) *Trade Unions: Purpose and Forms* (Oxford, Clarendon Press).

MBIKUSITA-LEWANIKA and C. CHITALA (ed.), (1990) *The Hour Has Come: Proceedings of the National Conference on Multi-Party Option* (Lusaka, Zambia Research Foundation).

MEEBELO, H. S., (1986) *African Proletarians and Colonial Capitalism* (Lusaka, Kenneth Kaunda Foundation).

MWANAKATWE, John M., (1994) *End of Kaunda Era* (Lusaka, Multimedia Zambia).

NINSIN, K., (1988) "In Precarious Balance: State and Society in Africa", in D. Rothchild and N. Chazan (eds.) *Precarious Balance: State and Society in Africa* (Boulder, Westview Press).

PETTMAN, J., (1974) *Zambia: Security and Conflict* (Sussex, Julian Friedmann Publishers).

PRZEWORSKI, A., (1992) *Democracy and the Market: Political and Economic Reforms in Eastern Europe and Latin America* (Cambridge, Cambridge University Press).

RASMUSSEN, T., (1974) "The Popular Basis of Anti-Colonial Protests", in W. Tordoff, (ed.) *Politics in Zambia* (Manchester, Manchester University Press).

ROTHCHILD, D. and N. CHAZAN (eds.) (1985) *Precarious Balance: State and Society in Africa* (Boulder, Westview Press).

SANDBROOK, R., (1985) *The Politics of Africa's Stagnation* (Cambridge, Cambridge University Press).

SCHMITTER, P. C., (1974) "Still the Century of Corporatism", *Review of Politics*, Vol. 36.

SKLAR, R. L., (1975) *Corporate Power in an African State: The Political Impact of Multinational Mining Companies in Zambia* (Berkeley and Los Angeles and London, University of California Press).

SIMUTANYI, N., (27 April-2 May, 1995) "The Politics of Structural Adjustment in Zambia", Paper presented to the Workshop on *Governance and Economic Policy Making* (ECPR Joint Sessions of Workshops, Bordeaux, France).

— (26 June-2 July, 1995) "Political Opposition and Democracy in Zambia: Problems and Prospects", *8th CODESRIA General Assembly on Crisis, Conflicts and Transformation Responses and Perspectives* (Dakar).

SORENSEN, G., (1993) *Democracy and Democratization* (Boulder, Westview Press).

TRANGRI, R., (1992) "The Politics of Government-Business Relations in Ghana", The *Journal of Modern African Studies*, 30, (i), 97-111.

TORDOFF, W. and R. MOLTENO, (1974) "Cleavage and Conflict in Zambian Politics: A Study in Sectionalism", in W. Tordof (ed.) *Politics in Zambia* (Manchester, Manchester University Press).

TORDOFF, W. (ed.) (1974) *Politics in Zambia* (Manchester, Manchester University Press).

VALENZUELA, J. S., (July 1989) "Labour Movement in Transitions to Democracy", *Comparative Politics*, 445-471.

ZCTU Files etc

(1992) Minutes of the General Council Meeting, Katilungu House (Kitwe, 18 October).

(1994) Submission of the ZCTU to the Zambian Constitutional Review Commission (29 September).

(1994) Report of the Secretary General, 9th Quadrennial Congress, QC/D No. 1, 2 and 3 (Livingstone, 26th-29th October).

(1996) ZCTU Chairman-General's Introductory Remarks, The Tripartite Consultative Labour Council Meeting (Lusaka, 18 January).

(1996) Minister of Labour and Social Security's Speech, The Tripartite Consultative Labour Council Meeting (Lusaka, 18 January).

(1996) ZFE Representative's Speech, The Tripartite Consultative Labour Council Meeting (Lusaka, 18 January).

(1996) Split Within the ZCTU: An Account of the Events as They Happened Before, During and after the 9th Quadrennial Congress in 1994 (Kitwe, ZCTU).

Labour and Industrial Relations Act (1993) (Lusaka, The Government Printer).

"Zambia, Implementation of Economic Recovery Programme — Efforts and Policies" (Report Presented to the Consultative Group for Zambia; 6-7 April 1993, Government of Zambia).

Times of Zambia.

Interview with Secretary-General and others (January-February 1996, Kitwe, Zambia).

Trade Union Congress Files

Trade Union Congress (Ghana), Report of the Executive Board (1st September 1992-7th June 1996, The 5th Quadrennial Delegates Congress, University of Cape Coast).

Interview with Secretary-General and others (August 1996, Accra, Ghana).

CHAPTER THREE

Cooptation, Control and Resistance: The State and the Nigeria Labour Congress

YAHAYA HASHIM

One Country, One Federation
One Industry, One Union
(COSATU, December 1985)

INTRODUCTION: STATE AND TRADE UNIONS IN CONTEXT

This chapter is an attempt to understand the labour regime established in Nigeria between 1975 and 1978. The point of focus is the relationship between the two most important parties that created that labour regime, namely the state and the trade unions. The second half of the 1970s heralded the first post-oil boom crisis in Nigeria. The unprecedented flow of foreign exchange that accompanied the oil boom was followed by a balance of payments crisis and inflationary pressures by the second half of the decade, necessitating stabilization measures by the then military regime under Generals Murtala and later Obasanjo. At about the same time the labour movement was also experiencing important shifts. Price inflation led to agitation for a wage review especially in the public sector, leading to the setting up of the Udoji Commission. The implementation of its recommendations in 1974/1975 led to a mass strike movement which was beyond the control of the unions (Peace, 1975). It compelled the then four labour federations into uniting in one union centre in December 1975 which the government failed to recognise, engineering instead another federation in 1978. It facilitated the formation of 'one union one industry' in the form of 42 industrial unions which replaced the hundreds of previous house unions. Changes were also made to other institutions of conflict resolution and industrial relations. The resulting labour regime has been referred to as corporatism in the literature (Onimode, 1982; Waterman, 1982; Lubeck, 1986; Fashoyin, 1990). This contribution, which draws largely on my 1994 thesis (Hashim, 1994), questions this characterization which tends to exaggerate the element of state incorporation, centralization and bureaucracy while underestimating the extent to which the new unitary labour regime was a product of aspirations within the labour movement itself.

By 1980 another influx of petrodollars was experienced, soon followed by a more enduring decline with major balance of payments deficit, a fall in manufacturing output and capacity utilisation, and a rise in unemployment. Price inflation, a crushing debt burden, and shortages became the norm. After two changes of political regimes, one in 1983 and another in 1985, a neo-liberal response to the economic and social decline was attempted in the form of a Structural Adjustment Programme (SAP), backed by the Bretton Woods institutions. The aim was to replace the state-driven development approach by a market-led one. It involved the de-nationalisation of policy making with policy dialogue becoming a transaction between the state and its international donors and creditors, further constraining the scope for the more participatory type of policy bargaining which a corporatist model would suggest.

Many of the current attempts at re-conceptualising the state in Africa have tended to be narrow and limited (see Beckman, 1988; Glickman, 1988, for a review). They are often snapshot views that isolate moments from complex processes. Such attempts have therefore not been very helpful to our understanding of the reconstruction of state-union relations. The literature on state-civil society relations has been more useful in this regard. However, there are two problems with this literature. The first is that state and society tend to be presented in binary opposition and a solid wall is often built between them (for a discussion see Beckman, 1993; Akwetey, 1994; Hashim, 1994). Secondly, there is a tendency to approach issues as if the state is a monolithic entity. However, both state and society are constituted by a variety of interests and there are different discourses for the different state-society relations.

In this contribution some of these problems are avoided by focusing on a specific state-society relation — that of state and trade unions — and by the use of corporatism as the framework of analysis. Corporatism poses no sharp divide between state and society, not even in advanced capitalist countries. On the contrary, it assumes an intricate and close link depending on the degree of incorporation. As a theoretical perspective therefore, corporatism is useful in the analysis of social formations, as found in Africa, where the state society divide is even more blurred than usual. This is probably why corporatism has become a common way of characterising state-union relations and sometimes even of state-society relations by scholars working on Africa (see for example Waterman, 1982; Shaw, 1982; Callaghy, 1984; Lubeck, 1986; Nyang'oro, 1987; 1989; Nyang'oro and Shaw, 1989; Fashoyin, 1990).

However, the literature on corporatism in Africa suffers from several problems. Writers assume that the phenomenon they are talking about in the African context is corporatism and proceed to discuss its variations between countries. The relevance of the concept is taken as given or self-evident. In contrast to 'societal-corporatism', reference is commonly made to 'state-corporatism' synonymous with state control of interest organisations, particularly of trade unions, drawing on the early literature on state-trade union relations in Africa where these were seen as essentially a matter of state control. This focus has continued to inform analysis even when the concept of corporatism was introduced. The empirical evidence and the theoretical premises are often weak. There is also a lack of understanding of the way in which the neo-liberal thrust has further undermined whatever element of corporatism that may have been there in the first place (for a general discussion of the African corporatist literature see Hashim, 1994).

This case study of the state and the Nigeria Labour Congress (NLC) seeks to challenge some of the assumptions on which such uncritical application of the concept of corporatism to Africa seems to be based. It seeks to distil some core aspects associated with the notion of a corporatist labour regime in the most authoritative literature, and operationalise and test them in the Nigerian case. To what extent has the Nigerian labour movement been incorporated and controlled by the state? Does it make sense to characterise the relation in corporatist terms? How has it been affected by economic liberalisation?

CORPORATISM AND SOCIAL ENQUIRY

Corporatism or neo-corporatism, as it is sometimes called in order to distinguish it from similar authoritarian practices in fascist regimes, is considered to be both a system of interest intermediation and a form of policy formation (Cawson, 1986). The emphasis in the literature is on interest organisation and representation (see the collections of Schmitter and Lehmbruch, 1979; Lehmbruch and Schmitter, 1982; Malloy, 1977; Collier, 1979). The most cited and most authoritative conceptualisation is one by Schmitter who termed it:

> A system of interest representation in which the constituent units are organised into a limited number of singular, compulsory, non-competitive, hierarchically ordered and functionally differentiated categories, recognised or licensed (if not created) by the state and granted a deliberate representational monopoly within their respective categories in exchange for observing certain controls on their selection of leaders and articulation of demands and supports (Schmitter, 1979b, 13).

Although Schmitter's definition refers to an ideal-typical corporatism, it has nevertheless provided the major indicators used in empirical studies of corporatist labour regimes especially from the intermediation school (see the studies of Wilensky, 1976; Schmitter, 1981; Schmidt, 1982; Streeck, 1982; Helander, 1982; and Cameroon, 1984). These indicators include a form of interest organisation (trade union) that is highly concentrated (that is monopolistic, centralised and bureaucratic), a state license or even the direct involvement of the state in creating the organization, and an exchange between state and the organization that involves restraints on the side of the latter.

Organizational concentration is the main aspect of the structure of union systems that is emphasised in the literature and it has been subdivided into monopoly, centralization and bureaucratization. The theoretical deduction made is that monopolistic unions ensure that all members of a sector are included in a corporatist bargain (often tripartite) and can be disciplined to comply with bargain outcomes without the threat of another union in the wings. Centralisation concentrates power in the hands of those who do the bargaining and disciplining while bureaucratization ensures that professional and technocratic competence is brought into the process.

Organizational concentration and restrained or even compliant behaviour on the part of the interest organisations are the distinguishing characteristics and the pre-requisite for corporatism (state or societal) and thus central to the theory. Therefore to ascertain whether or not the labour regime established in Nigeria between 1976 and 1978 was corporatist as is generally claimed, it is necessary to establish in the first instance the extent to which it was characterized by concentration, that is (a) monopoly (b) centralisation and (c) bureaucratization in the trade unions. Secondly, the significance of these three variables, even where they exist, for a corporatist labour regime has to be established. Using this analytical framework we can therefore seek insight into state-union relations in Nigeria and the resultant nature of the labour regime, from the earliest period of the economic crisis to the point when the neo-liberal policies of SAP were introduced and pursued.

CORPORATISM AND MONOPOLY

After the Nigerian civil war in 1970, the reconstruction and rehabilitation that followed was largely successful due to the oil boom. The Nigerian economy expanded rapidly. Its lapse into instability in the second half of the 1970s led to a change in political regime in the country and to a programme of rationalization. This extended to important institutions in society including the civil service and the trade unions. The manifold trade union system was replaced with monopolistic unions, an important requirement of a corporatist labour regime, in a state-led reform of the trade union movement.

Monopoly was established without significant dissension. A single union structure consisting of one union federation and 42 industrial unions was established by a government administrative and legal procedure following the unprecedented state intervention in the internal affairs of the unions between 1975 and 1978. This was enshrined in the trade union decree No. 22 of 1978 which amended decree No. 31 of 1973. The state intervention has been discussed in detail elsewhere (Hashim, 1987, 1994; Sachikonye, 1981; Eze, 1981; Umoh, 1980; Zasha, 1985). It can briefly be recounted here that the four central labour organizations which existed up to the first half of the 1970s voluntarily gave up their existence to come together, in December 1975, to form one central labour organization — the Nigeria Labour Congress (NLC) — the second to be called by that name in Nigeria's labour history. This followed the Apena Cemetery Declaration of September 1974 in which the leaders of the then existing four union centres who met to bury a colleague pledged to work for unity. They subsequently scheduled a congress for December 1975. The reason for the Apena Declaration can be found not only in the desire for unity but also in the independent pressure from workers for action over the government Udoji wage awards.

However, at the time of the coming together of the four union federations, in December 1975, the compromises required and the forces to be balanced proved too overwhelming as was indeed the case in the previous attempts at trade union unity. Thus the leaders met before the unity congress and drew up a slate of who will get which post at the 'elections'. Over 100 leaders were 'elected' at the inauguration in 1975. This led to protest from some union activists from across the four union federations, who considered the 'election' fraudulent and they unwittingly invited the new nationalistic military regime of Generals Murtala/Obasanjo to intervene. When the regime intervened it used these invitations as part of its justification. It not only refused to recognize the new union centre formed, but it also promulgated a decree (No. 44 of 1976) which banned the four centres that formed it and provided for the appointment of an administrator to oversee the affairs of the affiliate trade unions, rationalize them, and arrange for them to form another new centre. The government also set up a judicial commission of enquiry to investigate the banned union centres and their officers.

In the end, over 1,000 unions (mainly house unions) were organized into 42 industrial unions and a new centre, the third Nigeria Labour Congress, was formed all under the procedure stipulated by the government administrator. An automatic check-off system of dues payment as well as the compulsory recognition of unions were also instituted. This was codified in decrees No. 21 and 22 of 1978. The new central labour organization, the Nigeria Labour Congress, was named in the law and a schedule listing the member unions was included. These too were formed following the interventions of 1975-1978 and can therefore be said to be also state licensed or even created by the state. An important requirement for a corporatist labour regime seemed therefore to have been satisfied. However, the significance of such monopoly and of state licensed or created unions for state-union relations was not obvious. Two questions need to be addressed: (a) To what extent was the monopolistic union-system actually state imposed? and (b) To what extent did it produce compliant unions?

The monopolistic features of the new system cannot be explained primarily in terms of state imposition. They responded to pressures within the union movement itself. The decision to opt for one federation rather than a plural union system had already been taken by the unions themselves before the state intervened. The subject of controversy inside the union movement was the issue of leadership selection and the allegations of its non-democratic determination and not the philosophy of the unitary union system as such. This was the basis on which some union activists called for state intervention and it was the basis on which state officials claimed they intervened. Even the judicial inquiry into union affairs was justified on this basis (Adefope, 21 May 1976).

It was in the light of the above that the trade union leaders deliberately switched from a feeble opposition to state intervention, to active collaboration in the construction of the new union system. Those leaders who were interviewed preferred to view the restructuring as a state initiative that the union leaders took over and changed to their own long-sought programme of consolidation and unification. This might be an exaggeration as neither the unionists nor the state officials had their way completely in the restructuring. On some issues of dispute between the administrator and trade unionists the state ruled — though it did rule on the side of the unionists as well (Abiodun, 1978, 22). Waterman (1983) has pointed to the outcome of the rationalization of the dock industry which divided the unions into three so-called industrial unions and he questions the interests it served to divide workers that way. However, many union leaders regarded the outcome of the rationalization as a victory and something they had wanted for a long time.

Since the first trade union centre was established in 1943 and its subsequent break up, unions have repeatedly sought to unite in one centre more permanently. Ananaba (1969), Cohen (1971) and Otobo (1986) have all recorded the many attempts at unity, all of which failed. The division of the international trade union movement in 1949 and the cold war that followed reinforced the division in the Nigerian movement and the trade union internationals effectively used their financing capacity to maintain clients in Nigeria (ATR, 1977; Otobo, 1986). However, one conference resolution after another proposed unity and called for 'one industry one union' as a structure. As can be seen from the slogan from the Congress of South African Trade Unions (Cosatu) in December 1985, as quoted at the outset of this chapter, this urge was not limited to Nigerian unions. Cosatu at its very first congress adopted the same principle of 'one country one federation and one industry one union' and has since then rationalized its 35 affiliates to 12 industrial unions. Indeed Baskin (1991, 257) reports that 'by mid-1987, almost all Cosatu affiliates were committed in principle to centralised bargaining and participation in industrial councils'. Similarly as Bianchi (1986, 435) noted in Egypt:

> ... many labour leaders had been demanding greater centralization for years but Nasser's belated and ambivalent agreement in 1957 to permit the establishment of the Egyptian Confederation of Labour was ... delayed and nearly abandoned in Egypt when Nasser was confronted with strong police and military objections to the sudden concentration of union power.

Another reason why the single union system cannot be considered as having been simply state imposed was the fact that in times of crisis, unity had tended to be forced on Nigerian union leaders from the grassroots. Thus, 'Joint Action Committees' and other forms of coming together used to be established, though grassroots pressure to continue with the experiment after solving the immediate problem had not been successful (Cohen, 1974, 92). The 1975 NLC was in this respect only the latest in that long series of attempts at unity. It was an outcome of the independent and united action of workers across the federations during the Udoji strikes. It failed partly because of state hostility and largely because of the trade union movement's inability to handle — decisively and democratically — the internal dissensions and compromises required. That is probably why resistance to state intervention was not very dramatic but rather passive. A switch of tactics occurred in response to the state programme. Some of the unionists saw the state-sponsored restructuring as the chance to solve the problems of unity and finance, the two primary problems that writers have repeatedly noted as plaguing the trade union movement in Nigeria and elsewhere in Africa.

It is doubtful that the state-led rationalization would have succeeded without the cooperation of the trade union movement. The experiences from the second state intervention in 1988 seems supportive of this view. While the intervention on that occasion had many features in common with that of the late 1970s, the response was quite different. In 1988, as the government occupied the headquarters of the NLC and appointed an administrator to carry out its duties, most of the industrial unions refused to cooperate. For the initial duration of his assignment, the state administrator achieved nothing. The unions carried out a general strike which forced the government to recognize the fact that it could not determine matters unilaterally (Beckman, 1995). Moreover, when the mandate of the administrator was extended to include another rationalization of the unions, some unions refused and state officials were obliged to accept a court ruling against the plan. After the administrator's period was over and a new compromise leadership was installed in January 1989, the NLC produced a rationalization plan of its own, seeking to reduce the number of industrial unions through mergers and internal restructuring.

State intervention did not produce a compliant NLC and centrally controlled industrial unions. Indeed, shortly after the 1978 inauguration of the NLC, it was embroiled in a struggle against its 'creator'. It threatened to disrupt the programme for return to party politics in 1979 with its ultimatum to the Federal Government (in May 1979) to restore vehicle loans and transport allowances to employees, approve all pending negotiated agreements from the private sector, as the law required, and to repeal all punitive labour decrees. The military government was forced to respond and the Minister of Labour himself entered into negotiations and agreement with the unions before the expiry of the ultimatum. By the time the civilian regime was inaugurated in October 1979, or even earlier, serious considerations were entertained in government circles about breaking up the NLC. State officials tolerated or facilitated the establishment of a nucleus of a rival centre, the 'Centre for Democratic Trade Unions', contrary to the law setting up a single union system. A bill by one Senator Ibrahim Dimis of the governing party, National Party of Nigeria (NPN), was sponsored in parliament with the intention of removing the legal provision for monopoly. In response, unions campaigned intensely, including lobbying the OAU and OATUU, to protect the unity which they had achieved through state intervention barely three years earlier (see the NLC leaflet 'The Need to Sustain One Central Labour Organisation in Nigeria, 1981).

State licensed monopoly did not lead to state control of the trade unions or to union compliance as seems to be assumed in theories of corporatism. For the unions, monopoly was primarily a matter of unity and capacity for collective action, organization and finance. This was the reason why many unions in Africa, including Cosatu of South Africa, wanted it and this was why Nigerian unions collaborated with the state when it was introduced. While unity has come about 'voluntarily' in some countries and through state intervention in others, this can be seen more as a product of differences in historical experience. Its significance, as the Nigeria case has shown, is not simply one of co-optation or control.

CORPORATISM AND CENTRALISATION: UNION FINANCE AND THE AUTOMATIC CHECK-OFF

In corporatist labour regimes, centralisation of organisational and decision making structures is supposed to allow the monopolistic unions to exercise control over the constituent members and thus allowing for the state devolution of public policy-making that is associated with the corporatist model. Centralisation is often measured by the presence or absence of unitary or federal features. Common practices in Latin America and Africa include not only (a) the centralisation of union structure but also (b) centralisation of dues collection or check-off, (c) centralisation of decision-making and (d) centralisation of representation at negotiation. These practices are often regulated by law.

The two common central trade union structures among African trade unions are the federal and the unitary structures. Nigeria has the federal structure. In the unitary set up, the national unions or sectoral branches are controlled from the office of the central organisation. Indeed, they are often departments of the central union in charge of sectors of the national economy. In Tanzania, for instance, JUWATA had seven sectoral departments while UGTA of Algeria and ETU of Ethiopia had nine each. Sometimes the integration and supervision of the sectoral unions by the centre is even manifested in the physical sense that they are all located within one building. In Nigeria there were at first 42 affiliated industrial unions, all clearly distinguishable from the NLC and from each other.

Their identity, finance, and organization were not dependent on the centre. Instead it was the other way round. Their separateness was underlined by the state when in 1988 it did not interfere with the industrial unions while banning the NLC leaders and taking over their offices. In the 1994 intervention, the NLC and one of its affiliates, the oil workers' union (NUPENG) were banned while none of the other affiliate unions were affected.

The state legislated an automatic check-off payment of union fees with a provision for individual union members to opt out by signing a declaration to that effect. The industrial relations department of the NLC recorded very few cases of members signing out. It certainly represented some form of centralisation as compared to the pre-restructuring situation. At that time, union officials had to go directly to the workers to canvass for union dues. The union officials with whom we discussed this, recalled that period with animation, how little they were usually able to collect, and how each dues collection tended to turn into a confrontation with the workers who had to be convinced that they should be paying the union dues. Since the automatic check-off, managements simply deducted from the members' wages what was due to the unions and signed a cheque for that amount. The cheques were issued in the name of the national industrial union which retained the greater part and distributed the rest to the branches, the state councils, and to the NLC according to the union's constitutional formula (see Table 1).

Table 1: Dues Sharing Among Union Levels in Nigeria

Unions	Retained %	Branch %	State %	NLC %
1. Road transport	75	5	10	10
2. Public corporations	65	15	10	10
3. Hotels	70	10	10	10
4. Automobile	80	5	5	10
5. Footwear	70	10	10	10
6. Textile	78	10	2	10

Source: The various union constitutions and Aremu (1991, 13)

This arrangement strengthened the national unions against the branches, giving them first access to dues (disbursement powers) and allowing them to retain the greater portion. However, branch leaders were needed for the collection of the cheques from managements and delay and obstruction in passing them on were common. Branch leaders insisted that only they should be allowed to collect the cheques. In this way they acquired a 'withholding power', countering the disbursement power of the national officials. An employer who was interviewed spoke of the difficulty of keeping both branch and national union officials happy. In the case of his company, a strategy had evolved in which the company handed over the cheque to the branch officials while simultaneously notifying the national union.

Corporatist analysis tends to focus on labour centres as the political arm of the unions and thus as the vehicle and target for state control (see, for instance, Adu-Amankwah, 1990, on the experience of Ghanaian unions in this respect). The lack of NLC control over the system of check-off payments does not fit this assumed corporatist logic. There was no centralization of dues collection under the Nigerian system. Table 1 shows how limited was the NLC's share of the check-off. The industrial unions got the lion's share and, even more importantly, they, not the NLC, had the power of disbursement. The NLC's 10 per cent share may be compared to what was paid to other union centres in Africa. Moreover, these other national centres collected their own share directly at source and were thus not dependent on their affiliates. Some even collected all the dues, having the power of disbursement. The NLC had none of these possibilities as Table 2 indicates.

Table 2: Extent of Trade Union Centres' Financial Independence from Affiliates

Union centres	% of Union dues to centre powers	Disbursement dues at source	Can collect
JUWATA (Tanzania)	100%	Yes	Yes
ETU (Ethiopia)	50%	Yes	Yes
ZCTU (Zambia)	30%	No	Yes
TUC (Ghana)	30%	No	Yes
NLC (Nigeria)	10%	No	No

Source: Union constitutions and African Trade union officers

The NLC depended on the goodwill of the industrial unions for its funding. Even the ten per cent could not be relied upon as many unions withheld their payments altogether while others paid less than what was stipulated in the constitution. This made the question of membership dues a recurring source of acrimony in the union movement, especially during periods of approaching congresses as such payments were a basis for determining the number of delegates and votes assigned to each union. They also affected the distribution of foreign scholarships and training opportunities. Table 3 was computed on the basis of figures compiled by the NLC's Finance Department for discussion at the second NEC meeting in 1984. As can be seen from the Table, over 700 months' dues were owed to NLC by its affiliates and only four out of a total of 44 had paid their dues in full. The situation did not change much after 1984 and the non-payment of dues continued to be contentious.

Table 3: No. of Unions Owing the NLC and No. of Months Owed as at 30/6/1984

Number of months owed	0	1-5	6-18	24-66	1-66
Number of unions owing	(4)*	12	15	13	40
Total months owed	0	31	124	583	738

Fully paid from inception to 30/6/1984
Source: Computed from figures obtained from NLC secretariat

The failure to pay the NLC its share of union dues greatly undercut the financial position of the labour centre, undermining whatever role it was supposed to play in a corporatist arrangement. Many of the industrial unions were financially stronger and much better staffed and organized, as in the case, for instance, of the Civil Service Technical Workers Union (CSTWU), Textile Workers Union (NUTGTWN), and the Bank Workers (NUBIFIYE). Their officers were also better paid. The conclusion that can be drawn from this evidence is that, in the Nigerian case, state-legislated check-off payment of union dues did not lead to the centralization which is commonly assumed in the corporatist literature.

DECISION MAKING AND REPRESENTATION

In terms of centralization of decision-making, the NLC is a poor example of the assumed corporatist logic. The national centre had very limited control over the industrial unions and there were strong features of a collective leadership and representation. The national decision-making structures were enshrined in Article 5 of the NLC constitution (as amended in 1984), consisting of:
— The Congress-in-Session.
— The National Executive Council (NEC).
— The Central Working Committee (CWC).
— The National Administrative Council (NAC).
   The NLC had branches in nearly all the current 30 states of Nigeria which were called State Councils and had their own decision making organs. The 'Congress-in-Session' met every four years from 1984, being the highest decision making organ and responsible for the general policy of the movement. The congresses were the occasion for election of leaders and therefore noted for fierce competition between contending groups (broadly left and right) with a long history of their own in the union movement. Congresses tended to be preoccupied more with such power struggles and less, and mostly only indirectly, with contentious issues as is apparent from the extensive coverage offered by Nigerian dailies and weeklies (see, for example, media reports in February and March 1978, 1981, 1984 and 1988).
   The task of debating substantial policy issues was left to other organs. The NEC, which met at least twice a year, consisted of all the elected officials of the

NLC, the Presidents and General Secretaries of the industrial unions, the chairmen and secretaries of the state councils as well as the principal officers of the national secretariat who were non-voting members. There were specific decisions like general strikes, appointments, the firing and discipline of principal secretariat staff, budgets etc that were the primary domain of the NEC (see NLC Constitution as amended in 1984, Articles 6 and 7). Probably the most critical decision-making organ was the Central Working Committee (CWC), consisting of any one of the two NEC members of each affiliated industrial union, the elected officials of the NLC, as well as the principal officers of the national secretariat as non-voting members. It met at least once a month. The National Administrative Council (NAC) was the primary decision-making organ from which the national officers, including the President, operated. It consisted of the national officers and the principal full-time officers of the secretariat, that is, the Secretary General, the deputies, and the heads of departments. The NAC would normally meet at least twice a month and was essentially an administrative body. However, it had greater influence than that, given its power to set agenda, prepare briefs, position papers and meetings and to make decisions that required immediate response.

There was an articulated policy of abiding by the 'principle of collective leadership'. It had two important aspects. First, no NLC President or principal officer was supposed to enter into discussions with officials of the state or the employers' organizations on their own, even on minor issues. At least two or three colleagues were expected to be present. In the case of major issues, as for instance relating to the tabling of union demands or the negotiations that would follow, the CWC would be constituted into a delegation (as a constitutional right) for the purpose of the discussions. Such a delegation would always include national officers, both of the NLC and the industrial unions. The delegations often consisted of more than 20 members, to the annoyance of state officials. The leadership was not supposed to make any commitment in the course of such discussions without referring the offer or understanding reached to the CWC for endorsement. This second aspect was instituted more firmly in a dramatic manner in 1981. On 11 May 1981, a general strike was started by the NLC to back a demand for a minimum wage increase, among other things. On the second day of the strike, the government called for a negotiated settlement and an NLC delegation reached an agreement which all the parties signed. However, when the delegation returned to a waiting CWC meeting and informed it of the agreement reached, the CWC members rejected it as inadequate and chastised the leadership for signing without reference to the CWC. The members threatened to continue the strike and dared the NLC leadership to call it off if it was foolish enough to think that it could do that on its own. In the end, the CWC accepted the agreement but the lesson was learnt.

Collective leadership made it more difficult for state officials to co-opt key individual leaders in a informal clientelistic manner and thus undermine union demands. There is much evidence to suggest that state officials kept on attempting to establish such personal relations. For instance, when Chiroma was first elected national president of the NLC in 1984, he had a lot of conflict with the national administrative council (NAC) which sought to uphold NLC traditions in this respect. The conflicts, which were documented in NAC minutes, were over whether the President could consult with the Minister of Labour alone when seeking to thrash out issues of concern to the trade unions. The NAC insisted as a matter of principle that this should never be done, while the President thought he was not being trusted. The government sought to encourage direct, informal channels to the NLC Presidents. Brigadier Omojokun, when Minister of Labour, once advised a limited audience of trade unionists that an arrangement should be made for the NLC President to play tennis with the President of Nigeria for this purpose. He also suggested that the NLC President should tell him, informally, whenever he travelled outside the country and where he was going. These attempts by the government to establish personal avenues to the NLC leaders were intensified in the early 1990s while the NLC organs struggled to uphold the principles of collective leadership. Government officials kept being frustrated with the intimidating size of the NLC delegations to meetings and tried to prescribe, in their letters of invitation, an upper limit to the participants, using lack of space in committee rooms as a poor excuse. One NLC president also revealed that a government spokesman had told him that it was no point continuing discussion with him because he was unable to commit the NLC without consulting the organs of the Congress. What was the point, he asked, for the government to create one national union centre if it was unable to facilitate quick decisions.

The principle of collective leadership had a limiting effect on 'back door deals' and greatly facilitated transparency. Simultaneously, the low level of centralization in decision-making made the NLC less suitable for the role of transmission belt for state policies on the lines expected from national union centres in the corporatist model, at least of the state corporatist type. Having said this, the influence of the national officers and especially of the President of NLC, as a full-timer and the most visible single figure of the trade union in public media, should not be under-estimated. However, the NLC constitution sought to ensure that he would not be able to hold on to office, limiting his tenure to a period of four years. It can be concluded that the NLC was not characterized by the centralization of decision-making and representation typical of the state corporatist model. It had no control over the affiliated unions and their right to decide on industrial action or negotiation on their own. To achieve such control had clearly been an important objective of the ventures in corporatist direction attempted in other African countries. In Zambia, for instance, affiliated unions needed the approval of ZCTU for a number of decisions including the decision to embark on a strike or hold a strike ballot (rule 3g of the ZCTU Constitution). In Tunisia, a strike was illegal unless it had been approved by the only union centre — the UGTT (ILO Report of the Committee of Experts, 1985). Similarly, as Schiphost (1984, 4) has observed, national union negotiations in Ghana had to be carried out through the TUC. In Congo, the 1975 Labour Code provided that the decisions of the national centre superseded those of lower level organisations (ILO Report of the Committee of Experts 1986, convention 87). In other cases, affiliated unions had no powers whatsoever to decide or carry out any industrial action without the approval of the centre. None of these constraints had to be faced by the industrial unions in Nigeria. Indeed, as was shown above, the opposite was the case. The NLC could not call a strike or negotiate without the approval of the industrial unions, and only through the appropriate organs constitutionally so empowered, while the industrial unions were free to call a strike and represent their members as they saw fit. Whether in terms of check-off payments, decision-making or representation, the NLC could not be said to be regulating the activities of its member unions — it was the latter who exercised control not only of their own affairs but of those of the NLC as well.

BUREAUCRATIZATION

The third and final aspect of concentration to be considered here is the question of trade union bureaucracy, which has been a central feature of the state corporatist argument. What is suggested in the literature is basically that the corporatist arrangement facilitates the emergence of a centralized, bureaucratic structure, serving the purposes of government control and regulation while constraining or eliminating autonomy and participation from below. In the Nigerian case, 'bureaucratization' has been commonly used to characterise and explain union structures and their behaviour, actions and inaction, in the period after the restructuring of trade of 1978. Van Hear (1988, 159), for instance, talks of the 'centralization and bureaucratization of the labour movement' and argues that 'this hierarchically structured, bureaucratically managed labour movement contrasts with labour activity in the early 1970s which was carried on by more autonomous, accountable and local level unions and strike committees geared to local needs'. Primarily cited or implied as the proof of such bureaucratization seems to be the presence of more full-time staff engaged in regular office work, producing reports, accounts, minutes from meetings etc. Some of this is certainly more prevalent, for instance, regular correspondence with managements and government. Non-elected officials also do play a greater role than before 1978. For instance, in December 1988, full-time officials of the industrial unions, like Pascal Bafyau, Adams Oshiomhole, and E. U. Ijeh were for the first time elected to positions of national officers. At the State Council level, full-time union officers were also those most likely to be able to combine NLC work with other industrial union responsibilities. The spontaneous rallies and demonstrations of the 1950s and 1960s have become less common. Unionists claim that 'the days of table banging unionism are over' and argue that this has been replaced by responsible, 'scientific unionism'.

To what extent does such evidence of bureaucratization also suggest the emergence of bureaucratic forms of organization, functional division of labour, professionalism, hierarchical structures and specialization of tasks in the ideal-typical way assumed in the corporatist model? Has it generated a capacity for corporatist participation in policy-making which is thought to be a key feature of such a model? The evidence from the NLC does not support any such contention.

The NLC constitution provided for the functional division of the Secretariat into departments. Ten such departments were listed in the original constitution to which an amendment in 1984 added an eleventh, a women's department. The departments are broadly of two types, those which were supposed to facilitate the activities of the NLC itself like the Administration and Finance Departments and those that provided services for the whole labour movement like the Education, Research, Women's Affairs, Information and Industrial Relations Departments. Most of them have neither been functional nor functioning in the sense of specialised units — most have been one person departments with only the heads of department as staff. The provision in the budgets (to the extent that such were drafted) was often the salary of the head and nothing else. In general those departments which were supposed to provide services to the NLC Secretariat were more active and had more staff than those that offered services to the wider movement. Some departments, like the Legal Department, the Research Department and the Industrial Relations Department, were largely non-operational. The Women's Affairs Department, like the Legal Department, was never activated.

Similarly, while the number of full-time officers or professional unionists as they were called had increased, it is by no means obvious that this also meant an increase in professionalization as in the corporatist model. Compared to much smaller national labour centres like the Ghana TUC, the number of full-time officers were few, as can be seen from Table 4. The NLC had no full-time officers at the State Council levels. The responsibility for organizing State Council activities rested with the officers of the state branches of the industrial unions. At the end of 1991, the national Secretariat had only six staff members, including the President. At the peak of staffing in the early 1980s there had been 12 full-time officers.

Table 4: Number of Full-time Officers in Some African Unions

Unions	Total Employees	Full-time Officers	Regional full-time Officers	Union full Members
1. ETU Ethiopia	n.a.	66	120	370 000
2. TUC Ghana	140	28	10	600 000
3. NLC Nigeria	102	9	none	3 500 000
4. JUWATA Tanzania	800	n.a.	n.a.	470 000

Source: Union documents and union officers, 1991.

There was little specialization of tasks either between departments or their staff which made nonsense of the idea of a functional division of activities by department linked to the notion of a bureaucracy. In a memorandum to the General Secretary of the NLC calling for internal reforms in August 1986, the then Industrial Relations Officer observed:

> The situation where any head of department does the function of any other has greatly accentuated the lack of specialization. Though the intention is understandable — namely that noone is made indispensable — it does eliminate an important principle of making someone responsible for certain definite functions. This can only happen with specialization, and removing that person's indispensability should be by building up supportive functions within each department which can handle 80% of the department's function even without the Head and not by training replacements from across other departments. Otherwise the benefits of division of labour will continue to elude us (NLC Memorandum, 1986a, 3).

Similarly, the report of the trade union administrator imposed by the government in 1988, noted that from his discussion with the principal officers of the NLC,

> ... it was clear to me that the paid staff were not guided by any scheme of service which should describe jobs, qualification requirements for filling specific positions and spelling out career expectations. Another weakness in the personnel practice was that the promotion policy was not clearly spelt out to provide objective criteria for the guidance of management (Ogunkoya, 1989, 33).

He went on to castigate the record keeping or documentation system of the NLC calling it 'deplorable, stale and scanty' (Ogunkoya, 1989, 33-34). Moreover, while the NLC was hierarchical in the sense that there were positions placed one above the other and organs moving from shop-floor to the national level, such a hierarchy had little relevance in terms of bureaucratic organization. A hierarchy exists in most organizations. In the case of a bureaucracy, however, a hierarchy is supposed to be associated with a clear span of control, responsibility merging with authority, and the matching of job content with job requirement. There was little evidence of this in the NLC.

There is also no evidence that the NLC ever implemented a budget as noted in a 'brief' prepared for the new leadership of NLC in 1988 by the government-appointed administrator:

> It is regrettable to observe that the erstwhile management team responsible for the conduct of NLC affairs did not seem to appreciate the critical importance of budgeting as a tool of management for planning and control (Ogunkoya, 1988, 6). A few budgets had actually been prepared but never left the drawing board largely because the revenue that was expected was never realized. The 1984 and 1985 audited accounts of the NLC were typical of this financial predicament. Over half of the actual revenue collected was just enough to cover the small staff emoluments and this did not include pension which at that time did not even exist. Utility bills and secretarial costs consumed the rest (NLC Memorandum, 1986b).

Thus while some functional division of the NLC into departments and an element of hierarchical structure can be identified, at least on paper, as well as a few unionists with some professional training, on the whole, there was little evidence of the specialization, rationalization and professionalism which one would expect to find in a plausible corporatist arrangement.

LIBERALIZATION AND THE PROSPECTS FOR CORPORATISM

Since the mid-1980s and the moves towards economic liberalization, the prospects for a corporatist arrangement became even less substantial. With the introduction of the Structural Adjustment Programme (SAP) in 1986 the mode of public policy- making shifted decisively in favour of 'dialogue' between the state and international financial institutions rather than the exchange between state and incorporated national interest groups like labour, that was supposed to be characteristic of the corporatist model. The NLC became even less plausible than before as the co-opted partner in a state-led, national development strategy where the granting of organizational privileges, like 'monopoly' were supposed to be matched by 'good behaviour'. The lack of both participation and compliance was demonstrated most dramatically in the running battle between the government and the NLC over the removal of the 'petroleum subsidy' that culminated in two major strikes, one in 1988 and the other in 1993. The removal was part of the negotiated agreement between the state and the IMF/World Bank which was imposed on the Nigerian populace without debate. The support of the public made it possible for the NLC to resist and moderate the policy for a long time.

Although a full-scale restructuring of the labour market along the lines of the current neo-liberal project was not yet placed on the agenda, the few changes that were made nevertheless showed a move away from whatever corporatist tendencies were present from the late 1970s. As soon as General Babangida took power in 1985, his government went for a unilateral wage-cuts instead of a negotiated wage restraint policy. Income policy was discontinued from 1988 in favour of market determination of wages. Early in the 1990s government attempted, unsuccessfully, to abrogate the national minimum wage which has become increasingly unpopular with creditors and employers. However, it succeeded in abolishing the uniform national wage rates in the public sector. This action freed regions or states to set their own wage rates as they wished. Moreover, the banning and occupations of the offices of the NLC and some of its affiliates both in 1988 and 1994 suggested that the aim of the government was to exclude the unions rather than to co-opt them. The very emphasis of liberalization on markets, competition and deregulation was increasingly incompatible with a corporatist project based on co-optation and policy inclusion.

CONCLUSIONS

The Nigeria Labour Congress was organized on the basis of a state licensed monopoly and its leaders had a high media profile and public status, not unlike establishment elites. To use Offe's terms, it had been allocated some 'representation, resource, organization and procedural statuses'. However, it was neither centralized nor bureaucratic nor did it exercise much restraint in its relations with the state. Even if some aspects of the NLC may seem to fit the corporatist model, a closer look reveals a more complex picture than that envisaged in the theories of corporatism. For state licensing, for instance, to be effective as a means of ensuring compliance, there must also be the conditions for a quick withdrawal of the permission to operate. This did not exist in the Nigerian case. Similarly, the 'allocation of statuses' was not the outcome of a state design imposed on the unions but something that had been actively pursued by the labour movement from its own autonomous premises. They were therefore regarded as the achievements of the movement itself and defended when the government began to have second thoughts. The unity of the movement had been fought for — it was not a government gift, a 'bribe', which had to be reciprocated with compliance. This has remarkable resemblance with the history of unions in colonial times which the labour historian Frederick Cooper said 'turned the discourse of social engineering into the discourse of entitlements'.

So, if the state interventions in the Nigerian labour movement of 1975-78 and subsequently did not result in a state corporatist labour regime, how can the outcome be characterized? Our conclusions at this point can only be tentative. Elsewhere (Hashim, 1994), we have explored the notion of a 'balance of bargaining power' as a way of accounting for the relative weight of the power resources that were distributed among the parties to the labour regime, including the strength of organization, finance and the capacity to inflict damage on opponents as well as to protect one-self from them.

Before the intervention and restructuring of unions in the late 1970s, the state possessed major bargaining resources, both as a public sector employer and as the public authority. Private employers were powerful as well, given that bargaining was largely conducted at the level of the individual firm, where management could employ its power resources against weak local unions. International actors used their financial resources to influence the divided trade union movement. Unity depended on their support and it was not forthcoming unless these actors were sure that their own local clients were in control of the process. The Nigerian trade union centres before 1978 were financially and organizationally weak, unable to collect much in union dues and relying on foreign funding for their programmes. Their organizational weakness was partly compensated for by their capacity to obstruct opponents. They were also able, to some extent, to defend themselves against opponents as the state's or the employers' only leverage on them was to withhold recognition for bargaining. Since collective bargaining was not widely accepted, the use of that leverage only led to new union demands backed by 'lightning strikes', as testified by G. C. Okogwu, the then Director of Industrial Relations, before the Adebiyi tribunal (ATR, 1976, 88).

After the 1975-78 restructuring, it would seem that the balance of bargaining power shifted in favour of the unions. Although state licensing may have added to the power resources of the state, unions were also empowered (see Aremu, 1991; Adrae and Beckman, 1996; 1998, on the experience of the textile workers' union). They acquired new organizational and financial resources: automatic check-off, unity, and compulsory recognition. It represented a real shift in the balance of power in favour of the unions, something which did not escape leading members of the business community who complained that the state had created a 'Frankenstein's monster' (see Odunaike, 1983, 8; Ubeku, 1983, 192-3).

The employers were temporarily weakened. Negotiations with small house unions were replaced by national collective bargaining where they confronted big industrial unions. In a survey of management and union views on bargaining levels covering some 110 firms and almost 1,000 employees, Fashoyin (1982, 87) found on a smaller sample of 47 firms, that 45 per cent of the firms preferred to deal with their employees, another 36 per cent with their company unions. Only 19 per cent of the responding managements preferred to negotiate with the industrial unions formed since 1977. All of the latter were large employers, falling within the top three of the six categories of company sizes. The international union actors were also weakened as they were deprived of their leverage and clients after the restructuring, filing complaints against the reforms with the ILO, especially against the ban on foreign affiliation. Subsequent state interventions, in 1988 and 1994, did not affect the balance of bargaining power as significantly as the first. The basic structures were maintained, even if the government sought to enhance its influence. They were both attempts by liberalising political regimes to secure temporary advantage over the unions which they perceived as obstructing their political agenda. Rather than abolishing the inherited arrangement, they sought to exploit its scope for control, drawing on both the precedent and structures of the first intervention.

Corporatist models of analysis fail to capture these successive shifts in the balance of bargaining power, the nature of the evolving conflicts, and the strategies pursued by unions as well as the state. As we have attempted to show in the Nigerian case, such models tend to presuppose either too much of state control — incorporation, co-optation — or too much convergence of interests ('societal corporatism') to do justice to the contradictory nature of state-union relations.

BIBLIOGRAPHY

ABIODUN, M. O. (1978) *Restructuring of Trade Unions in Nigeria 1976-1978* (Jos, Salama Press).

ADEFOFE, Brigadier (1976) "Speech by the Minister of Labour", Appended in Umoh, J. U. (1980) "Politicians, Unionists, Employers: Enemies or Partners?" (Unpubl.).

AKWETEY, E. O. (1994) "Trade Unions and Democratisation: A Comparative Study of Zambia and Ghana" (PhD Thesis, Stockholm, Stockholms Universitet).

ANANABA, W. (1969) *The Trade Union Movement in Nigeria* (Benin, Ethiope Publishing Corporation).

ANDRAE, G. and B. Beckman (1996) *Bargaining for Survival: Unionized Workers in the Nigerian Textile Industry* (Geneva, UNRISD Discussion Paper No. 78).

— (1998) *Union Power in the Nigerian Textile Industry: Labour Regime and Adjustment* (Uppsala, Nordiska Afrikainstitutet; Somerset, New Jersey; Transaction Publishers, Kano Centre for Research and Documentation).

— (1984) 'Labour and Industrial Crisis in The Third World: The Case of Nigerian Textile and Cotton' *Project Outline* (AKUT, Uppsala).

— (1991) 'Textile Unions and Industrial Crisis in Nigeria: Labour Structure, Organisation and Strategies' in I. Brandell (ed.) *Workers in Third-World Industrialisation* (London, Macmillan).

AREMU, I. (1991) 'The Social Relevance of Trade Unionism: The Case Study of National Union of Textile and Garment Workers in Nigeria' (M.A. Research Paper, The Hague, ISS).

ATR (1977) *Justice Adebiyi Tribunal Report on Trade Unions* (in 70 volumes) (Lagos, Federal Government Publishers).

BASKIN, J. (1991) *Striking Back: A History of COSATU* (London and New York, Verso).

BECKMAN, B. (1993; 1995) 'The Politics of Labour and Adjustment: The Experience of the Nigeria Labour Congress' in T. Mkandawire and A. Olukoshi (eds) (1995) *Between Liberalisation and Oppression: The Politics of Structural Adjustment in Africa* (Dakar, CODESRIA Books).

— (1996) 'Interest Groups and the Construction of Democratic Space', in Jibrin Ibrahim (ed), *Expanding Nigerian Democratic Space* (Dakar, CODESRIA Books).

— (1997) 'Explaining Democratization: Notes on the Concept of Civil Society', in Özdalga and S. Persson (eds) *Civil Society, Democracy and the Muslim World* (Istanbul, Swedish Research Institute).

CAWSON, A. (1986) *Corporatism and Political Theory* (Oxford, Basil Blackwell).

COHEN, R. (1971) 'Nigeria's Central Trade Union Organizations: A Study Guide' *Journal of Modern African Studies*, 9 (3): 456-8.

— (1977) 'Michael Imoudu and the Nigerian Labour Movement' *Race and Class*, 18 (4): 345-62.

— (c1974, 1981) *Labour and Politics in Nigeria, 1945-71* (London, Heinemann).

COLLIER, R. B. and D. Collier (1979) 'Inducements Versus Constraints: Desegregating "Corporatism"', *The American Political Science Review*, 73 (4): 967-86.

COLLIER, D. (1979) 'Overview of the Bureaucratic-Authoritarian Model', in D. Collier (ed.) *The New Authoritarianism in Latin America* (Princeton, Princeton University Press).

COSATU (1985) *Slogan of the 1985 Congress of Cosatu* (Johannesburg).

EZE, O. (1981) 'The New Labour Reform', in O. Oyediran (ed.) *Survey of Nigerian Affairs 1976-1977* (NIIA and Macmillan Press).

FASHOYIN, T. (1982) 'Incomes Policy, Pay Expectation and Wage Determination in Nigeria: A Survey' *Research for Development, NISER* 2 (1) January.

— (1990) 'Nigerian Labour and the Military: Towards Exclusion?' *Labour, Capital and Society*, 23 (1): 1237.

'FGN Decree 31, 1973 Decrees (also Acts)', in *Laws of the Federation of Nigeria, 1990* (Federal Ministry of Justice, Lagos).

'FGN Decree 44, 1976 Decrees (also Acts)', in *Laws of the Federation of Nigeria 1990* (Federal Ministry of Justice, Lagos).

'FGN Decree 22, 1978 Decrees (also Acts)', in *Laws of the Federation of Nigeria 1990* (Federal Ministry of Justice, Lagos).

HASHIM, Y. (1987) 'State Intervention in Trade Unions: A Nigerian Case Study' (M.A. Research Paper, The Hague, ISS).

— (1989) 'The State in Africa' (PhD Research Seminar, The Hague, ISS).

— (1994) 'The State and Trade Unions in Africa: A Study in Macro-Corporatism' (PhD Thesis, The Hague, Institute of Social Studies).

HELANDER, V. (1982) 'A Liberal-Corporatist Sub-system in Action: The Incomes Policy System in Finland', in G. Lehmbruch and P. C. Schimitter (eds) *Patterns of Corporatist Policy Making* (London, Sage).

ILO (1985) *Report of the Committee of Experts on the Implementation of Recommendations and Conventions* (Geneva, ILO).

— (1986) *Report of the Committee of Experts on the Implementation of Recommendations and Conventions* (Geneva, ILO).

LEHMBRUCH, G. and P. C. Schimitter (eds) (1982) *Patterns of Corporatist Policy-Making* (London, Sage).

LUBECK, P. (1986) *Islam and Urban Labour in Northern Nigeria: The Making of a Muslim Working Class* (Cambridge, Cambridge University Press).

MALLOY, J. M. (1977a) 'Authoritarianism and Corporatism in Latin America: The Modal Pattern' in J. M. Malloy (ed.) *Authoritarianism and Latin American Corporatism* (London, University of Pittsburg Press).

NLC (1986a) Memorandum from Assistant General Secretary (Industrial Relations) to General Secretary, 28 August 1986.

— (1986b) 'Congress 1985 Audited Account' Memorandum from Assistant General Secretary (Industrial Relations) to General Secretary, 28 August 1986.

NYANG'ORO, J. E. (1987) 'On the Concept of "Corporatism" and the African State', in *Studies in Comparative International Development*, 22 (1).

— (1989) 'The State of Politics in Africa: The Corporatist Factor', in *Studies in Comparative International Development*, 24 (1): 559.

NYANG'ORO, J. E. and T. M. Shaw (eds) (1989) *Corporatism in Africa: Comparative Analysis and Practice* (Boulder, Westview).

ODUNAIKE, S. O. (1983) 'Introduction', in *Industrial Relations Forum, Series No. 1* (Lagos, NIPM).

OGUNKOYA, M. (1989) *Report of the Sole Administrator of the NLC* (Lagos, Federal Government Press).

— (1988) 'Brief on the Management of the Nigeria Labour Congress' Prepared by the Sole Administrator of the NLC Mr. M. O. Ogunkoya for Mr. Pascal Bafyau, The New President of the NLC', 30 December.

ONIMODE, B. (1982) *Imperialism and Underdevelopment in Nigeria* (London, Zed).

OTOBO, D. (1986) *Foreign Interests and Nigerian Trade Unions* (Ibadan, Heinemann).

PEACE, A. (1975) 'The Lagos Proletariat: Labour Aristocrats or Populist Militants', in R. Sandbrook and R. Cohen (eds) *The Development of an African Working Class* (Toronto, Longman).

SACHIKONYE, M. L. (1981) 'State and Trade Unions in Nigeria: A Study of the Restructuring of the Nigeria Labour Congress (M.Sc Thesis, Zaria, ABU).

SCHIPHORST, F. (1984) 'Trade Unions, Politics and Participation' OOATUU/FNV Seminar, 12 March-19 April (The Hague, ISS).

SCHMIDT, M. G. (1982) 'Does Corporatism Matter? Economic Crisis, Politics and Rates of Unemployment in Capitalist Democracies in the 1970s', in G. Lehmbruch and P.C. Schimitter (eds) *Patterns of Corporatist Policy-Making* (London, Sage).

SCHMITTER, P. C. and G. Lehmbruch (eds) (1979) *Trends Towards Corporatist Intermediation* (London, Sage).

SCHMITTER, P. C. (1979a) 'Introduction' in P .C. Schmitter and G. Lehmbruch (eds) *Trends Towards Corporatist Intermediation* (London, Sage).

— (1979b) 'Still the Century of Corporatism' in P. C. Schmitter and G. Lehmbruch (eds) *Trends Towards Corporatist Intermediation* (London, Sage).

— (1981) 'Interest Intermediation and Regime Governability in Contemporary Western Europe and North America', in S. Berger (ed.) *Organising Interests in Western Europe* (Cambridge, CUP).

SHAW, T. M. (1982) 'Beyond Neo-colonialism: Varieties of Corporatism in Africa' *Journal of Modern African Studies*, 20 (2).

STREECK W. (1982) 'Organisational Consequences of Neo-corporatist Cooperation in West German Labour Unions' in G. Lehmbruch and P. C. Schmitter (eds) *Patterns of Corporatist Policy-Making* (London, Sage).

UBEKU, A. K. (1983) *Industrial Relations in Developing Countries: The Case of Nigeria* (London, Macmillan).

UMOH, J. U. (1980) 'Politicians, Unionists, Employers: Enemies or Partners?' (Unpubl.).

VAN HEAR, N. (1988) 'Nigerian Labour in the 1980s', in R. Southall (ed.) *Trade Unions and the New Industrialization of the Third World* (London, Zed).

WATERMAN, P. (1982) 'Division and Unity Amongst Nigerian Workers', *Research Report Series 11* (The Hague, ISS).

— (1983) 'Aristocrats and Plebians in African Trade Unions? Lagos Port and Dock Worker Organisation and Struggle' (PhD Thesis, Nijmegen).

WILENSKY, H. L. (1976) *The New Corporatism, Centralization and the Welfare State* (London, Sage).

ZASHA, J. (1985) 'The State and Trade Unions', *Nigerian Journal of Political Science*, 4 (i and ii): 120-33.

CHAPTER FOUR

Whose Civil Society? Trade Unions and Capacity Building in the Nigerian Textile Industry

BJÖRN BECKMAN

CIVIL SOCIETY VERSUS THE UNIONS: A CONTEXT OF DEBATE

Where does institutional capacity come from? This chapter discusses the institution-building potential of trade unions in a global conjuncture where they are undercut by economic crisis and beleaguered by a liberalizing state and its transnational sponsors. It explores an alternative empirical logic which credits unions with a more positive role in the process of economic and political reconstruction. The chapter summarizes findings from a joint study with Gunilla Andrae on the textile industry and the Textile Workers Union in Nigeria (Andrae and Beckman, 1998; 1996; 1991) and adds reflections on institution building in civil society, state-civil society relations, and democratization.

The textile industry was badly hit by crises and adjustment and the union had to fight an essentially defensive struggle in an attempt to minimize workers' losses in income and employment. Simultaneously, however, the union was surprisingly successful in advancing workers' and union rights. Companies which in the past had violently resisted unionization were made to accommodate to a union-based labour regime. Collective bargaining was increasingly respected. The union played an important role in enforcing legality "from below", not only within work places but also in disciplining police, courts, and other state agencies involved in regulating conflicts in the labour arena.

The experience of the Nigerian textile union is used to illustrate a general argument about workers and structural adjustment which was first raised in a joint text with Yusuf Bangura (Bangura and Beckman, 1991). Aspects of the argument have been developed in a critique of liberal theories of civil society and "empowerment" (Beckman 1992; 1993; 1997b) and in work on interest groups and democratization (Beckman, 1997a; Beckman and Jega, 1995).

Economic liberalizers tend to see trade unions as part of the problem rather than as part of the solution. Their political impulse is that unions should be undercut, disorganized and disarmed. Politically, this is justified, not just in terms of the imperative of economic reforms, supposedly in the interest of all, but also because of an overall vision for an emerging "civil society" which needs to be liberated from the shackles of statist and corporatist development models. The freeing of market forces, they say, will generate a new set of social agents, a new civil society, as opposed to the "vested interests" of the old order. These new forces will organize themselves autonomously from the state, put pressure on the latter to become more responsive, accountable and representative, thus laying the groundwork for democratization. Theories that link capitalist development and democratization are invoked and supported by empirical evidence: The more advanced a capitalist society becomes economically, the more likely it is to be a liberal democracy.

Even those who do not share the economic and political visions of the liberalizers may find virtue in their promotion of organizational autonomy, especially in a context where unions and other interest groups have been under the thumb of an authoritarian state. It may be welcomed not the least by local activists who see a corporatist union bureaucracy as an obstacle to democratic mobilization within the unions. The rationale of the anti-corporatist impulses differ. The liberalizers have their own reasons for breaking up a corporatist pact which, historically, is linked to statist and welfarist projects that are seen to be standing in the way of the freedom of the market. The main worry of the anti-corporatist unionists is usually the opposite. To them, union bureaucrats, as a result of their corporatist links to state and employers, are too willing to strike compromises with the liberalizers, and too timid in their defence of wage employment, industrialization and social welfare.

But where are the political institutions that will deliver the economic growth which in its turn is expected, in due course, to generate democracy? What will happen in the meantime in societies which are on the brink of national collapse and disintegration? The failure of structural adjustment programmes are attributed to institutional failures. Governments have been "too weak" to adhere consistently to the reforms, especially when these hit at populations which are already suffering. The liberal vision, in giving priority to the economic reforms, tend in practice to be tolerant of authoritarian politics. Reformers worry, for instance, that "premature" democracy in Eastern and Central Europe may cause the abandoning of economic liberalization as politicians bend in to disgruntled electorates. Key decision-makers, they argue, must be insulated from popular pressures. The authoritarian impulse is reinforced by the success stories of countries like Chile, South Korea and Taiwan, where authoritarian but apparently efficient regimes have laid the foundations for rapid economic growth and thereby, simultaneously, it seems, generated the social forces that are capable of transforming society in a democratic direction.

Those who are branded "vested interests" by the liberalizers are, of course, particularly unimpressed by the supposed political benefits of economic liberalization. More often than not, the economic reforms go hand in hand with a general assault on trade unions and other organized groups. In such a context, unions often feel that they have a legitimate claim to be representing broad popular interests in opposition to the manner in which the reforms are designed and implemented. They may also in many instances have contributed significantly to wider democratic political alliances (Valenzuela, 1989; Rueschemeyer, Stephens and Stephens, 1992). On the contemporary African scene, there is evidence of unions participating in democracy movements and in responding courageously to political repression imposed on society as a whole (Akwetey, 1994; Bangura and Beckman, 1991; Beckman, 1995; Webster and Adler and other contributions to this volume).

The economic reformers, however, are more concerned with the capacity of unions to obstruct liberalization than with their potential as a democratic force. Moreover, the scope for ignoring the political claims of the unions widens as the wage economy sinks into serious crisis. Irrespective of the designs of the liberalizers, the material base of unions is eroded as wage workers face a sharp decline in market and workplace bargaining power and their numbers and income are decimated. It is particularly devastating in the African case because of the prolonged period of economic decline. The process is reinforced by economic liberalization as industries are deprived of protected markets and foreign debt payments eat deeper into what remains of the public sector economy. It is therefore not surprising that the liberalizers feel free to consider unions as increasingly irrelevant to their own project, except as a possible nuisance, an obstacle which needs to be eliminated or neutralized.

INSTITUTIONAL CAPACITY, LABOUR REGIME AND SOCIAL CONTRACT

There is an awareness among economic reformers of all shades about the need to develop institutional capacity to sustain reforms. It is not enough to "get your policies right"; you must ensure that they are institutionally grounded, sustained and reproduced. There is also a realization that the political problem lies as much with the institutions of civil society as with those of the state and that the two are, in fact, intimately connected.

Central to our understanding of institutional capacity is the ability to regulate conflicts of interests in the allocation of resources. This is always a problem but it becomes particularly acute when a society undergoes major transformations or are under pressure from the surrounding world to do so. The institutions of the state are at the centre of such conflicts, both because of the resources they appropriate and distribute and because of the way they intervene in the balance of forces which underpin a particular mode of conflict regulation in society. Society contains numerous overlapping arenas in which conflicts over resources are enacted and resolved. These arenas and their institutions and procedures for self-regulation are constituted in close interaction with the formation of the state. The latter may emerge from the former but even where states, as in the colonial context, are imposed from outside, their effective presence in society is a function of their insertion into these arena-specific regulatory processes, either intervening in the name of some external project or responding to demands from actors within the arenas themselves.

The formation of states and civil societies needs to be understood in the context of this mutual determination. The dialectics of the process is obscured in the current dominant liberal preoccupation with the need to disengage civil society from the state. The propagation of disengagement, however, seems less a matter of the undesirability of a close link-up between the state and certain interests in society than of preventing the wrong sort of state from linking up with the wrong sort of interests, that is, interests hostile to aspects of the liberal economic project. This can be seen clearly in the lack of inhibitions on the side of the liberal reformers when it comes to advocating state intervention in support of those organized interests and social agents that are considered helpful in ensuring a political basis of the reforms, that is, the vested interests of the preferred new social order. The seeming disjuncture in such thinking between undesirable "vested interests" and the vision of a liberated civil society can be understood in that pragmatic context. Civil society is defined in terms of the institutional requirements of a particular ideological project. In consequence, however, alternative ideological projects as well as "empiricist" concerns with state-civil society dynamics, need to liberate and disengage their own conceptions of civil societies from their incorporation into the liberal agenda.

We prefer to think of institutional capacity in terms of the relationships that govern a policy arena, rather than as qualities that are attributable to a governing institution. The "regimes" which govern such arenas are the critical "institutions". We use the term regime to refer to an assemblage of institutions, organizations, rules and practices through which the governance of the arena is effectuated. The extent to which the interests can assert themselves in the constitution and the operation of the regime reflects the balance of power both in specific arenas and in society at large. That balance is not constant, it is continuously shifting, both as a result of circumstances (e.g. changing market conditions, state intervention etc) and as a result of the efforts by the contesting parties (organization, leadership). As the regimes involve relations of domination (management, discipline, authority), they are potential arenas of democratic struggles as far as those who are being subordinated have an interest in changing the regime itself as to enhance their say in the way in which they are ruled.

We speak of a "labour regime" in referring to the regulation of the conflicts of interests between employers and employees in work places and in the labour market. In developing the concept we seek to integrate discussions of the development of labour processes, regulation regimes (Lipietz, 1986), labour practices and strategies (Brandell, 1991), including theories of "factory regimes" (Burawoy, 1985) and corporatism (Cawson, 1986), as well as the political economy critique of conventional "industrial relations" literature (Hyman, 1989). A labour regime contains formal or informal rules and practices that define rights and obligations. It may be more or less arbitrary (despotic) or constitutional, authoritarian or participatory, imposed or agreed (contractual). It can be more or less democratically constituted in terms of rights of organization and expression and the extent to which workers are given a say in decisions which affect them. Even if disciplinary rights rest with managers and authorities, the process by which such rights are exercised may or may not be organized in a way as to protect against arbitrary treatment. The scope and limitations of the disciplinary rights may themselves be subjected to negotiation.

We may speak of a labour regime as more or less "contractual" to indicate the extent to which it is based on some form of accord between the parties. The contract imposes constraints on the exercise of power on all sides, including restrictions on the use of obstruction and non-cooperation by the subordinate party, as in the case of the regulation of the rights to strike. The expansion of constitutional forms of conflict regulation is therefore as much a struggle for the definition and recognition of the "legitimate interests" that are to inform such contract. As with all contracts, it is bound to reflect the differences in strength (resources, organization, leadership, alliances etc) of the contracting parties. There is nothing necessarily "fair" about it and the democratic content, in terms of influence, may be limited. Still, the contract may allow the subordinate party some element of legal protection on which to build the strength from which future, more advantageous contracts can be negotiated.

In many instances, a formal set of rules may exist in the statute books, as required, for instance, by international conventions or as influenced by legal practices elsewhere. This is true of much labour legislation. But such rules are often of little consequence for the way in which authority is actually exercised. It underscores that formal rules have no more meaning than can be asserted and defended by the contending forces. The renunciation of the use of force as part of the social contract is conditional. Unless the ultimate sanction of non-constitutional force is retained, subordinate groups cannot expect their interests to be respected, either when establishing or seeking to uphold the new legality.

Trade unions are central to the construction of contractual labour regimes. They have an interest in constitutionalizing conflict resolution in a way that opens up for the recognition of their rights to organize and represent the workers. To this end, unions are prepared to enter an accord with employers and the state, on behalf of the workers, a contract, which implies the partial renunciation of the use of force and the acceptance of outside arbitration and adjudication. The contract may be instituted at the national level, leaving its application to individual workplaces open to negotiation and contestation. It may also be initiated in a particularly "advanced" sector of the economy, having its frontiers expanded to include a widening range of work places. The state may play a more or less active role in formulating the legal framework that provides the institutions, procedures and sanctions but its effectiveness depends on the extent to which it is accepted as legitimate by the immediate parties of a conflict. Otherwise it will be dodged, circumvented, and subverted.

Our study of the Nigerian textile industry suggests the consolidation of a contractual, union-based labour regime, a process of deepening constitutionalism, premised on the evolution of a social contract, involving state, employers, unions and workers. The achievement questions our intuitive understanding that crisis and liberalizing adjustment should be expected to weaken the union. What was the logic of this "counter-cyclical" assertion of organizational capacity and successful institution building? What was the historical configuration of social forces which sustained it? The bulk of this chapter is concerned with summarizing the empirical evidence. Simultaneously, however, the achievement opens up for a wider discussion of policy regimes and organized interests and their significance for the constitution of alternative civil societies, capable of sustaining alternative economic and political reforms. To this we return in the concluding sections of the chapter.

THE NIGERIAN TEXTILE INDUSTRY

All over Africa, the manufacturing industry has been hit by crises and adjustments. Industry depended on imported inputs, state subsidies and protection and was therefore seriously affected by decline in import capacity, indebtedness, and fiscal crisis. Liberalizing adjustment policies further exposed its vulnerability in market terms. In Nigeria, textiles is the most important manufacturing industry. It was an ideal case for import-substituting industrialization in the de-colonization phase. A commercialized peasantry and an expanding public service sector ensured a domestic market. Colonial commercial firms invested in manufacturing in order to get a share of the protected market. Textiles were a priority for regional and federal state investors, drawing on the accumulated surplus of the marketing boards. State investments were undertaken in partnership with transnational firms and international finance institutions. Indigenous private entrepreneurs went for their share, often as the junior partners of state and foreign private capital.

Nationalist economic policies during the Civil War (1967-1970) offered new incentives, including a ban on the importation of textiles. After the war, an even stronger incentive was the expanding income from petroleum. Despite waste and bottlenecks, Nigerian industrial markets expanded fast. By 1980, the Nigerian Textile Manufacturers Association (NTMA) had some 70 members, covering most of the large firms, one-third with more than one thousand workers, ten with 3,000 or more. The textile union, NUTGTWN, claimed some 75,300 members, a figure based on check-off payments of membership dues. In its own estimate, the union organized some 75 per cent of the industry which may suggest an industry of some 100,000 workers, leaving out the informal sector. While the highest number of factories were in Lagos, some of the largest plants, were in Kaduna, the administrative centre of the north, and a favoured site for large-scale public investment. Kano, the other major northern city with its long commercial history, was also an important textile centre with a strong input of indigenous Nigerian and naturalized Lebanese capital.

The first half of the 1980s was a period of decline. By 1985, the textile union had lost one-third of its members and capacity utilization had sunk below 30 per cent. Much of the decline occurred before the national economic crisis was generalized with the drop in petroleum prices and export earnings. New textile companies mushroomed and old ones expanded to meet demand in a booming, oil-fuelled domestic market. The realization of the market potential, however, was undermined by the distortions which accompanied the boom. Externally the Naira was strong, but domestically it was eaten by oil-fed inflation. While the procurement of foreign machinery and inputs should have been facilitated by the over-valuation of the Naira, the rush for imports caused serious congestion and corruption, including in import licensing, customs and ports handling, adding heavily to import costs. Production costs were exacerbated by numerous bottlenecks, not the least in power supply. Also wages were a stop-go affair, with government intervening intermittently either to impose wage freezes or to concede, administratively, big wage hikes. High domestic production costs and a strong Naira were, of course, an invitation to the importers for whom tariffs and other restrictions, including outright bans on textile imports were obstacles that could be overcome through informal and parallel channels. A vastly expanded textile industry was therefore unable to reap the fruits of its investments, facing a serious cost and market crisis, precipitating strategies of adjustment including closures, take-overs, mergers, retrenchment as well as efforts to introduce more competitive products and up-grade technology and productivity.

The peak in oil fortunes in 1980 was followed by a steep decline. Industry was hit by the contraction of purchasing power and local markets. The most immediate problem was the supply of imported raw materials and other inputs. The textile industry, drawing on Nigerian produced cotton, had in the past been less import-dependent than other industries. But the impact of the oil-boom and the strength of the Naira had redirected demand towards external sources of supply, including a growing share of synthetic yarn (Andrae and Beckman, 1987). Although bred on protection and wary of liberalization, the textile industrialists welcomed, at least in principle, the "homegrown", although World Bank-sponsored, structural adjustment programme (SAP) which was introduced in 1986 by the Babangida government. Trade liberalization and devaluation radically altered the operating conditions of the protected and import-dependent Nigerian manufacturing sector. The devaluations reinforced the strong recessionary tendency of the economy. The textile industry, however, was in a better position than most to adjust to changing conjunctures and policies. It had already gone through a phase of technological upgrading and take-overs had created more integrated and less vulnerable production cycles.

Cutting labour costs was central to the restructuring. The share of labour in the cost structure of the textile industry declined, both due to the drop in real wages and because of the rising costs of other inputs. The suppression of wages was actively promoted by the state which imposed wage freezes and wage controls. In real terms the 1981 minimum wage had been cut to one-quarter by the end of the decade. But the share of wages in total production costs dropped even more drastically. It fell from some 50 per cent at the beginning of the decade to less than 10 at the end.

Domestic markets were shrinking. The continued decline in purchasing power restricted the scope for raising prices. The contraction, however, was partly compensated for by the increase in exports, primarily to the West African region where the CFA Franc was supported by the French Central Bank. As the value of the Nigerian Naira was slashed, the differential to the CFA Franc widened and Nigerian textiles became the cheapest in the region.

At the beginning of the new decade, average capacity utilization had risen to over 50 per cent. Employment which was at its lowest point in 1986/87 had risen by at least 10 per cent by 1990. The textile industry had demonstrated a notable capacity for restructuring, including the upgrading of technology, backward integration, raising domestic value-added and labour productivity, and reorganizing management and finance. How sustainable was the recovery? Domestic markets continued to decline and the export success was precarious as it depended on the over-valuation of the CFA Franc. A 50 per cent devaluation was imposed in 1993. Although Nigerian producers continued to have a competitive edge, exchange rate policies in the region could be expected to be further adjusted.

More fundamental worries, however, were caused by the continued decline of the Nigerian economy. Economic policies were undermined by the inability of the regime to maintain some minimum of fiscal control. The repeated postponement of the transition to civilian rule created uncertainties about the whole institutional arrangements, even threatening national unity.

The workers were nearly all male, mostly in age groups with family responsibilities, and with a high level of formal basic schooling. The few women were mostly in small garments firms which were not covered by our survey which was undertaken in Kano and Kaduna. As the crisis deepened, workers said they consumed less and depended more on supplementary income from other sources, including both urban type income (crafts, trade etc) and farming. Most workers were first generation non-farmers. Their parents were in most cases farmers and they themselves had undertaken agricultural work, often as their only previous job experience. Especially before the upturn in the industry in the late 1980s, many workers left employment because they could not cope. Temporary closures and compulsory leave induced many to look for alternatives. Accumulated gratuities and other end-of-service benefits provided starting capital. However, lay-offs throughout the wage economy caused overcrowding in the informal sector and workers became less willing to leave voluntarily. Company employment records show a marked decline in labour turnover. While agriculture and returning to the village continued to be seen as a safety valve, workers were increasingly anxious to hold on to their jobs and to dig in their heels in defence of their work-place interests. By narrowing the options, the crisis had reinforced working class identity, despite the growing inability of workers to reproduce themselves as wage workers alone.

UNIONS AND COLLECTIVE BARGAINING

The textile workers were organized in the National Union of Textile, Garment and Tailoring Workers of Nigeria (NUTGTWN) which was established in 1977 as a result of a reorganization initiated by the state (Otobo, 1987; Hashim, 1994; Beckman, 1996). The 1976-78 labour reforms created one central organization, the Nigeria Labour Congress (NLC), and 42 industrial unions, amalgamating previous rival industrial and house unions. It was a corporatist arrangement where the union was granted the right to be the sole organizer of the textile workers (Cawson, 1986; Hashim, 1994). It allowed for the compulsory deductions of union dues ("check-offs") by management, once a majority of workers had joined the union, giving it a strong financial basis which was used to hire staff, rent offices, pay for transport, print information material, and organize meetings, seminars, conferences and rallies. Special levies were deducted to fund the building of the central secretariat in Kaduna and a sub-secretariat in Lagos.

In most major companies, union branches held regular and competitive elections. Many had a tradition of competitive branch politics from before the new national union and participation in elections and other union activities was often high. In big firms, branch executives had their own offices provided for by management. Key officers were allowed to take time-off for union work without loss of pay.

The 1976-78 labour reforms facilitated industry-wide collective agreements, generalizing conditions of service from the better organized firms to the unionized part of the industry as a whole. In addition, branch executives and zonal officers pushed local demands. The labour laws made it difficult to engage in strikes "officially" (Fashoyin, 1980; Otobo and Omole, 1987). Disputes were supposed to be resolved through compulsory arbitration and in the final instance adjudication by the Industrial Court. Such laws predated the imposition of the new consolidated union structure of the late 1970s. In combination, they held the authoritarian and repressive potential of corporatist labour regimes from elsewhere in the third world, where states "grant" unions monopolistic rights of representation in exchange for effective state control (for the Latin American experience in this respect, see Malloy, 1977). In the Nigerian case, it did not prevent unions from encouraging workers to engage in unofficial industrial action to put pressure on management.

What could the union do protect the interests of the workers? It negotiated higher redundancy payments to discourage employers from lay-offs. Companies were induced to hold on to excess workers while waiting for better times, rather than paying them off. Both closures and retrenchments had to be subjected to collective bargaining at the plant level, according to the Procedural Agreement. The scope for making companies show restraint in retrenching workers was enhanced by the latent threat of a violent breakdown if the aggrieved workers felt badly treated. The firms would have to consider possible damage and disruption of production when calculating the costs. The pressure in this respect affected both union and management. Firms sought to escape by expanding the number of casual, temporary workers. This was effectively resisted by the union. Attempts by firms to use sub-contractors with non-unionized labour were also defeated. A major frontier of local bargaining was the terms on which workers accepted to be sent on "compulsory leave".

Real wages were declining fast as consumer prices rose while government imposed a wage-freeze (1983-1988). The union sought to dodge it by negotiating allowances, bonuses, incentives and other "non-wage" or fringe benefits. The spectrum of compensatory demands kept expanding and the proportion of fringe benefits in total take-home pay increased from less than one-third to more than half. The most important and hotly contested fringe benefit was the annual end-of-the-year bonus. Strikes and go-slows were commonplace during the last months of the year. Unionists spoke of an "annual bonus fever". The government sought to restrict bonus payments as part of the wage freeze but the union refused to comply. The employers were in most cases obliged to accept whatever the local balance of forces seemed to suggest as a reasonable outcome. Special "incentives" were offered to compensate for the restricted bonus.

The rate of inflation made the wage freeze increasingly untenable, especially with the introduction of "structural adjustment" in 1986, a supposedly liberal economic policy regime. The modest consolidation of the textile industry, at a reduced level of output, provided openings for a union wage offensive. Despite a defensive barrage, employers made major concessions.

Achievements at the bargaining table, however, continued to be undermined by inflation and the union looked for political solutions. As the decade of the 1980s drew to a close, the revision of the minimum wage became the rallying point for a campaign led by the General Secretary of the textile union. After protracted negotiations the state finally accepted a major increase, although far from giving full compensation for the erosion in real wages. Implementation had to be negotiated at the sectoral level. Here too, the textile union led the way. The employers insisted that there should be no "across the board" increases, that is, for workers above the stipulated minimum, but the union issued an ultimatum in open defiance of government directives and the employers conceded. The agreement in 1991 meant that the textile workers on the average may have recovered roughly half of what they had lost in purchasing power over the past decade.

Developments in the first half of the 1990s underscored the limited scope for making sustainable gains through collective bargaining in a context of extreme macro-economic instability and decaying public institutions. The system of orderly, periodic collective bargaining was disrupted and new proposals for fresh negotiations had to be drafted as soon as an agreement had been signed. The textile union was notably successful in the new type of bargaining game. It continued to be ahead of other unions both in reaching and implementing agreements and in terms of actual wage gains. However, the credibility of collective bargaining was undermined by inflation running out of control, sparking off a chain of events that escalated into a full scale rebellion within the textile union in May 1993 (for a full discussion, see Andrae and Beckman, 1998).

THE ORIGIN OF A UNION-BASED LABOUR REGIME

The hard won gains in wages and other payments, achieved for Nigeria's textile workers by their union from the early 1980s to the early 1990s, were never anywhere close to restoring real wages. At one point, in the mid-1980s, and before the stabilization and modest upturn, these had been reduced to as little as one-quarter of their 1981 value. The successful wage offensive of the late 1980s and early 1990s reduced the gap considerably, to something more like one-half. The modest recovery in employment was also sustained into the mid-1990s, largely due to unofficial exports to the West Africa region.

The unresolved institutional and policy crisis of the late-1990s suggests that Nigeria was in for further de-industrialization. The instability of the situation was aggravated by the judicial murder of the Ogoni activists in November 1995. However, looking back at the period of study, from the late 1970s to the mid-1990s, we see a remarkable capacity of both industry and union to restructure and adapt to new market constraints in a volatile and disruptive policy environment. In particular, we note the ability of the workers to sustain a continued and deepening process of unionization — a union-centred labour regime — founded in the militant self-organization of the workers, and providing an autonomous political basis for union bargaining power. It related in particular to the upper echelons of the industry, the large, integrated textile mills which dominated in terms of output and formal employment and who controlled the textile employers' association. The achievements at that level, however, tended to be diffused further down the scale, to smaller, single-process firms which were more hostile to the union. The diffusion was promoted by industry-wide collective bargaining, in combination with active union enforcement in the face of such hostility.

Looking at the period as a whole, our examination of union records, interviews with officials, and participation in union meetings suggests a paradoxical expansion and vitality at all levels of the organization at a time marked by overall economic decline as well as by labour's diminishing share in the cost structure of the industry. Production was reorganized, with more machines managed by fewer workers ("overloading") and work discipline and labour control were stepped up. All this points to a decline in labour's bargaining power, both in the workplace and in the labour market (for the distinction, see Arrighi, 1983). Simultaneously, however, it provided for the emergence of a better organized and more qualified workforce. The upgrading of competence and work discipline went hand in hand with the generalization of collective bargaining. The union assisted managements in disciplining labour, but achieved simultaneously the extension of workers' rights in the workplace. The union's ability to intervene in, what Burawoy (1985) calls, the "political apparatuses of production" at the work-place level, supervising and challenging managerial practices of labour control was enhanced. The generalization of collective bargaining at national and company levels accelerated the modernization of the industry. Confronted with a powerful union, weak companies were obliged to either restructure themselves in line with industry "standards" or fold up.

Our evidence suggests that the union had a genuine base in the self-organization of the workers. It was reflected in its mode of responding to workers' grievances and what it achieved in these respects. It also manifested itself in political process at the branch level, and the scope it offered for influence and control from below. We saw evidence of accountability, rooted in the militancy of the cadres at the shop-floor and their preparedness to challenge and defy union officials when feeling shortchanged. It constrained co-optation by state and management while simultaneously providing the union with a basis for confronting the latter and exact genuine concessions on behalf of the workers. The union had to be accommodated. It could not simply be repressed. The prevailing conditions of crisis and shifting policies reinforced the imperatives of accommodation as the firms faced dislocations and shortages and the need to restructure production. Rather than to risk provoking "spontaneous", unpredictable, and potentially violent forms of labour resistance, the employers sought to enlist the co-operation of the union.

Union autonomy vis-à-vis the employers was thus backed by militant self-organization at the work-place level. It contrasts with the stereotypes of submissiveness commonly associated with third-world workers. It is also at odds with conventional narratives of labour movements where effective organization is assumed to emerge from the sustained formation of working class identity and consciousness as part of the process of proletarianization. Certain features distinguish the Nigerian industrial workforce encountered by us from the notoriously subordinated workers in, for instance, the early textile industries of East Asia, who were mostly very young, poorly educated, often women, being subordinated not only at the workplace but also by patriarchal control outside it (Munch, 1988). In the Nigerian case, we meet an overwhelmingly male workforce, usually from the most active age groups with family responsibilities, and with a remarkably high level of education. Their autonomy may partly be explained by their standing in society, and the dignity and respect that they could claim for themselves on such grounds. But autonomy was rooted also in a political economy dominated by small producers with independent access to land and other means of production. Not only were the levels of formal proletarianization low, which is of course true for all early industrializing countries, but also other modes of labour subordination outside the household were weak. This is in contrast to European, Latin American and Asian societies where rural labour was subordinated to land owners and feudal lords and therefore "available" to the new industrial masters in an already subordinated form. In these other cases, they had been deprived of the autonomy, which, in the Nigerian-type of context, seems to encourage workers to resist submission to authoritarian factory regimes. Here, the commodification of production relations in agriculture and the concentration of private control over land were still limited.

Militant self-organization benefitted from this relative autonomy. Workers were weakly socialized into the role expectations associated with factory work, less accustomed to the indignities of authoritarian factory regimes, more prone to defy what they perceived as unacceptable working conditions and offensive managerial practices. In particular, they were more prone to withdraw their labour if offended, either temporarily in some form of industrial action, or by leaving the factory. Society outside the factory gates held prospects of alternative modes of making a living, if not in practice, at least in the world view of the workers. It provided escape routes which made the possible disciplinary consequences of defiance look less intimidating. Union leaders spoke of the mentality of "damning the consequences". Again, our surveys show important differences between Kano and Kaduna in these respects. The Kano workers were more urbanized and integrated into local clientele networks, while the Kaduna workers were more agrarian in background, making them more autonomous and more available for unionization.

The insertion of industry in a surrounding culture of independent production made the moulding of workers to fit the requirements of factory work more difficult. In that sense, we can speak of an unconsolidated industrial working class. However, it did not make workers "half-peasants" — another popular stereotype. Their level of education and aspirations had set them on a course of emancipation from the peasantry and factory work was part of that advance.

The peasant environment contributed to assign a high status to factory work. This does not follow naturally from the insertion of industry in a predominantly agrarian context. Elsewhere, both historically in Europe and contemporarily, for instance in much of South Asia, early industrialization is associated with social degradation, oppressive factory regimes, and human misery. What explains the higher status of factory work in the Nigerian context? The differences between the surrounding agrarian societies are only part of the story. We also need to look at differences in the history of wage work and the formation of industry itself. Nigerian factory workers required education to a certain level partly because of the foreign origin of industrial enterprise. Especially in the early plants, managers, technicians, and supervisors were mostly foreigners and they preferred to employ workers who understood English. This, of course, applies more to the large plants owned by the state and multinationals. Even as middle-management and supervisory cadres were indigenised, English remained a natural means of communication in large factories where workers came from different indigenous language groups. Moreover, several years in school served as a preparation for work-place discipline, especially in a context were the culture of factory work was not well developed.

An industry based on an educated, high-status workforce, however, would have been unlikely in Nigeria at this point in time had it not been made economically feasible by the policies of import-substitution, pursued by the post-colonial state and supported internationally, and where industry produced for heavily protected domestic markets. In that context, the cost of labour mattered less, at least originally. The high-status profile of industrial labour was also supported by the dominance of the state as the major employer of wage labour in the economy. A pattern of wage work modelled on the public services was diffused to other "modern" sectors of economic activity, most directly through the role of state ownership in industry, but also more generally, for instance, in the decisive role of public sector wage awards for wage setting in the private sector.

Trade unions played a key role in this dissemination. The union movement originated largely in the public sector and it remained predominantly one of public sector employees. When manufacturing employment grew at a later point, the impetus to unionization was already there, reinforcing models of wage work originating in an expanding public service, the backbone of modernization and nation-state formation. It carried with it expectations of conditions of service, salary scales, promotions and incremental steps unheard of in manufacturing workplaces in other early industrializing societies.

The militant self-organization of the workers was conditioned by the way industry was situated simultaneously as islands of wage work in a sea of independent producers, and, within the wage economy, as the junior partner to the dominant public service sector. Without the unions, however, this autonomy may as well have generated a mode of workplace behaviour marked by individualized strategies of coping and resistance, hidden or otherwise (cf. Cohen, 1991), or more anarchic modes of collective behaviour, including the "rampaging" so often quoted by unionists as the typical "infant disease" of the labour movement. The strength of the union lay in its ability to give organizational cohesion to the forces on the ground. The acceptance of its leadership by the workers, at least for most of the time, was assisted by their understanding that unions were natural participants in the organization of the workplace, also in striking contrast to other early industrializing regions of the world. It was based on expectation derived from already established patterns in the public services, as further reinforced and generalized by the corporatist pact of 1978, and efficiently implemented by competent union leaders.

Far from being a hindrance to industrial restructuring, the union played an active part in the upgrading of the industry. The unconsolidated nature of the industrial working class reinforced the centrality of union mediation in the labour regime, making the union itself a crucial agency of class consolidation. The process had two sides. On the one hand, it involved the formation and qualification of labour in terms of the requirements of the production process. New workers were educated about proper behaviour in the workplace by union cadres. Managers appealed to the union for help when they themselves failed to control unruly workers. On the other hand, the union was an instrument of the development of a collective identity, expectations of rights, and the promotion of collective interests. The two sides went together; rights and duties. In both respects, it involved asserting leadership, enforcing discipline, and providing cohesion in a workforce which was readily provoked into outbursts of independent, militant industrial action.

The centrality of the union was reinforced by the extreme strains on industrial relations imposed by the successive crises of the early 1980s and the subsequent changes in economic policy. The combined vulnerability of both labour and capital in this situation enhanced the dependence of both on the union as a mediator. To the workers it offered a defence in a situation where their bargaining position was extremely weak. To the managers, the union provided an unofficial ally in the difficult process of adjusting the industry and its workforce to the drastic changes in markets and production conditions. Their reluctant dependence on the union in this respect boosted its bargaining position. We may therefore argue that the drastic fall in workers' market bargaining power, to use Arrighi's (1983) terms, was partly compensated for by an increase in workplace bargaining power.

Externally supported unionization interacted with the autonomous militancy of unsubordinated labour in boosting the workplace bargaining power of the workers. Their commitment to collective forms of action was enhanced, offering evidence of working class formation at a time when the class was experiencing decomposition, in terms of declining numbers as well as in its capacity to reproduce itself from wages. The process reflected the logic of industrial adjustment itself, where world market exposure forced not only cuts in employment and wages but also the upgrading of labour, both in terms of skills and in its adjustment to the labour process.

TRADE UNIONS, INSTITUTIONAL CAPACITY, AND DEMOCRACY: CONCLUSIONS

The chapter began with a critique of liberal theories which eulogize the new civil society that supposedly will emerge from the liberation of market forces and thus become the source of institutional renewal and capacity building. The problem with the liberal vision is that it is unable to identify the social carriers of their programme, except in terms of right-thinking technocrats who are supported by international finance institutions and insulated from local political pressure that threatens to derail the reforms. Most existing organized interests, and trade unions in particular, tend to be dismissed as vested interests of an old, discredited social order.

It is not improbable that most ordinary people in poor countries would be willing to tolerate autocratic and technocratic governments as long as the latter performed reasonably well in terms of peace, order and economic development. But it may not be an option which is likely to be available to most. What will prevent fractious, incompetent, and repressive autocracies to continue to obstruct serious change, as in Nigeria? Nigeria is not unique in having central state institutions that lack the competence and legitimacy to carry out meaningful economic and political reforms. Attempts by international finance institutions to push the leadership in the direction of reform have tended to aggravate the situation. Illegitimate regimes have been further undermined politically and responded to opposition by a combination of intransigence, repression, and erratic policy changes. Until the return to democracy under Obasanjo in 1999, the country had slipped into decay.

So, where do good institutions come from? How will the impetus for reform be sustained politically? This chapter has argued that the search for institutional capacity may find a point of departure in the experience of conflict regulation in society and the organization of interests to which such conflicts give rise. Viable institutions are those which recognize and respect these conflicting interests and assist in developing agreements among the parties concerned around procedures for conflict management. The institutionalization of such agreements can be seen as premised on a social contract where the parties commit themselves to abide by certain rules. The formalization of these rules and the sanctions by which they are backed is a process of constitutionalizing the relations.

The experience of the Nigerian textile workers union obtains its wider significance in the context of such wider process of capacity building from below. We saw how the institutions for regulating conflicting interests in the industry interacted with and reinforced capacity building at the level of the state. The constitutionalization of labour relations in industry placed pressures on the institutions of the state, the police, the courts, and the labour ministry officials, to abide by the rules and respect the contractual relations entered into by workers and employers. There was a clear link between the politics of the workplace and a process of institutionalization at the level of the state, reinforcing the reluctant support of the latter for organizational rights and interest group autonomy.

This is also where we see the link to the wider issues of democratization. Basic rights at the workplace, such as rights of organization and representation, had to be secured and defended at the national political level as they posed a threat to state authoritarianism and a potential basis for democratic opposition. For much of the 1980s and the early 1990s the Nigerian trade union movement had succeeded in defending those rights. With the abortion of the political transition programme in 1993 and the deepening of the political crisis, it came increasingly under fire from the state as the unions were among the few sources of autonomous power and opposition which successive military dictators had failed to suppress. The defence of union rights and autonomy was an important frontier of the wider democratic struggle.

REFERENCES

AKWETEY, E. O. (1994) *Trade Unions and Democratisation: A Comparative Study of Zambia and Ghana* (Stockholm, Department of Political Science).

ANDRAE, G. and B. BECKMAN (1991) "Textile Unions and Industrial Crisis in Nigeria: Labour Structure, Organisation, and Strategies", in I. Brandell (ed), *Workers in Third World Industrialization* (London, Macmillan).

— (1996), "Bargaining for Survival: Unionized Workers in the Nigerian Textile Industry", Discussion Paper 78 (Geneva, UNRISD).

— (1998), *UNION Power in the Nigerian Textile Industry: Labour Regime and Adjustment* (Uppsala, Nordiska Afrikainstitutet; Somerset, New Jersey; Transaction Publishers, Kano; Centre for Research and Documentation).

ARRIGHI, G. (1983) "The Labour Movement in Twentieth-Century Western Europe", in I. Wallerstein (ed), *Labor in the World Social Structure* (Beverly Hills and London, Sage).

BANGURA, Y. and B. BECKMAN (1991) "African Workers and Structural Adjustment With a Nigerian Case Study", in Dharam Ghai (ed), *The IMF and the South: The Social Impact of Crisis and Adjustment* (London, Zed Books). Also in A. O. Olukoshi (ed), *The Politics of Structural Adjustment in Nigeria* (London, James Currey, 1993).

BECKMAN, B. (1992) "Empowerment or Repression? The World Bank and the Politics of Adjustment", in P. Gibbon, Y. Bangura and A. Ofstad (eds), *Authoritarianism, Democracy and Adjustment: The Politics of Economic Reform in Africa* (Uppsala, Scandinavian Institute of African Studies. (Also in *Africa Development*, XVI, 1991:1).

— (1993) "The Liberation of Civil Society: Neo-Liberal Ideology and Political Theory", *Review of African Political Economy*, 58.

— (1995) "Interest Groups and the Construction of Democratic Space", in J. Ibrahim (ed), *Expanding Democratic Space in Nigeria* (Dakar, Codesria Books).

— (1996a) "The Politics of Labour and Adjustment: The Experience of the Nigeria Labour Congress", in T. Mkandawire and A. Olukoshi (eds), *Between Liberalisation and Oppression: The Politics of Structural Adjustment in Africa* (Dakar, Codesria Books).

BECKMAN, B. and A. JEGÁ (1995) "Scholars and Democratic Politics in Nigeria", in *Review of African Political Economy*, 64.

BRANDELL, I. (ed) (1991) *Workers in Third-World Industrialization* (London, Macmillan).

BURAWOY, M. (1985) *The Politics of Production: Factory Regimes and Capitalism and Socialism* (London, Verso).

CAWSON, A. (1986) *Corporatism and Political Theory* (Oxford, Basil Blackwell).

COHEN, R. (1991) "Resistance and Hidden Forms of Consciousness Among African Workers", in R. Cohen, *Contested Domains: Debates in International Labour Studies* (London, Zed Books).

FASHOYIN, T. (1980) *Industrial Relations in Nigeria* (London, Longman).

HASHIM, Y. (1994) 'The State and Trade Unions in Africa. A Study of Macro-Corporatism' (The Hague, Institute of Social Studies. Ph.D. dissertation).

HYMAN, R. (1989) *The Political Economy of Industrial Relations* (London, Macmillan).

LIPIETZ, A. (1986) "New Tendencies in the International Division of Labour: Regimes of Accumulation and Modes of Regulation", in A. Scott and M. Storper (eds), *Production, Work and Territory* (Boston, Allen and Unwin).

MALLOY, J.M. (red) (1977) *Authoritarianism and Corporatism in Latin America* (Pittsburgh, University Press).

OTOBO, D. (1987) *The Role of Trade Unions in Nigerian Industrial Relations* (Oxford and Lagos, Malthouse).

OTOBO, D. and M. OMOLE (eds) (1987) *Readings in Industrial Relations in Nigeria* (Oxford and Lagos, Malthouse).

RUESCHEMEYER, D., E. H. STEPHENS and J. D. STEPHENS (1992) *Capitalist Development and Democracy* (Cambridge, Polity Press; Chicago, Chicago University Press).

VALENZUELA, S. J. (1989) "Labor Movements in Transitions to Democracy: A Framework for Analysis", *Comparative Politics*, 21 (4).

CHAPTER FIVE

Liberalization and Labour Regimes: The Case of Senegalese Industrial Relations

BASSIROU TIDJANI AND AFRED INIS NDIAYE

INTRODUCTION

This contribution examines the extent to which economic liberalization policies first introduced in 1979 have shaped labour regimes in Senegal. Contrary to what occurred in most sub-Saharan African countries, political democracy and union pluralism preceded structural adjustment in Senegal. The late 1970s and 1980s were a turning point. This era witnessed the breakdown of traditional industrial relations in Senegal due to the negative impact of adjustment programmes on labour's living and working conditions, the emergence of autonomous unions and the internal crisis of the integrated central union because of its failure to defend labour's interests. The 1980s opened an era of liberalisation of Senegalese industrial relations setting the stage for the 1990s during which, thanks to decreasing subordination of organized labour to political parties, unions operated as 'private interest groups' essentially preoccupied by the defence of their group interests. This trend, reinforced by the privatization of monopoly public enterprises, went hand in hand with decentralized collective bargaining, concertation and participation schemes. However, in these latter schemes the state and employers played the major roles with constant attempts to put labour on the ropes in order to realize two goals: the improvement of firms' competitiveness and the implementation of economic programmes.

The limitation in analysing how labour regimes have been influenced under liberalization in Senegal is that it may provide an inconclusive account of what has happened. This is because liberalization is still in process. The privatization of the most important public enterprises is far from being completed. Autonomous sectoral unions continue to be created (for example, during the last week of September 1996, the Port of Dakar, one of the largest in West Africa and up to now dominated by the central union related to the ruling party, witnessed the birth of an autonomous union). So we need a framework of analysis which allows us to capture current developments and to integrate more or less predictable changes in labour relations.

Using Krasner's work (1983) as a conceptual point of departure, we define labour regimes as 'sets of implicit or explicit principles, norms, rules and decision-making procedures' which allow us to understand and explain labour relations outcomes as well as actors' behaviours and expectations. The central questions of this contribution are: how has liberalization stimulated or limited the emergence of labour regimes in Senegal? What are the basic features of these labour regimes? We are interested in an empirical characterization of labour regimes under liberalization, and we provide an analysis of related changes in the balance of power, actors' interests and social values. These three factors are taken as the basic causal factors influencing labour relations outcomes: namely laws, rules, decision-making processes and actors' behaviours. In order to capture the stability of the labour regime as well as processes of change, we attempt an examination of the two first decades of the post-independence period.

Despite the critique of his work as conventional, we still consider Dunlop's framework of analysis as a useful one for interpreting changes in labour relations under economic liberalization in Senegal. Dunlop explained that industrial relations (IR) have three major components: the main actors (state, employers and their associations and workers and their organizations); the establishment of industrial relations laws and rules; and the overall context. The context as defined by Dunlop includes three elements, namely technological characteristics, markets and budgetary constraints, and the control and distribution of power in the larger society. Evidently, this approach was influenced by certain features of the American labour regime especially business unionism. The norms were that the management of the firm was the employers' prerogative while the unions' role was to press for a better redistribution of resources with the state overseeing rules and procedures. Under this regime, collective bargaining was the principal decision-making procedure and mechanism of conflict resolution.

Despite the specific character of US business unionism, we believe that this framework provides the main elements to look at in order to understand and explain changes in labour regimes in national contexts. In the case of Senegal, from the 1960s to the 1990s, the Code of Labour as the main regulatory instrument of labour relations has constantly been a contested terrain between actors. From the 1960s to the late 1970s, both opposition politics in the larger society, markets and budgetary constraints shaped labour relations which reflected to a large extent the control and the distribution of power in the larger society. However, from the late 1970s, markets and budgetary constraints have become dominant causal factors. Liberalization and structural adjustment programmes (SAPs) accelerated processes of change. Autonomous unions emerged at a time of political democratization so reflecting the balance of power in the larger society. Their number continued to rise despite the collapse of opposition parties, especially after the February 1993 presidential elections.

LABOUR RELATIONS AND STATE CORPORATISM PRIOR TO ADJUSTMENT

In African countries, national development was the major issue during the immediate post-independence years. Politically, it took the form of state control over the civil society. Economically, an absolute priority was given to production. In labour relations, unions were to contribute to achieving these goals because their members' interests were assumed to be the same as the interests of the nation. State corporatism was the best way of reaching such objectives. Unlike elsewhere in Africa, at least up to the late 1970s, in Senegal the ruling party could never stabilize its domination over organized labour. From 1960 to the first adjustment programme introduced in 1979, there were three failed attempts to stabilize a regime of state corporatism in Senegalese industrial relations.

The first attempt at state corporatism occurred in 1961. Senegalese workers had inherited the French pluralistic and political tradition and around 40 trade unions existed. For the ruling party, national development required a re-configuration of labour organizations and a re-definition of their agendas. Unions were required to focus exclusively on the defence of their members' interests through a central organisation, the National Union of Senegalese Workers (UNTS) borne from the forced merging of unions with different traditions. Failure to establish the first elements of state corporatism soon became apparent. In May 1963, diversity in the composition of UNTS provoked internal conflicts accentuated by internal divergences in the ruling party. This led to a split in the union and finally to the emergence of the doctrine of "Responsible Participation".

This doctrine, which still underlies the relationship between the dominant central union and the state, although in a weaker mode, was the second attempt to institutionalize state domination over labour. It included economic, political and repressive elements the theoretical basis of which was set at the ruling party October 1963 Congress. Economically, the issue was about increasing production and national revenue, and unions were deeply involved in it (Lô, n.d.). Politically, the central union was to be integrated into the ruling party. Finally, the state expanded its repressive apparatus to unions by introducing in 1965 a law against any organization (union or party) which represented a threat to its domination over the civil society. This repressive pattern later took the form of changes in the labour code and was maintained throughout the 1970s.

In a labour movement characterized by a pluralistic tradition, the imposition of a single center for organized labour had a downside. Many workers who were not members of the ruling party entered UNTS and saw in it not an arm of the state but an instrument which could be useful for the defence of their rapidly decreasing purchasing power. In May 1968, in the same period as the student revolt, the central union launched a general strike against basic commodities' price increases and unemployment. The gains were important: a 15% increase of the minimum wage, a reduction of deputies' and ministers' and ministers' advantages, and demands made by UNTS members for a review of state-union and party-union relations. The state responded by promoting in 1969 the emergence of a new center, the National Confederation of Senegalese Workers (CNTS) which replaced UNTS. Thus May 1968 marked the failure of the integration strategy as another attempt to introduce state corporatism.

The third attempt was first formalized at the ruling party's December 1969 Congress which suggested a new integration strategy based on the co-optation of labour leaders into both the government and the national assembly. However, in the early 1970s, the combination of continuing student and labour unrest and the first signs of the economic crisis forced the state to considerably revise its attitude towards labour and the civil society. In 1971, the state once again mobilised its state apparatus; in addition to the dissolution of UNTS, Article 249 of the Code of Labour was modified and compulsory arbitration imposed in all labour conflicts. For the third time, an attempt to establish total state domination over organized labour failed.

The state was nonetheless pushed to make major economic concessions (two wage increases in 1973 and 1974), and its strategy shifted at its December 1976 Congress from union integration to affiliation as an ultimate way of implementing its conception of labour relations. On the one hand, the concept of labour integration (although never really implemented) was that all working people members of the ruling party had to be automatically members of the central union, and that all union members should belong to the ruling party. On the other hand, labour affiliation presupposed that although the ruling party constituents were automatically members of the central union, other unions' members could belong to other political parties. However, this major concession on the part of the ruling party was compensated by the modification of Article 6 of the Labour Code: in order to restrict the emergence of competing unions, recognition procedures were made more complex.

The two major reasons for this changing strategy on the part of the state and the ruling party were firstly the rise of internal conflicts in the central union and secondly shifts in the balance of power in the larger society during the 1970s. In the face of rapidly growing economic problems requiring the defence of workers' interests, lack of consensus among members on the interpretation of their organization's responsibilities *vis à vis* the state led to fractions in the CNTS. In the larger society, the long struggle of opposition parties for the legal recognition was partially successful. With the recognition of three political parties by 19 79, Senegal entered the first stage of multi-partyism. It was also the first stage of union pluralism. However, the trade unions created were subordinated to opposition political parties.

Politically, a tradition of pluralism and search for independence among workers did not allow for the construction of a single labour center. A regime of corporatist concertation where many labour organizations representing different interests have access to government would have probably led to better results for the state. Economically, the honeymoon between the state and labour expected from the national construction programme was very short indeed because for labour it meant high commodity prices, low wages and unemployment. So state corporatism proved difficult to root deep into Senegalese labour relations.

Opposition parties were divided between those who advocated "entrisme" in the CNTS to build their bases and those who advocated the creation of alternative central unions. These two positions respectively explain internal debates in the CNTS on ruling party-union relations and the emergence during the 1970s of trade unions subordinated to opposition parties. The doctrine of "Responsible Participation" was revised. Autonomous unions were created. Democratization expanded. During the same period, the economic crisis deepened. International funding agencies became major players in the Senegalese political economy.

LABOUR UNDER ADJUSTMENT: THE BREAKDOWN OF TRADITIONAL LABOUR RELATIONS

For workers, the central issue during the 1970s and 1980s continued to be the defence of their working and living conditions. In 1980, for example, labour's purchasing power was only 73% of its 1960 level, 3,000 workers lost their jobs in the agro-business sector; strategic public enterprises were liquidated (Diop, 1992). This constituted the basis for teachers', students' and industrial workers' unrest. Organized labour, dominated by CNTS despite its weakening by the birth of autonomous unions, made significant legislative gains during the early 1980s. These were the signing of an inter-professional national collective agreement, and the suppression of Articles 80-01 and 199 of the Labour Code. The first one set a limit to payments due to employers in case of unfair lay-offs. The second allowed employers to hire workers without following recruitment procedures established by the Code. However, as we moved towards the 1990s, labour began to experience significant losses on other fronts. In 1987, Article 35 of the Labour Code (replaced in the early 1990s by Article 47 to which we will return) was amended in order to permit employers to engage in short-term contracts renewable for unlimited periods of time. Two years later, in 1989, the Investment Code [in its Articles 12, 22 and 23] allowed employers to fire at will.

These losses were partly related to the fact that, contrary to previous years, organized labour had to face not only the state but also an empowered employer community and international funding agencies, all three frequently operating as an anti-labour coalition. Because adjustment programmes had no social dimensions of safety nets, trade unions encountered negative effects from their implementation.

The first elements of economic liberalization and structural adjustment appeared in the late 1970s. Senegal implemented successively in 1979 a Financial Stabilization Plan; from 1980 to 1984 a medium-term Economic and Financial Adjustment Plan; and from 1985 to 1992 a long-term Adjustment Plan. These plans were accompanied by state economic disengagement and privatization. At the industrial level, the New Industrial Policy (NPI) introduced by the Ministry of Industry in 1986 included tariff revision, price liberalization, the simplification of import and export procedures, the reform of the Code of Labour (employment flexibility), the reform of the Investment Code, and other measures in favour of employers.

From 1982 to 1987, six sectoral autonomous unions entered the industrial relations arena. These unions had two important characteristics. First, they were from diverse origins, thus proving the extent to which social discontent had spread in the society: doctors, lawyers, journalists, university professors, school teachers and other public sector workers in electricity, telecommunications and water supply sectors created their autonomous unions. Second, and this was an important novelty, they were not subordinated to political parties. Thus, the 1980s in Senegalese industrial relations were an era of union autonomy. In addition to the state strategy of allowing workers to use different channels of expression given growing discontent, the emergence of autonomous unions resulted from the combination of several factors: the failure of a particular form of political unionism (i.e. the control of unions by political apparatuses); and the incapacity of CNTS as the arm of the ruling party in the labour movement to seriously defend workers' interests.

The birth of sectoral autonomous unions which led to the creation of the National Union of Autonomous Syndicates in Senegal (UNSAS) in 1990 was one of the most important transformations of Senegalese labour relations during the 1980s. First, evidently it fostered competitive unionism and raised the issue of labour unity during struggles against SAPs. Second, it created the conditions for the "civilization" of Senegalese industrial relations and the end of union subordination to political parties. The "civilization" of industrial relations can be defined as its organization based on the mutual recognition of actors and the establishment of a legal framework to regulate the relations between the actors. Third, it generated more debates in CNTS around the need to rethink practices of "Responsible Participation" in a context of economic crises and liberalization which considerably reduced state resources and thus its capacity to subsidize the central union leaders' practices of clientelism. Towards the end of the 1980s, in a major statement, CNTS admitted that "Responsible Participation" means domination, domestication, subordination, and class collaboration between unions' directions and state institutions at the expense of labour's interests although it continued to operate within the framework of that doctrine (CNTS, 1987). This was a major change in discourse.

WORKING CONDITIONS AND SHIFT IN DISCOURSE ON LABOUR RELATIONS

Although economic crises and structural adjustment programmes were not the source of democratization and the restructuring of labour relations in Senegal, they definitely accelerated these two processes. Interestingly, labour organizations' greater focus on the defence of their members' interests did not prevent the implementation of SAPs, as expected by radical autonomous unions and critics of "Responsible Participation". This was to a certain extent due to the fact that the civilization of industrial relations in Senegal had at its center the transformation of labour organizations into private interest groups.

What is the fixed set of interest organizations in Senegal? They are on labour's side CNTS and UNSAS, and on employers' side the National Council of Employers (CNP), the most representative employer organization and later the National Confederation of Senegalese Employers (CNES) who split from CNP in 1993 on the basis of a nationalistic agenda directed against the subordination of Senegalese employers to their European counterparts. What are the bases for an interdependence between actors' interests under economic liberalization? The response is that despite diverging interests unions, employers and the state agreed explicitly or implicitly that the consequences of the economic crises and of SAPs had been so negative for the structure of labour markets, workers' conditions and performances of firms that they needed to combine their efforts to find adequate solutions.

Our analysis of CNTS' First of May grievance book from 1980 to 1995 shows a shift from a grieving and distributive logic to a productive and participative one. In 1984, CNTS leaders emphasized the fact that they were spending more time on issues relating to companies restructuring than on the elaboration of grievance books. According to them, frequent threats of enterprise closing created among workers a participative mentality ("conscience autogestionnaire") (CNTS, 1985). Between 1991 and 1995, CNTS's demands for workers' participation in companies' management and boards of directors and in policy making shifted from 16 per cent of its total demands to 28 per cent. This was based on the rejection of the idea that the management of the firm was the exclusive domain of employers (CNTS, 1987).

Given the conditions of its emergence which also made its specific character (i.e. a radical opposition to CNTS's "Responsible Participation"), UNSAS, the autonomous central union has had to maintain its orientation towards the defence of its members' interests and the rejection of any compromise with the state and employers. However, its demands for concertation in 1993 during the workers' struggle against the Austerity Plan and later its participation in tripartite and bipartite committees along with CNTS were clear indications of its search for a social pact. Later, during the 1990s, UNSAS's attitude on the issue of privatization of public enterprises (telecommunications, water supply) shifted from radical rejection to accommodation ("accompagnement").

On their side, employers reinforced this trend towards the search for compromises. In 1987, CNP introduced its "Social Pact" (Pact Social) which presented its conception of the partnership between employers and labour in a context of economic crisis and liberalization (CNP, 1987). The main point of this document was the need for new labour relations which excluded grievances not grounded in the real difficulties which are central to companies' survival and job security. This was to be realized through the institutionalization of periodic bipartite dialogue and a shift from the traditional opposition between capital and labour to a positive synergy materialized by a pact between them.

The central question is the following: has organized labour's shift toward concertation and participation been the result of a conscious and independent choice or the outcome of a relationship of power in favour of employers and/or the state, and eventually international funding agencies? The concept of 'private interest group' is not synonymous with equity, justice or equilibrium concerning social actors' interests. It includes relationships of power, especially in hard times. We argue that this shift by labour resulted more from its declining bargaining power than from an unconstrained choice.

By the end of the 1980s, there was evidence of failure (both economically and socially) of the adjustment programmes implemented in Senegal (Lachaud, 1987, Duruflé, 1988; Dia, 1988; Kassé, 1990; Berg, 1990). In his work on the resistance of Senegalese workers to the consequences of SAPs, Ndiaye (1992) showed how badly they were hit. The majority of them (60.5 per cent) had four children on the average but had to satisfy the needs of more than 10 people in their household. Most workers (96.8 per cent) could not satisfy their basic needs such as daily expenses, school fees, medical care and housing rent anymore . Official statistics show that between 1976 and 1990, while the minimum wage index shifted from 100 to 187.81, the price index went from 100 to 242.49. It also appeared from these statistics the existence of a large gap between the growth rate of taxable revenues (7.36 per cent) and tax increases (31.26 per cent) from 1980 to 1990.

Workers' deteriorating working and living conditions brought up two major consequences. First, changes occurred in their traditional salaried status: a great number of them engaged in some informal activities in and out of the workplace in their daily life to supplement income. Second, in the firm, labour depended more and more on employers both individually and collectively for the satisfaction of their immediate needs. The employers provided individual loans which reached up to 41 per cent of workers' monthly wages. They also allowed for the creation of solidarity associations (based on religion, ethnicity or villages) in the workplace. These associations were substitutes for unions' actions although most workers remained union members. While the rate of unionization reached between 80 per cent to 90 per cent in the firms investigated, only 6 per cent of their workers relied on labour organizations to increase their wages.

These associations exhibited characteristics which contributed to the weakening of unions in the workplace. Their members were wage workers and management and their operating mode was exclusively consensual as opposed to trade-union grieving strategies. Their relations with employers were based on class collaboration, not on the relations of production; their existence depended totally on employers' will.

The 1990s accentuated the trend of the 1980s. It appeared more and more clearly that despite discourses on the search for compromises, labour relations were increasingly becoming a relationship of power between workers protecting their working and living conditions, employers facing the insecurity of market competition and the state trying to maintain its political capabilities and legitimacy. International funding agencies' formal recommendation that the civil society be involved in national level policy-making through concertation (Government du Senegal, 1992) was too idealistic to be implemented in a structural adjustment context worsened by devaluation.

NEW ELEMENTS IN THE LABOUR REGIME: TOWARDS CONCERTATION AND PARTICIPATION?

The 1990s have been characterized by a number of notable developments. Economically, SAPs continued to be implemented. Their central elements were the 1993 Austerity Plan (Plan d'Urgence), the January 1994 devaluation of the currency, and the privatization of monopoly public enterprises. Politically, the ruling party again won in the February 1993 elections. Opposition parties lost most of their political capabilities and autonomy by being integrated into a government coalition. Organized labour shifted from opposition to SAPs to accommodation. More specifically, labour organizations' reactions to government and employer policies was one of initial opposition, then demand for participation, finally bargaining in tripartite or bipartite committees. However, in most cases, they were involved in the implementation of state or employer agendas.

Moreover, during the 1990s, the centrality of the state became more obvious. If the discourses on state disengagement had any basis in the 1980s , the 1990s showed that the state was back in the vogue given demands for its intervention by the civil society (Tidjani, 1993). Citizens expected the establishment of control mechanisms and coercive rules to guarantee commodity price stability. Because of the failure of the NPI, employers expected state intervention on issues relating to customs, taxes and production costs. Unions demanded the end of their members' decreasing wages through indexation to the cost of living. Furthermore, due to their declining bargaining power in many workplaces, unions tended more and more to consider national level bargaining as a substitute for workplace level bargaining. This automatically made the state an obvious contender on labour relations issues. Although they toned down struggles against the implementation of SAPs (at least for some time), civil society organizations called for controlled de-regulation and saw in the state the most effective regulatory institution despite critiques of its failure.

Requirements for state intervention by different groups in the Senegalese civil society confirmed the view that

> groups in civil society are also dependent on the state for their very functions and liberties. The freedom, individuality and social justice associated with civil society can be obtained or secured only within the framework of legal equality, plurality and unrestricted public spheres guaranteed by the state (Beckman and Sachikonye, 1996, 2).

This made the 1990s an era of discourses on tripartite and bipartite concertation and participation although in practice most attempts still need to show some success.

However, the first major test of the 1990s was undoubtedly the 1993 Austerity Plan supported by international funding agencies. According to the government, this plan was inevitable because of a structural disequilibrium in public finances which led to a deficit of 180 billions CFA (1 dollar US is about 500 CFA). Implementation of this plan was the condition for a World Bank loan of 60 billion CFA for Senegal's debt repayment. The strategy contained in the Austerity Plan sought to increase state revenues and reduce its expenses. Additional resources were to come from tax increases, customs duties and the establishment of new fiscal obligations for businesses to raise revenue. The reduction in government expenditure especially in the public sector where salaries amounted to 60 per cent of state resources was aimed at the 40 per cent norm set by the government. Although the plan involved cuts in government officials' privileges, workers and their organizations as well as all opposition parties massively rejected any attempts to reduce their wages. Employers' associations were also radically opposed to it.

The most important and unexpected aspect of the struggle against the plan was the construction of the "Intersyndicate", a united front of all unions whether linked to the ruling party or autonomous. For the first time, since independence, unions with radically different orientations mobilized their members to oppose government economic policies. Given its long relationship with the ruling party, CNTS was at first hesitant in its reaction to the plan. Then, it joined the coalition under the combined pressure from UNSAS and from its own members. Finally, it became for a while the spearhead of the coalition given its numerical domination over the Senegalese organized union movement and its easy access to government institutions. For example, its deputies voted against the Austerity Plan in the National Assembly.

The second most important aspect of unions' actions against the plan was their capacity to protect their independence, thanks to autonomous unions involved, *vis-à-vis* opposition political parties whose credibility had been severely weakened by their integration into the government coalition. However, opposition parties were also mobilized and actually their collective opposition against the plan came before the unions' "Intersyndicate" and played a major role in the total success of the September 2nd general strike against a proposed wage reduction, and a demand for concertation between the "Intersyndicate" and the government. This major success was even acknowledged by government officials. This general strike was the first one since the May 1968 events. Significantly, unions were the leaders of this strike; opposition parties came in support of it after failed attempts to organize it jointly with the "Intersyndicate". Thus, a central characteristic of the "civilization" of Senegalese industrial relations, namely the independence of unions from political parties, was reinforced.

However, this success was only partial because after three weeks of negotiations with government officials, the "Intersyndicate" broke down. This showed the limits of unions' cohesion in Senegal. The main reason for this break were CNTS ambivalence due to its reliance on "Responsible Participation," and its loyalty to the ruling party to which the large majority of its leaders belonged. It would be too lengthy to give a narrative of the negotiation process and how it led to the end of the "Intersyndicate" as this has been analyzed in full detail elsewhere (see Ndiaye and Tidjani, 1995). Although this first national level concertation between unions and government brought limited gains to workers, wages were still reduced, and the plan implemented. Nevertheless, this concertation set the stage for other ones.

We observed above that organized labour was at the center of the opposition to the Austerity Plan. However, employers from both the formal and informal sectors were also opposed to it but for different reasons. The former were concerned by what they construed as the anti-business measures of the plan, especially tax increases. For the first time in the history of Senegalese labour relations, employers' associations (particularly the CNES) drew unions into a coalition against government policies. Informal sector employers also effectively participated in the success of the September 2 strike by closing their shops. This was on the basis of an agenda against monopoly businesses protected by the state in economic activities such as sugar and rice production and processing, critical to the wealth of the nation. Such initiatives, although ephemeral, facilitated the establishment of concertation and participatory structures following the 50 per cent devaluation of the CFA.

The devaluation was also an issue during the struggle against the Austerity Plan in 1993. Among other reasons, unions rejected wage reduction because they anticipated the devaluation. It occurred in January 1994 and was a major attack on workers' purchasing power. Improvements expected from it especially for businesses and for labour markets never really materialized. In fact, the momentum towards privatization of many public enterprises and over the flexibilization of labour in the workplace in addition to the negative consequences of the devaluation further weakened the position of organized labour. It also considerably reduced their chances of being serious contenders in concertation and participative structures, even though unions saw in them, for lack of better strategies, a potentially useful innovation in labour-capital-government relations in Senegal.

Mass discontent over the devaluation and demands for wage adjustment by workers led to the tripartite "Comité de Suivi de l'Aprés Dévaluation" in charge of managing all the social and economic consequences of the devaluation. Then came the Tripartite Concertation Committee "Comité de Concertation Tripartite" for a periodic examination of workers' grievances. Also set up were the bipartite structures between employers' associations and unions to preserve social peace, firms' survival and to improve labour markets. The National Committee on Employment Policy, "Comité National de Suivi de la Politique de l'Emploi" was established to take charge of the evaluation of government employment policies.

None of these committees actually realized its objectives, and at this point, none of them functions. An explanation of this failure requires an analysis of social actors' attitudes in national level concertation and participative structures and in workplaces participative processes (for example, in cases of privatization).

In theory, organized labour's involvement in concertation and participative structures can be viewed as a form of social control aimed at a better defence of their members' interests. Devine defines social control as "a process through which decisions about social life are taken and implemented, directly or indirectly, by the people who are affected by them" (1991, 205-206). Elaborating on Devine's definition, we argue that social control in the case of Senegalese unions was a strategy aiming at participating in decision-making processes on national economic policy instead of merely reacting to the consequences of the policy. However, if participation and concertation are to be more substantive from the viewpoint of unions, two conditions must be met. First, government and employers have to demonstrate political readiness to accept unions' input. This condition depends on the mutual recognition by social actors of their contributory capacities. Second, an agreement must exist among actors on the participatory framework and the mechanisms through which it operates.

Although UNSAS was present in all tripartite and bipartite committees, it preferred concertation to participation because it considered the latter as a form of "class collaboration". CNTS advocated ideas of concertation and participation but rejected any sort of bipartite schemes (e.g. the CNP's Social Pact) which did not involve the state as an arbitrator. The reasons were that although the CNTS criticized "Responsible Participation", it still found it a comfortable framework to work within. The framework allows for easy access to government institutions and resources and for resistance to the rise of autonomous unions generally feared by the state. Thus, for the state, CNTS is an arm against UNSAS.

Given the context of liberalization, employers' associations did not perceive the state as a major player in the type of labour relations they wanted to promote. For them, the state could at most be a distant arbitrator. In effect, while unions tended to focus more and more on national-level bargaining, employers looked at the bilateral partnership in the workplace as one of the better ways of improving the performance of firms. Actually, employers' attitudes towards workplace collective bargaining somehow matched the position of the state which pursues a disengagement strategy.

In national level bargaining where it plays a major role, the state has had attitudes which have largely contributed to the failure of tripartite structures, and these attitudes were criticized both by employers and unions. First, it constantly manipulated these latter to make its decisions acceptable to other actors. Second, in cases where decisions were taken collectively, it reneged on their implementation. Finally, on central issues, it "forgot" to seek other actors' opinions, especially those of labour.

Workers have been the losers in this new trend towards de-regulation, concertation and participation. Employers control the workplace. The state can manipulate national level bargaining. Labour has barely been able to link workplace level with national level bargaining. The superior political capabilities of employers and the state are related to their superior organizational capacities compared to labour.

However, there are divergences between the two major employers' organizations. The CNES split from CNP in 1993. Furthermore, while CNP favoured long-term stable and institutionalized pacts with labour, CNES preferred ad-hoc arrangements and structures dealing with limited agendas. However, they both agreed on the need to make the firms more competitive, and to take advantage of opportunities for labour flexibility through the state's initiative to revise Article 47 of the Code of Labour. This revision gives employers more powers to lay off workers for economic reasons. This has directly contributed during the past few years to an increase in temporary employment at the expense of permanent jobs (Sud-Hebdo, 1996).

Structural adjustment programmes have led to several discourses on the disengagement and weakening of the state in Africa. Obviously, in the case of Senegal such discourses contradict the civil society's calls for state intervention. According to Wade (1990), three elements are central to the capacity of a particular state to govern a country. They are (1) the competence and coherence of the state bureaucracy and (2) the degree of institutionalization of its political authority which both determine (3) its relationships with the civil society, especially employers and investors in periods of economic crisis during which any solution depends on the restructuring of the production apparatus.

Besides the support which it has received from international funding agencies, the superior organizational capacity of the Senegalese state is related to its control over economic data and information, and its ability to distribute them to other actors in a selective way even when its bureaucratic apparatus appeared to be disorganized. The bases for this control are the higher level of institutionalization of its structures and thirty six years of bureaucratic experience which have led to an operating mode inaccessible to their partners, especially non-collaborative unions such as UNSAS. Control over information is a key bargaining advantage in a period when the complexity of the context requires solutions based on a certain level of expertise on the part of social actors. The weak expertise of labour is particularly obvious on issues related to privatization, an essential aspect of liberalization.

The weak expertise does not automatically mean the end of collective actions. However, by promoting the weakening of some regulatory mechanisms, it has stimulated the decline of large scale collective bargaining, for example, at the national level, to a certain extent. As liberalization led to decentralized collective bargaining, the gap between workplace and national level negotiations began to widen. For example, while the "Intersyndicate" was breaking away during the struggle against the Austerity Plan, in many firms (e.g. railways, telecommunications, water supply), the unity of labour was maintained on the basis of work-place related grievances. The on-going case of the National Society of Telecommunications (SONATEL), a public enterprise in a monopoly position and now involved in a privatization process is a perfect illustration of that.

SONATEL is a case where, while at the central level UNSAS and CNTS have not been able to build any unity since the 1993 Austerity Plan, their two affiliated sectoral unions (respectively the SNTPT and the SYTS) built a firm level "Intersyndicate" to face the expected negative consequences of privatization on wages, employment and other working conditions. Concertation and participation based on loyalty to the company have been at the center of the Intersyndicate's agenda. Because concertation with the state and top management required a certain level of expertise which it did not possess, the "Intersyndicate" extended its membership to middle management. The outcome of this collaboration has been high quality documents based on national data and international comparisons.

Because for the "Intersyndicate" one of the important issues was to defend the acknowledged prestige of SONATEL as "a success story" in the Senegalese economy, participation in the capital of the emerging private firm was to be central in its strategy. In order to achieve such a goal, workers involved in the "Intersyndicate" created an independent financial entity whose aim was to buy shares in the privatized SONATEL. The most recent offer the government made to workers has been to give them 10 per cent to 12 per cent of the new society's capital shares. Finally, a social pact elaborated by the "Intersyndicate" and focusing on issues of anticipated requirements, lay-offs, outplacement, financial help for small firm creation by employees to cite but a few, is now the object of negotiations between management and workers.

Workers' attitudes towards privatization is a learning process. For instance, the privatization of SONATEL was preceeded by other privatizations, especially the one that occurred at the National Society of Water of Senegal (SONEES), another public enterprise with a monopoly in water supply. In that firm, unions created an "Intersyndicate" and first rejected any kind of privatization of the company. This was based on the argument that the firm was profitable. However, seeing that their opposition was a lost battle they decided to be accommodating. Their gains were, however, minor compared to what SONATEL's "Intersyndicate" (which also first rejected privatization) obtained.

What has happened in privatized companies, especially in large ones such as SONATEL and SONEES who play the role of locomotives in national industrial relations, is an important indication of new developments in relations between labour, capital and state because it encapsulates most of the changes occurring. Unions are more and more operating as private interest groups. Reliance on pacts, concertation and participation mechanisms are important features of industrial relations. Unions' acceptance of concertation and participation has resulted from a shift in the balance of power in favour of employers and the state. Expertise on economic and social issues has become central to labour relations. There is a declining interest in coordination between national level and workplace level bargaining. Political parties are no longer central actors in the emergence of new labour relations as was the case during the late 1960s and the early 1980s, for example. Although labour is not totally on the ropes, it is in a less militant shape than it was in the early 1990s concerning collective action.

LABOUR REGIMES AND LIBERALIZATION IN SENEGAL: A SYNTHESIS

During the first period examined — from 1960 to the late 1970s — labour relations debates and practices were about constant re-arrangements of rules and procedures following changes in power and economic interests. Workers' reactions to their declining conditions and discontent with their social position *vis-a-vis* the ruling party were at the origin of most conflicts to which the state responded in various ways: satisfaction of demands, integration or affiliation, repression, changes in the labour code, each of them corresponding to a particular arrangement. However, the state could not stabilize state corporatism, as its preferred regime given its economic and social objectives. In other words, during this period there were no established and generally accepted principles and norms (to all actors) as intervening variables between shifts in power and interests on one side and labour relations outcomes on the other. This was due to the fact that while for the state and the central union leadership the establishment of state corporatism mattered, for the rank-and-file union members it did not matter as much.

The conditions for the emergence of a different labour regime began to exist during the 1980s with the "civilization" of labour relations. There was a coherence between the progressive transformation of unions into private interest groups, their presence in concertation and participatory structures in national-level bargaining, and their demands for social pacts and co-management in the workplace. Returning to the main components of regimes, we characterize as causal factors the weakening of labour by employers and the state (power issue), and the negative impact of SAPs on workers' conditions (economic interests); and as the most important outcomes the introduction of employment flexibility in the Code of Labour and collaborative attitudes aiming at establishing social pacts . Using Dunlop's concepts, it can be stated that power, markets and budgetary constraints have affected rules and the relationships among actors from the late 1970s to the 1990s.

We argue that actors' egoistic interests in a structural adjustment context, the end of union subordination to political parties and the search of knowledge and expertise on the part of organized labour are playing a major role in the shaping of the labour regime in Senegal. Egoistic interests may stimulate the creation of regimes when their satisfaction involves risks of Pareto-suboptimal outcomes. It was mentioned earlier that although the state, workers and employers had divergent interests, they understood the need for collaborative arrangements in order to exit the crisis.

However, because collaborative arrangements do not exclude relationships of power and may be a step towards a labour regime, the creation of a labour regime involves relationships of power. "Dominant actors . . . may compel other actors to act in conformity with a particular set of principles, norms, rules and decision-making processes" (Krasner, 1983, 15). The fact that unions lost some of their political capabilities under liberalization underscored that Senegal was moving towards a labour regime heavily weighted in favour of the state and employers.

As a dynamic factor in the development of a labour regime, the birth of autonomous unions and their independence *vis-a-vis* political parties, was central to the transformation of organized labour into private interest groups in search of pacts. Pacts require elaboration which goes beyond simple grievances, and they have made knowledge and expertise central aspects of Senegalese unions' activities. Knowledge and expertise stimulate actors' collaboration because they uncover "complex connections" and hidden convergent views. In Senegal, during the 1990s, greater collaboration between autonomous unions and intellectuals for expertise (e.g. the case of the "Intersyndicate" (see Ndiaye and Tidjani, 1995), the creation of a data bank "observatoire" by unions for negotiation purposes, and the unity between blue-collar and white-collar workers in the workplace on issues of privatization opened the way to concertation and participation schemes.

REFERENCES

BECKMAN, Bjorn and Lloyd M. SACHIKONYE (1996) 'Labour Regimes and Liberalization: The Restructuring of State-Society Relations in Africa. Towards an Analytical Framework', *Workshop on Labour Regimes and Liberalization*, jointly organized by the Department of Agrarian and Labour Studies, Istitute of Development Studies and the Department of Political Science, Stockholm University, 16-18 May, 1996, Harare.

BERG, E. (1990) *Adjustment Postponed: Economic Policy Reform in Senegal in the 1980s* (Report prepared for USAID/Dakar).

CONFÉDÉRATION Nationale des Travailleurs du Senegal, (1987) *La Participation des Travailleurs Comme Strate'gie de development* (Dakar, Senegal).

CONSEIL National du Patronat, (1987) *Pacte Social* (Dakar, Senegal).

DELANEY, J. Thomas and Marick F. MASTERS, (1991) "Unions and Political Action", in George Strauss, Daniel G. Gallagher, and Jack Fiorito (eds) *The State of the Unions* (Industrial Relations Research Series, Madison), 313-346.

DEVINE, Pat. (1991) "Economy, State and Civil Society", *Economy and Society*, 20 (2), 205-216.

DIA, M. (1988) *Le Senegal Trahi: un marché d'esclaves (du verbalisme socialisant au libérlisme non libertaire)* (Sélio, Paris).

DIOP, B. Babacar, (1992) "Les Syndicats, l'Etat et les Partis Politiques", in Momar CoumbaDiop, (ed) *Senegal Trajectoires d'un Etat* (Dakar, Série des livres due Codesria), 479-500.

DURUFLÉ, Gilles, (1988) *L'ajustement Structurel en Afrique (Senegal, Côte d'Ivoire, Madagascar* (Karthala, Paris).

DUNLOP, T. John, (1958) *Industrial Relations Systems* (New York, Holt).

GOUREVITCH, P. A. (1986) *Politics in Hard Times: Comparative Responses to International Economic Crisis* (Ithaca, Cornell University Press).

GUÉYE Ousseynou, (1996) "Les Temporaires ont la cote", *Wal Fadjiri*, Lundi 16 Septmbre, 1349, 5.

KASSÉ, Moustapha, (1990) *Senegal: Crise économique et Ajustement Structural* (Editions Nouvelles du Sud, Paris).

KONE, D, (1990) *Genése du Syndicat Unique des Travailleurs de l'Electricité (SUTELEC)* (Mémoire de DEA, Université Cheikh Anta Diop, Dakar).

KRASNER, D. Stephen, (1983) "Structural Causes and Regime Consequences: Regimes as Intervening Variables", in Stephen D. Krasner, (ed) *International Regimes* (Ithaca, Cornell University Press), 1-21.

LACHAUD, J.P. (1987) *Restructuring des entreprsise publiques et les ajustements sur le marché due travail au Senegal: des possibilities à la mesure des experiences* (IIES, Geneva).

LÔ, MAGATTE, (1987) *Syndicalism et Participation Responsible* (L'Harmattan, Paris).

MINISTÉRE de l'Economie, des Finances et du Plan, (9-12 Janvier, 1992) *Séminaire Banque Mondiale-Autorités Sénégalaises* (Dakar, Senegal).

NDIAYE M. I. Alfred, (1992) 'Crise économique prolongée et formes de réponses des travailleurs: Etude de la résistance du travailleur Séngalais' (Theése de Doctorat Troisiéme Cycled' Anthropologie, Université Cheikh Ana Diop, Dakar).

NDIAYE I. Alfred and Bassirou TIDJANI, (1995) *Mouvements ouvriers et crise conomique. Les syndicats Sénégalais face à l'ajustment structural* (Série de monographies 3/95, Codesria, Dakar).

SACHIKONYE, Lloyd M, (1996) 'The State and the Union Movement in Zimbabwe: Cooptation, Conflict and Accommodation', Workshop on *Labour Regimes and Liberalization*, jointly organized by the Department of Agrarian and Labour Studies, Institute of Development Studies and the Department of Political Science, Stockholm University, 16-18 May 1996, Harare.

STREECK, Wolfgang and Philippe C. SCHMITTER, (1985) "Community, Market, State and Associations? The Prospective Contribution of Interest Governance to Social Order", *European Sociological Review,* 1 (2), 119-137.

TIDJANI, Bassirou, (29 Janvier, 1994) "Le consensus plutôt que l'unité", *Sud Quotidien,* Samedi , 248, 1 et 4.

TOURAINE, A, (1960) "Contribution à la sociologie du mouvement ouvrier: le syndicalism de contrôl", *Cahiers Internationaux de Sociologie,* XXIII, 57-88.

WADE, R. (1990) *Governing the Market: Economic Theory and the Role of Government in East Asian Industrialization* (Princeton University Press).

CHAPTER SIX

Economic Liberalization, Authoritarianism and Trade Unions in Egypt

OMAR EL-SHAFEI

INTRODUCTION

In the midst of deep socio-economic crises and escalating foreign debts, many countries in Africa and elsewhere in the Third World embarked on programmes of structural adjustment from the early 1980s onward. These consist of economic "reform" measures introduced under the auspices of the IMF and the World Bank, and constitute a radical departure from policies pursued by post-colonial regimes in much of Africa during the preceding two decades.

By the early 1990s, these measures were accompanied by a wave of democratization, in a way that seemed to confirm the neo-liberal assertion that economic and political liberalization tend to go hand in hand. Trade unions played a significant role in this democratization. These developments in Africa coincided with the democratic revolutions that led to the collapse of the Stalinist regimes of Eastern Europe, and that invariably led to the emergence of regimes committed both to a market economy and liberal democracy.

While the democratic transformations have often been hesitant, half-hearted, and subject to negative reversals, the orthodoxy everywhere has become that economic efficiency requires a market orientation, and that the latter is a precondition for democratic government. It is in this context that "the 'liberation of civil society' from the suffocating grip of the state has become the hegemonic ideological project of our time" (Beckman, 1993, 20).

This ideological project is dominant in Egypt today not just among neo-liberals, but also among many leftists. Paradoxically, the prevalence of the discourse of civil society does not reflect the actual course of Egyptian politics, where the application of structural adjustment in recent years has been accompanied by more authoritarianism. This chapter examines developments in the labour regime in Egypt within the broader structure of the state-civil society relationship during the period of economic liberalization that started in the mid-1970s and acquired a new momentum in 1991. We attempt to: (a) argue that Egyptian trade unions have been fully incorporated into the authoritarian corporatist structure of the state, despite the erosion of the material base of Egyptian corporatism over the past two decades; (b) provide an explanation for the fact that deeper economic liberalization in the 1990s has been accompanied by an increase, rather than a relaxation, in authoritarian rule; and (c) suggest a strategy of workers' contribution to the "liberation of civil society" that does not envisage the separation of civil society from the state, but the restructuring of the state-civil society relationship.

ECONOMIC LIBERALIZATION AND THE LABOUR REGIME

Egypt witnessed a general increase in the level of workers' struggles from the late 1960s onward. This needs to be understood in the context of the crisis of Nasser's populism at that time. In the aftermath of the 1952 coup that brought the Free Officers to power, the Nasser regime attempted to incorporate the workers' movement within the structure of the state through a mixture of reform and repression (Beinin and Lockman, 1988).

On the one hand, many of the long standing demands of the trade union movement were granted, the most important being the improvement of job security by sharply limiting employers' right to dismiss workers arbitrarily for economic reasons. In addition, work hours were reduced in industrial establishments, the minimum wage was doubled, a social insurance was introduced and the government committed itself to the provision of administrative jobs to all university graduates and manual jobs to all graduates of secondary schools (Posusney, 1991, 182).

On the other hand, strikes were outlawed and violently repressed, leftist influence within the trade union movement (substantial during the 1940s and early 1950s) was eliminated through repressive means and the trade unions themselves were denied independence and fully incorporated within the structure of the state. The institutionalization of the corporatist trade union structure took place between the late 1950s and mid-1960s. The regime announced the formation of the General Federation of Egyptian Trade Unions (GFETU) on January 30, 1957. Beinin notes that

> the government did not take any chances on the political composition of the leadership of the federation. The government submitted the names of the seventeen members of the executive board of GFETU to the founding conference. There were no nominations from those attending the conference, and no election was held (Beinin, 1989, 75).

The transformation of the union movement from pluralist to corporatist structures was completed by the Unified Labour Law Code of 1959 and the Trade Unions Law of 1964. These laws centralized the union structure around a small number of national industrial federations under the supervision of the GFETU and the newly-created Ministry of Labour. The new centralized structure was open to direct and indirect government manipulation. Moreover, membership in the ruling party became a necessary condition for candidacy in the trade union elections at all levels (Bianchi, 1989, 128).

The populist measures taken by Nasser's regime led to a rise in the real wages by roughly 60% between 1952 and 1966 (Posusney, 1991, 182-92). This however, was not matched by an equivalent increase in labour productivity. As a result, by the mid-1960s Egypt faced a serious economic crisis, an important component of which being a fall in the profitability of the industrial sector (Bradley, 1983, 80-92). This crisis reflected the difficulty of combining high levels of investment and consumption, and exposed the social contradictions embodied in the Nasserist project. The effect of the economic crisis was exacerbated by the military defeat of 1967. Together, the military defeat and the economic crisis undermined Nasserism. They contained the seeds of the "post-populist transformation". In the words of Raymond Hinnebusch:

> the decline of Nasserism spawned the forces which would give rise to Saddatism. Widening contradictions between the radical populist policies pursued by Nasser and the dominant bourgeois segments of the regime's social base, was perhaps the ultimate factor in the undermining of Nasserism (Hinnebusch, 1988, 29).

While the first modest steps of economic liberalization were taken by Nasser in the late 1960s, Sadat embarked on a fully fledged "post-populist" transformation following the October 1973 War. In 1974, Sadat declared an Open Door Policy — welcoming foreign investment and encouraging the private sector — and dramatically altered Egypt's foreign policy by adopting a pro-Western stance. Sadat's new course involved an abandonment of Nasser's implicit "social contract" with the workers. It represented an attempt by the state to solve its economic crisis at the expense of the living standards of the masses in general and the working class in particular.

The years 1967-1977 witnessed a rising wave of class struggle through which workers expressed both their disillusionment with Nasserism and their objection to their exploitation under the open door policy. This rising wave culminated in the mass uprising that engulfed nearly all Egyptian cities in January 1977, in which workers played a leading role (Beinin, 1992). Paradoxically, Sadat's "liberalization" did not entail a relaxation of state domination of the trade union movement. On the contrary, Sadat's regime further tightened the corporatist union structure, making the top union leadership increasingly self-recruiting and more isolated from the rank and file workers.

The union laws of 1976 and 1981 rendered the union structure more hierarchical than before (Bianchi, 1986, 432). These laws also continued the Nasserist principle of outlawing strikes.

Bianchi provides a convincing explanation for this seeming paradox:

> Sadat's policies of economic liberalization were bound to generate greater working class discontent by reversing earlier trends toward social equity and exposing the economy to greater international competition. It was against the backdrop of mounting labour unrest, including the violent strikes in Mahalla al Kubra in 1975 and culminating in the "bread riots" of January 1977, that Sadat enacted several reforms designed to strengthen the union confederation, to alienate its leaders from the rank and file and to co-opt them more effectively as junior members of the authoritarian elite and privileged partners in the new capitalist economic order (Bianchi, 1986, 438).

The tightening of bureaucratic control over the labour movement led to a specific pattern of workers' struggle during the 1980s. Shop-floor militancy was combined with extreme hostility on the part of the trade union bureaucracy towards the rank and file movement. While the strikes and sit-ins of the 1970s were sometimes led by labour unions, the struggles of the 1980s expressed in a much clearer way workers' lack of confidence in "their" trade unions, including the local union branches. At the same time, the state's response to the big strikes and sit-ins has invariably been very violent and repressive. Elsewhere we have examined the interaction between workers, trade unions, and the state in five salient strikes and sit-ins that occurred in Egypt's industrial and transport sectors during the mid to late 1980s (El Shafei, 1995). My conclusion included the following assessment:

> The pattern of worker's struggle in today's Egypt is linked to the particular form of "post-populist transformation" that Egypt experienced after the early 1970s. As economic liberalization coincided with the strengthening of the corporatist structures in the trade union movement, this movement has increasingly diminished in significance. Today, Egyptian unions neither lead workers in struggle as their proper role would seem to require, nor manage to contain workers as the state would like ... Worker's unions are increasingly becoming part of the state structure in Egypt. In the West, trade unions are generally regarded as intermediaries between workers and capital (both state and private capital), defending workers' interests within the framework of the existing capitalist social order. The situation in Egypt is rather different. Egyptian trade unions act as agents of the state inside the workers' movement. Even the lowest level of the trade union bureaucracy — the local union committee — is quite isolated from workers' struggles. Since the members of the union committees are nearly powerless visa-a-vis higher levels of the trade union structure, they tend to distance themselves from militant workers' action in order to avoid punishment by their superiors (El Shafei, 1995, 37-38).

THE DESPOTIC MARKET OF THE 1990S

Structural Adjustment: The Economic and Social Content

Between the mid-1970s and mid-1980s, Egypt witnessed a relatively high growth rate (an average 9 percent per annum) and thus steady improvements in per capita income (despite deterioration in the distribution of income). Following the fall in oil prices in the mid-1980s, however, rapid decline started to occur. Inflation reached 20 percent by 1986 (up from an average level of 12 percent during the preceding five years). There was a sharp reduction in the growth rate and an increase in the foreign debt from about US$20 billion dollars in 1980 to about US$50 billion dollars in 1990. Budget and balance of payment deficits reached record levels and unemployment reached about 20 percent in 1989/90 (El Biblawy, 1992, 188-89).

The deepening economic crisis convinced the Mubarak regime of the need for more systematic reform. The regime thus endorsed a "stabilization and structural adjustment programme" on the basis of two agreements with the IMF and the World Bank in 1991. The stabilization component of this programme aimed at restoring fiscal and monetary balance. The structural adjustment component "dealt with the real economy and aimed at eliminating structural distortions" (El Naggar, 1996, 10). While the first three years of the reform programme witnessed remarkable success under the first (macroeconomic) part of the programme, this was achieved at the cost of a sharp reduction in growth and living standards. According to one analyst,

> macroeconomic performance has improved dramatically, but microeconomic performance has deteriorated sharply. Unfortunately for the government, it is performance at the micro-economic level that shapes individuals' perceptions. While economists are persuaded by data on balance of payments, levels of indebtedness, budget deficits and other macro-economic indicators such data means little to ordinary people concerned about the scarcity of jobs, low wages, and inadequate profits (Cassandra, 1995, 11).

The structural adjustment component of the reform programme has been moving much slower than agreed. The government reshuffle in January, 1996 however, clearly aimed at providing both privatization and structural adjustment with a fresh push. Dealing as it is with the "real economy", this component of economic reform is much more vital than the fiscal and monetary stabilization. While the last few years witnessed a reduction of per capita income, a deterioration in income distribution and an increase in unemployment, structural adjustment is threatening the very basic social gains of the Nasser era for both the urban and rural masses.

For the urban masses the Nasserist "social contract" amounted to this: the provision of important economic and social concessions to organized workers, especially in the public sector, in return for insuring the loyalty of workers to the state, denying them the independence of their movement, and inhibiting strikes. The most important of the Nasserist concessions, as we have seen, was job security. Structural adjustment is explicitly targeting the retreat from this concession. According to most estimates, the Egyptian public sector — which accounts for about 35 percent of the total labour force — has excess labour of between 20 and 30 percent (Khawaga, 1993). This applies to both workers in public sector companies and government employees. The programme of structural adjustment aims at getting rid of excess labour in public sector companies within the next few years. The obstacle, however, lies in the "rigidity" of labour legislation. Hence the concern by the government over the last few years to introduce a new labour code.

After prolonged negotiations, hesitation and delay, the government ultimately drafted a final version of the Unified Labour Law. This is expected to be approved by the government-dominated parliament during its current session. The new law makes it much easier for employers (in both the public and private sectors) to resort to mass lay-offs. It states that they "have the right to adjust the work-force according to economic conditions" (Pripstein, 1995, 52). The law also facilitates individual dismissals in numerous ways. More importantly, it nullifies the very meaning of the work contract concept by giving employers the right to reduce wages and/or change work conditions "for economic reasons" (Pripstien, 1995, 53).

Public sector workers previously had special privileges that were denied to them when the special law covering their conditions was cancelled in 1991. Formally then, the same labour law (Labour Law Number 137/1981) has been applied to private and public sectors during the past five years. In practice, however, important differences remained between the two sectors in terms of job security for workers, since private sector employers were able to use several devices to evade the legal protections against firing. By removing these protections, the new labour law effectively dissolves the disparity in job security between the two sectors, with the aim of reducing labour opposition to privatization (Prispstein, 1995, 55).

In return for employers' right to fire, the law legalizes strikes for the first time since 1952. The right to strike, however, is qualified by many conditions which make its legal practice rather impossible (El Hilali, 1994).

Discontent about the new law among rank and file workers did not prevent the leaders of the GFETU from endorsing it. In fact, they were an important partner in the negotiations that produced the law. If job security was the major Nasserist gain for urban workers, agrarian reform has been its counterpart in rural Egypt. While the redistribution of land itself has been relatively modest benefiting only about 12 percent of Egyptian peasants, the agrarian reform law provided "some one million families with 'quasi-property rights". These rights consisted of secure tenancy at fixed rent for more than 1.5 million of Egypt's six million feddans of agricultural land" (Hinnebusch, 1993, 21). However, this gain has also been eroded as part of structural adjustment when the parliament passed an amendment to the agrarian relations law in June 1992.

The new law, for which the government has been campaigning for many years, increased rent from seven to 22 times the land tax per feddan. More importantly, the law stipulates that "all contracts will be terminated by 1997-98 and thereafter owner-client relations will be governed by the free market" (Hinnebusch, 1993, 22). The aim of the new law, as Hinnebusch rightly notes, is to give a boost to the "replacement of small peasant production by larger scale capitalist agriculture" (1993, 22). This is being done at the expense of the interests of millions of small peasants.

Structural adjustment constitutes then a qualitative turning point in the Egyptian regime's attempt to solve the acute economic crisis by intensifying the exploitation of both the urban and rural poor. In this sense, it both reflects and affects a shift in the balance of class forces in Egypt against labour and in favour of capital (local state and private capital as well as foreign capital).

The Political Framework of Structural Adjustment

The application of structural adjustment policies in Egypt went hand in hand with increased coercion and authoritarianism. The absolute and relative deprivation suffered by most Egyptians during the first half of the mid-1990s translated into more political support for the Islamists — militants and moderates alike. As the government has been raising prices, removing subsidies and cutting spending on welfare, Islamists have been able to win support through easing some of the pressure on the poor by providing cheap health services and education. As Stanley Reed notes,

> a high percentage of both the Gamaa [an eminent militant Islamist group] rank and file and its leaders come from such upper Egyptian cities as Asyut, Sohag, and Beni Suef. The people in these regions tend to be poorer and more alienated from Cairo than those in the North (Reed, 1993, 99).

While it was precisely the Egyptian state that first unleashed the Islamists against its Nasserist and leftist opponents in the early to mid-1970s, the strategy of Mubarak *vis-a-vis* militant Islamists in the early 1990s has been very simple: a qualitative escalation of coercion. It is estimated, for instance, that "about 86 percent of the causalities resulting from civil disorder in the 41 years up to 1993 occurred during the Mubarak era, 92 percent of which occurred in the four years 1990-93" (Cassandra, 1995, 19). The excessive violence used against militant Islamists involved systematic resort to torture of detainees and widespread reliance on military courts.

Having been relatively successful in crushing militants who aim at the violent overthrowing of the regime, Mubarak then directed his crackdown on the

Muslim Brotherhood who are moderate Islamists willing to abide by the rules of the political game in Egypt. Unlike militant Islamists with their base among the urban and rural poor, the Brotherhood "is rooted in the traditional establishment of professionals and businessmen" (Reed, 1993, 102). They also managed to widen their support in Egyptian society during the early 1990s, as the policies pursued by the regime were alienating many people. This wider support was reflected in their relative success in local elections and their control over many professional syndicates. Alarmed by the growing influence of the Brotherhood in these syndicates, the government enacted the Law to Guarantee Democracy within the Professional Syndicates. This law requires a minimum voter turnout of 50 percent of the members in the professional syndicates, or, failing this 33 percent in a second round. If these electoral thresholds are not met, voting results are void and syndicates fall under the supervision of a panel of government-appointed judges (Cassandra, 1995, 15). As Ahmed Abdalla notes, the quorum of one-half of all voting members "does not exist for — and has never been achieved in — national elections for members of parliament or for the president of the republic" (Abdalla, 1993, 298). He adds that the law "was instantly nicknamed the "Law of Nationalizing Unions", contrasting it with the privatization campaign under way in the economy". The government responded to widespread anger among members of the professional syndicates with excessive violence (Beinin, 1994, 29).

The intensification of authoritarianism was not only directed at Islamists, however. Aware of the unpopularity of its reversal of agrarian reform in the countryside, the government introduced a law in March 1994 terminating the

> century-old practice of villagers electing their mayors and deputy mayors.
> Not even Nasser has meddled with this vestige of democracy. For the
> Mubarak regime to have done so suggests that it is anxious about rural
> political instability (Cassandra, 1995, 16).

With regard to the labour regime, trade union leaders at the national level, as we have seen, supported the new labour law which removes protection against firing. They are aware, however, of widespread hostility to the law among workers and local trade unionists. In order to further insulate themselves from pressure from below, they proposed in 1994, an amendment of trade union law allowing board members of the upper and middle levels of the trade union bureaucracy to maintain their membership in the general assembly of the level they occupy (upper or middle) without being re-elected at their workplaces. The law was quickly passed by Parliament.

Another symptom of further restrictions on Egypt's limited democratic space is the new legislation passed in May 1995 — a few days before the end of the five year term of parliament — imposing restrictions on press freedom. While the law triggered massive anger among journalists, the regime managed to defeat journalists' opposition through its manipulation of the conservative and corporatist journalists' association.

Last but not least, the parliamentary elections in November/December 1995 confirmed the regime's insistence on liquidating any significant legal opposition. While many commentators were hoping that these elections might constitute a positive turning point in the direction of democratization, the outcome was rather shocking. Ruling party candidates resorted, with the help of police officers, to brutal violence and the elections were crudely rigged in a way that exceeded the average pattern of electoral life in Egypt (Legal Aid Center, 1996). As a result, opposition representation in parliament declined from about 20 percent to less than four percent. Only one Islamist was able to win a seat in the parliament.

The Chinese Model: An Attempt at an Explanation

Events in Egypt over the past five years are moving in the direction of the Chinese model: economic liberalization and deeper integration into the world economy accompanied by more authoritarianism. Why did Egypt not participate in the wave of democratization that swept Africa in the 1990s?

To begin with, it is important to note that at a fundamental level, and contrary to the assertions of the ideologues of neo-liberalism, economic liberalization and democracy are not compatible. The unpopular measures of structural adjustment and the class biases of economic "reform" programmes tend to increase mass discontent and the tendency of the regimes to resort to authoritarian measures to ensure stability. We need to explain those cases where economic liberalization has been accompanied by political liberalization. Historically, democratization was the product of pressure from below on the regimes. These found themselves forced to concede liberal democratic changes in order to avoid more radical challenges to the status quo. More importantly, however, the initiative in democratization was sometimes taken by the regimes themselves. This reflected a recognition by reform-minded elements within African and Eastern European regimes that the best way to enhance the chances of success of the unpopular neo-liberal policies is to get the backing of sections of the very opposition they previously persecuted. For only the oppositionists have the popular prestige to control the masses and ensure the transition is a smooth one (Harman, 1990, 69).

In Egypt, the pressure from below on the regime was not systematic nor strong enough to force democratic concessions. One important reason for this is that trade unions, as we have seen, have been effectively incorporated inside authoritarian state structures. Militant activity by rank and file workers, despite its significance, failed to develop a sustained institutional challenge to the state and the corporatist trade unions. At the same time, both radical and moderate Islamists fundamentally lack a democratic vision capable of mobilizing their supporters in the direction of forcing the regime into making democratic concessions.

If the government did not face strong pressure for democratization, it did not opt to initiate a democratization process for reasons not difficult to understand. The regime finds sharing power with the Islamists too dangerous. At the same time, since the uprising of January 1977, it has marginalized and domesticated all sorts of liberal, nationalist and leftist opposition. Hence the option of sharing power with the non-Islamist opposition was not an attractive one, precisely because the government is well aware that this opposition lacks "the popular prestige to control the masses and ensure the transition is a smooth one".

THE STATE AND CIVIL SOCIETY IN EGYPT: WHAT IS TO BE DONE?

The "liberation of civil society" discourse is widespread in Egypt today. Perhaps the best representative of this discourse is the New Civic Forum (NCF), an association of Egyptian liberal-minded businessmen and neo-liberal economists and intellectuals. For the head of NCF, the eminent economist Said El Naggar, "democracy in the political realm is the counterpart of the free market in the economy — each a necessary condition for the other" (Naggar, 1996, 10). The aim of "democracy", however, is nothing else than dismantling the "vested interests" hostile to structural adjustment. In El Naggar's words;

> The question arises as to the best way of overcoming opposition to [economic] reform on sectional or sectoral grounds. There are reasons to believe that in the Egyptian context a greater measure of democratization may well be the most effective way of dealing with this kind of opposition. It could serve to break up unholy alliances in the present political set-up. No less important is the fact that a greater measure of democratization would probably bring to power a government with a clear-cut mandate to implement the economic reform program" (El Naggar, 1996, 10).

The basic assumption of El Naggar is that the "public" is in favour of economic liberalization. The problem, however, is that the "public" is not organized. The aim of promoting civil society is to create structures and organizations capable of expressing "popular" support for economic liberalization, while dismantling the "vested interests" hostile to reform.

Neo-liberals are not the only supporters of "civil society liberation" in Egypt. The left is also obsessed with civil society. For the legal left, represented by the National Progressive Unionist Party (NPUP), the main danger facing Egyptian society is an Islamist takeover. Thus the NPUP is prepared to practically ally with the regime against the Islamists. In this context, "defending civil society" basically means defending the authoritarian status quo against Islamism. For the more radical left, "liberation of civil society" means promoting the autonomy of democratic popular organizations active in defending human rights, women's rights, trade union rights, etc. Unfortunately, however, even this "radical" left seems to have been domesticated over the past few years. Increasingly, the emphasis is on building "professional" civil society organizations. By this they basically mean non-popular and non-political organizations that can be tolerated by an increasingly more authoritarian regime.

It looks as if there is hardly any room for optimism concerning the prospects of democratization and civil society liberation in Egypt. One has to remember, however, that the current programme of structural adjustment represents a massive socio-economic turning point. The fact that the regime is basically relying on coercion alone in promoting its plans for economic reform, implies that there are indeed prospects for higher levels of social protests than we have been witnessing in recent years. What is needed then is systematic rank and file work aiming to articulate the opposition of the oppressed and exploited to structural adjustment and authoritarianism.

While Egyptian trade unions are highly dominated by the state, rank-and-file workers — given their strategic position in the economy, their history of struggle and the current challenges they are facing — might well play a significant role in creating a dynamic civil society in Egypt, provided they manage to translate their militancy into an institutional challenge both to the authoritarian state and the corporatist unions. The aim of this civil society will not be to separate itself from the state, but rather to combine autonomy and freedom with democratic access to decision-making.

REFERENCES

ABDALLA, A. (1993) "Egypt's Islamists and the State", *Middle East Report*, July-August, 28 -31.

BECKMAN, B. (1993) "The Liberation of Civil Society: Neo-liberal Ideology and Political Theory,", *Review of African Political Economy*, 28: 20 -33.

BEININ, J. (September-October, 1994) "Terrorism, Class and Democracy in Egypt", *Middle East Report*, 20-23.

— (1992) "Will The Real Egyptian Working Class Please Stand Up?" (Unpublished Paper, Stanford University).

— (1989), "Labour, Capital and the State in Nasserist Egypt, 1952-1961", *International Journal of Middle East Studies*, XXI, 72-90.

BEININ, J. and LOCKMAN, Z. (1988) *Workers on the Nile* (London, Tauris).

BIANCHI, R. (1989) *Unruly Corporatism: Associational Life in Twentieth Century Egypt* (New York, Oxford University Press).

— (1986) "The Corporatization of the Egyptian Labour Movement", *The Middle East Journal*, 40: 423-439.

BRADLEY, C. (1983) "State Capitalism in Egypt: A Critique of Patrick Clawson", *Khamsin*, X, 80-92.

CASSANDRA. (1995) "Impending Crisis in Egypt", *Middle East Journal*, Winter, 9-27.

EL-BIBLAWY, H. (1992) *al Taghyeer min agl el istikrar (Change for Stability)* (Cairo, Dar el Shorouq).

EL-HILALI, N. (1994) *Hatha el mashru'lan Yamur (This Draft law will not Pass)* (Cairo, Dar el Khadamat el niqabiyya).

EL-NAGGAR, S. (1996) "Development, The liberal Way", *Al Ahram Weekly*, 11 April.

EL-SHAFEI, O. (1995) "Workers, Trade Unions and the State in Egypt: 1984-89", *Cairo Papers in Social Science*, 18 (2).

HARMAN, C. (1990) "The Storm Breaks", *International Socialism*, XXXXVI, 3-93.

HINNEBUSCH, R. (September-October, 1993) "Class, State and the Reversal of Egypt's Agrarian Reform", *Middle East Report*, 20-23.

— (1988) *Egyptian Politics Under Sadat* (Colorado, Lynne Reinner Publishers).

LEGAL AID CENTRE (1996) "et Taqrir al niha'i' an el intikhabat" (Final Report on Elections) (Unpublished Report, Cairo).

POSUSNEY, M. (1991) "Workers Against the State: Actors, Issues and Outcomes in Egyptian Labour/State Relations, 1952-1987" (Unpublished PhD. dissertation, University of Pennsylvania).

PRISPSTEIN, M. (July-August, 1995) "Egypt's New Labour Law Removes Worker Provisions", *Middle East Report*, 52-53.

REED, S. (September -October, 1993) "The Battle for Egypt", *Foreign Affairs*, 94-107.

CHAPTER SEVEN

Exodus Without a Map? The Labour Movement in a Liberalizing South Africa

EDDIE WEBSTER AND GLENN ADLER

INTRODUCTION

The second anniversary of South Africa's new democracy was celebrated in two sharply contrasting public events. On Saturday 27 April 1996 country-wide celebrations were held to mark 1994's founding election. President Nelson Mandela and the senior leaders of the Government of National Unity gathered near a neo-fascist statue of arch-apartheid Prime Minister J. G. Strijdom in Pretoria where they officiated over a parade asserting the theme of national reconciliation. This odd combination of military strength and cultural diversity featured tribally-dressed children perched atop the security forces' armoured vehicles. The new "rainbow" flag was prominently displayed, most strikingly in the now-familiar sight of a flyover by air force jets trailing smoke plumes in the new national colours. This pageant of reconciliation seemed to capture the oft-cited South African "miracle": the tenuous but nonetheless secure harmonisation of strongly conflicting interests.

Yet, three days later a country-wide celebration of a different sort of democracy occurred when millions of workers heeded a strike call by the Congress of South African Trade Unions [COSATU] that saw more than 200,000 workers participate in street marches in the major cities. This was the first national one-day strike in South Africa's new democracy, called in support of COSATU's long-held demand that a clause protecting management's right to lock-out striking workers not be included in the country's new constitution. Indeed, labour won the demand, and there is no reference to the lockout in the final constitution (Constitutional Assembly, 1996). However, underlying this strike is labour's deeper dissatisfaction with the transition process in South Africa.

The labour movement and the democratic opposition more broadly were historically sceptical of liberal parliamentarianism as too limited a form of governance that tended to reinforce elite privileges. By contrast they articulated a participatory notion of democracy, which they saw as a superior form enabling all citizens to participate continually and actively in community and political affairs. However, the transition consolidated in the 1994 election produced a pacted Government of National Unity that included representatives from the old regime and from the democratic movement. It yielded an imperfect liberal democracy that conferred legitimate decision-making power on parliament and on the state bureaucracy.

While this is an exceptional feat in a deeply divided society where the alternative may well have been civil war, it reinforced the familiar separation of state and civil society, premised on the sovereignty of parliament, a concept never before endorsed by the internal democratic opposition. Furthermore, it left intact the pillars of the capitalist market economy: it was a transition in the political system, not a transition in the political economy (Saul, 1996). Indeed, the economic policies so far adopted by the new government demonstrate considerable continuity with those of the previous regime. The new ANC Minister of Finance Trevor Manuel, maintains his predecessor's commitments to fiscal discipline, reducing the government's deficit and high real interest rates. The ANC has recently embraced privatisation as a "fundamental principle", along with the gradual elimination of exchange controls, and the reduction of tariffs to encourage export-led growth. Furthermore, in the talks over an interim constitution the ANC accepted that the Governor of the Reserve Bank, appointed by the apartheid government, would remain independent and would continue in office until August 1999. The new liberal democracy has thus yielded a politics of reconciliation — symbolised by the Pretoria parade — premised on neoliberal macro-economic principles that are increasingly hegemonic in government economic policy-making.

However, the transition also produced a range of new institutions which are not comfortably contained within the ambit of parliamentary democracy or neoliberalism. Foremost amongst these is the National Economic Development and Labour Council [NEDLAC], a multi-partite body designed to establish consensus on economic and social policy. For the first time in South African history, NEDLAC provides civil society formations — including labour, business associations, and civic movements — with an institutionalised role in policy-making. In addition to their normal possibilities of lobbying parliamentarians and the bureaucracy, civil society formations may now through NEDLAC propose and oppose policies before they go to parliament. This formal purchase on policy-making gives autonomous organisations in civil society, including the labour movement, the possibility to participate directly in economic and social policy formulation.

Approaches to transition that emphasise elite pacting — popular in American political science — have considerable difficulties explaining that such possibilities have emerged in South Africa. From this tradition, unions and other civil society organisations are primarily seen from a functionalist perspective in their relation to pacting: they may be called upon by the pro-democratic negotiators to put pressure on the regime, or alternatively, to restrain unruly masses and to prevent the disruption of political arrangements worked out above their heads in elite pacts (Adler and Webster, 1995, 90). Jeremy Cronin, Deputy General Secretary of the South African Communist Party [SACP] has elsewhere labelled this the "tap" theory of mobilisation, turning mass action on or off, based on the requirements of the negotiations (Cronin, 1992).

Elsewhere we have proposed an actor-based theory of transition that "does not present movements merely as potential threats to order, but recognises the central role of social movements in the origin, development, and outcome of the transition process" (Adler and Webster, 1995, 90). The labour movement as a social movement is thus an important — and largely overlooked — participant in transitions. By virtue of its large membership and tight shopfloor-based organisation, the labour movement may have the power to disrupt the economy; when tied to a political strategy this capability confers on labour the potential to shape the transition.

Elsewhere we have used the concept "social movement unionism" to account for the particular form taken by COSATU. The term describes trade unions that transcend the narrow confines of collective bargaining and workplace demands to engage with the wider political struggles for democratisation in all spheres. Social movement unionism describes a blurring of the distinction between trade unions as formal organisations and social movements as loosely structured networks of social action (Adler and Webster, 1995, 89). In South Africa, it was the twin grievances of capitalist exploitation and apartheid that compelled trade unions to seek both economic and political solutions to their members' problems.

As will be seen below, NEDLAC emerged through a combination of negotiations and social movement mass action, a labour movement strategy that we have elsewhere identified as "radical reform" (Adler and Webster, 1995). Labour has used its social movement power in pursuit of radical reform: "disciplined and sophisticated social movements may be able to inject more progressive content into the democratising process and wrest important concessions from the elite" (Adler and Webster, 1995, 76). In this respect, labour is not pursuing a programme of revolutionary rupture, indeed, it has operated in the context of established institutions; however, its programme has been inspired by a broad commitment to radical and socialist economic and social transformation.

The movement has sought to promote a more participatory notion of democracy and an alternative to neoliberalism. The 30 April general strike, with its focus on changing the constitution, is part of an attempt by COSATU to reassert its organisational autonomy and force its ally — the African National Congress — to adopt an economic policy in the interests of labour and the poor. Labour has recently released its own economic programme articulating an alternative to neoliberalism, one based on social equity influenced by left-Keynesianism. The programme has been submitted to NEDLAC, where labour will oppose competing agendas from government and capital. Whether COSATU can fully realise the possibility of remaining autonomous yet participating in policy making in the new conditions of a democratic South Africa is explored in this chapter.

South Africa is in a process of transition from a despotic labour regime based on a racially segmented labour market, restrictions on union rights, and limited social welfare. The core struggle in NEDLAC and elsewhere is over the successor to the apartheid labour regime. On the one hand, business is promoting a market-based regime in the interest of flexibility and competition. It rests on a two-tiered labour market aimed at a low-wage regime and reductions in government social spending. There are increasing resonances between these ideas and those produced in the government's new macroeconomic strategy. On the other hand, labour and sections of the government are promoting a corporatist/co-determinist labour regime based on a negotiated class compromise. This vision would be underpinned by a social pact in which labour may trade off wage growth for increased public and private investment in training, expansion of the social wage, and participation over economic decision-making.

Labour's campaign places its ally in a dilemma: does the ANC try to accommodate labour's demands and promote the interests of its mass base or does it respond to increasingly assertive pressure from domestic and international capital to pursue neoliberal economic and social policies? The consolidation of democracy in South Africa is thus at a crossroads, notwithstanding the display of unity in the Pretoria parade. This dilemma raises a fundamental question about the future of the Triple Alliance between the ANC, the SACP and COSATU. What is at stake, in short, is the class content of democratisation in South Africa. Will the ANC through the Alliance discipline and marginalise COSATU, or will COSATU be able to use the Alliance to promote a class compromise between labour and capital: in other words, a social pact that promotes equitable growth and job creation?

In Part One we will describe the structure and power of the contemporary labour movement, tracing its emergence in the 1970s and 1980s as a central actor in the South African political economy. In Part Two we will trace the labour movement's increasing political role in the 1980s, culminating in an alliance with the ANC and SACP, through which labour was able to influence the origins, development and outcome of the transition process. In Part Three, we will examine labour's role in the consolidation of democracy, where it has experienced serious difficulties realising the opportunities to influence policy making. These difficulties stem from a growing marginalisation from the centres of policy-making, and problems internal to the labour movement in developing its policy programme.

In moving from apartheid to democracy, labour has embarked on a journey into unexplored territory best captured by the phrase an "Exodus without a map".[1] This term was coined by Enoch Godongwana, General Secretary of the National Union of Metalworkers of South Africa, in criticising the form of COSATU's 1993 decision to participate in parliament (Webster, 1996). However, we feel this phrase captures COSATU's general difficulty in re-defining its role in the consolidation of democracy. Labour — along with the rest of South Africa — has left the bondage of apartheid, but it has not yet arrived fully in the "promised land". More fundamentally, the labour movement lacks a clear vision of the "promised land" as well as of the means to get there: for the first time in its history it has no clearly articulated alternative to capitalism and the new democratic terrain requires somewhat different strategies and tactics from those used against the apartheid state. Labour thus has new opportunities to influence policy but profound problems in realising them. However, recent events indicate a resurgence of labour's role in politics and economics, which opens up the potential for a more contested democratisation and a re-definition of state-civil society relationships leading to a more radical outcome to the transition process.

PART ONE: THE GROWTH OF THE CONTEMPORARY SOUTH AFRICAN LABOUR MOVEMENT

While labour movements in much of the world have experienced declines in membership and influence during the 1980s and 1990s the South African labour movement has grown rapidly. The membership of trade unions grew dramatically from more than 700,000 in 1979 to nearly 3,000,000 in 1993. This involved a growth in union density from slightly more than 15% to 58% over the same period.

There are 213 registered trade unions, many of which are small craft unions or professional associations that are declining in membership (Department of Labour, 1995). However, the broad trend is towards nation-wide industrial or sectoral unions in the core of the economy, including mining, metal, textile and clothing, retail and commercial, chemical, food, and the public service. Thus, although there are many unions in the country, the majority of union members are concentrated in the large national industrial unions in these sectors.

Many of the unions are affiliated to one of six federations [see Table]. On the face of it this suggests a degree of fragmentation in the labour movement, though the largest federation, COSATU has more members than all the other federations combined. However, the labour movement in South Africa is deeply divided on grounds of race and political orientation. Historically South Africa had a dualistic industrial relations system, as had other settler colonies in Africa. Trade unions with non-African membership were recognised under the Industrial and Conciliation Act of 1924, while Africans were excluded from the formal industrial relations system and subject to tight control through the pass system. The dualistic system ended in 1979 when the Act was amended to cover all employees except migrant workers, farm workers, domestic servants and employees in the public sector.[2] The granting of formal trade unions rights to African employees legitimised the then emerging black trade union movement, and membership figures sky-rocketed.

Table 1 : Union Federations, Number of Affiliates and Membership, 1994

Federation	Affiliates	Membership*
Congress of SA Trade Unions (COSATU)	15	1 317 496 (45%)
National Council of Trade Unions (NACTU)	18	334 733 (12%)
Federation of SA Labour (FEDSAL)	16	257 258 (10%)
Federation of Independent Trade Unions (FITU)	24	236 000 (8%)
SA Confederation of Labour (SACOL)	4	54 290 (2%)
United Workers Union of SA** (UWUSA)		

*The percentage in the membership column reflects the federation's membership as a proportion of total membership.
**Estimates of UWUSA membership fluctuate between 30,000 and 100,000, but reliable figures are not available.
Source: Macun, in press.

COSATU and NACTU are essentially industrial unions of African semi-skilled workers, although COSATU is firmly committed to organising workers regardless of race, and has always had a significant number of coloured and Indian members. In recent years it has made some inroads among white workers as well. Indeed, its leadership has always included non-Africans in key positions.

These demographic differences express themselves in the two major political traditions within the democratic movement. COSATU has always subscribed to the national-democratic tradition, led by the African National Congress. NACTU's origins lie in the Black Consciousness political tradition, and the federation has more recently aligned itself with the Africanist tradition articulated by the Pan Africanist Congress, which broke away from the ANC in 1959 because of the latter's multi-racial definition of the nation.

The other major federations, FEDSAL, FITU, and SACOL have their origins in the old white-dominated labour movement, and are themselves divided in terms of skill and ethnicity. FEDSAL represents white-collar workers, and recently has taken on a larger number of black members. FITU and SACOL, on the other hand, represent skilled and semi-skilled white workers respectively, while SACOL is essentially a movement of Afrikaans-speaking workers. FEDSAL and FITU are both politically unaffiliated, though they have been historically hostile to the democratic movement, while SACOL has been linked with the far-right wing Conservative Party.

UWUSA was launched in 1986 with covert funding by the apartheid state. Its membership is almost entirely confined to Zulu-speaking semi-skilled and unskilled workers affiliated to the Inkatha Freedom Party led by Chief Mangosuthu Buthelezi. It has virtually no organised presence in the workplace, but it has often played a divisive role acting as scab labour undermining efforts by COSATU or NACTU (Harvey, 1996).

The massive growth in membership mentioned above has been largely confined to the unions within the democratic movement, principally those affiliated to NACTU and COSATU. COSATU in particular developed a strong shopfloor presence exemplified by the central importance of the shopsteward.These unions emphasised the development of factory-level leadership democratically elected by rank-and-file workers and directly accountable to them (Pityana and Orkin, 1992). This particular strategic innovation came about in the early 1970s when the then emerging black unions in Durban sought to avoid the growth of top-heavy office-bound leaderships. They were inspired by a programmatic commitment to worker control and to the need to survive state repression, which tended to be directed in the first instance at highly exposed national leaders. Furthermore, these unions were committed to building industrially-based structures, concentrating on shopfloor issues while remaining — for reasons of survival — unaffiliated to the exiled liberation movements.

The Durban unions ultimately merged in 1974 to form the Trade Union Advisory Coordinating Council [TUACC], the first progressive trade union centre to emerge since the repression of the early 1960s. In 1979 TUACC joined with other emerging unions from the Eastern and Western Cape to form the Federation of South African Trade Unions [FOSATU] (Friedman, 1987). In fact, the legal proscription of the nationalist movements meant that in their formative years these embryonic unions were able to develop leadership, organise their constituency, and define their strategies and tactics relatively independently from the ideological orientations and models of the ANC, SACP, and especially their labour arm, the South African Congress of Trade Unions [SACTU]. The space created by virtue of banning and exile, meant that the new unions could develop innovative approaches to organising that differed from the populist strategies and tactics of the nationalist-linked unions of the 1950s.

By 1991 COSATU unions alone included more than 25,000 shopstewards, giving an average ratio of one steward to 50 workers. The shopsteward system gave workers power in production, a capacity to intervene directly in struggles challenging managerial control over wages, working conditions, and the organisation of production (Webster, 1986). Furthermore, as shopstewards constituted the pool from which more senior union leaders were drawn, the system enabled rank-and-file members to exercise an unprecedented degree of control over their officials.

As the democratic struggle gained momentum in the early 1980s, these shopstewards moved beyond the factory into the community. The organisational manifestation of this movement was the emergence of joint shopsteward councils that cut across workplaces uniting workers as a class and creating the embryo of a working-class politics in particular communities (Webster, 1985). At the same time that shopstewards from the new industrial unions were being drawn into community politics, the national-democratic tradition re-emerged through community-based unions linked to the African National Congress. These competing thrusts brought sharply to the fore the form and content of labour's participation in the democratic struggle, which will be the focus of the next section.

PART TWO: THE ORIGINS OF THE TRIPLE ALLIANCE

There are three major traditions within the democratic labour movement which structure the differing perspectives on labour's relationship to politics: the national democratic tradition, the shopfloor tradition, and the black consciousness/Africanist tradition (Fine and Webster, 1989).

The national democratic tradition has the deepest roots in the labour movement, originating in the creation in 1955 of SACTU, which combined most of the then-existing unions organising among black workers. SACTU's alliance with the ANC involved a redefinition of its trade union role along the lines of political unionism. Lacking a strong power base on the shopfloor and faced with an increasingly hostile state and intransigent employers, SACTU mobilised the oppressed — across class lines — around the demands of the ANC's popular programme, the Freedom Charter, adopted in 1955. SACTU's involvement in the Congress Alliance was premised on the assumption that South Africa could not be understood in class terms, but that political change necessitated a national democratic struggle to liberate South Africa from white rule that was seen as a form of "colonialism of a special type" (Wolpe, 1988). To this end, the Congress Alliance was a multi-class movement of organisations representing the broad oppressed groups in South Africa under the leadership of the ANC and aiming to establish a national democracy. In form and content, the Alliance — and particularly the relations between unions and the nationalist party — parallelled other national liberation movements on the African continent.

SACTU's participation in the Congress Alliance facilitated the rapid growth of trade unions in certain regions (Lambert, 1988). But it also brought SACTU into direct conflict with the state and the organisation felt the full force of repression in the 1960s. By 1964 it had ceased public activities in South Africa and operated in exile until the unbanning of the ANC in 1990.

When union activity re-emerged before and after the Durban strikes of 1973, SACTU and the other formations of the Congress Alliance were in exile and their internal operatives were deep underground. The unions that first emerged in the early 1970s scrupulously avoided political involvement and concentrated on developing factory-based structures, including shopstewards, as outlined in Part I. The approach of their leading strategists was informed by an assessment of SACTU's errors, arguing that its close identification with the Congress Alliance and its political campaigns caused its demise: political engagement, in this view, led to a neglect of workplace organising while inviting repression. By contrast, these emerging unions developed what has come to be known as the shopfloor tradition, best captured in 1982 in a prominent speech by the FOSATU General Secretary, who proposed the development of a workers' political movement under worker control as an alternative to the national democratic tradition (Foster, 1982).

The picture of unions and politics in South Africa is often incomplete, as it neglects a third tradition competing for workers' loyalties during the 1970s: the Black Consciousness Movement. This tradition has similarities to the national democratic tradition, in that it holds that racial oppression is a manifestation of national oppression; its emphasis on racial structures and identities virtually excludes class relations from its analysis. In this respect, the unions that developed under the Black Consciousness umbrella were a labour arm in a multiclass movement. Certain emerging unions clustered around the Urban Training Project, which through a variety of mergers and splits developed into the Council of Unions of South Africa [CUSA]. Though CUSA was politically unaligned, it later recombined as NACTU, with alliances with the PAC and black consciousness organisations. This political tradition is distinguished from both the national democratic and shopfloor traditions in its emphasis on black leadership and its corollary hostility to the leadership of white intellectuals in the labour movement. Notwithstanding their radical political affiliations, these unions in their organisational form tended to emulate the old-line white unions with their emphasis on office-bound leadership. They tended not to develop the shopsteward structures at the core of the shopfloor tradition.

In the late 1970s the national democratic tradition re-emerged in the labour movement, inspired by the ANC's and SACP's re-invigorated efforts to rebuild their internal structures in the wake of the Soweto uprising of 1976. In the Eastern Cape in particular, new community-based unions such as the South African Allied Workers' Union [SAAWU] were established that explicitly followed the organising tradition of SACTU. These community unions argued that workers' struggle in the factories and townships was indivisible and that unions had an obligation to take up pressing community issues, such as housing conditions (and by implication the national democratic struggle). The shopfloor unions were criticised for "economism" and "workerism" due to their apparent abstention from politics. In re-asserting political unionism, the community unions revived another tradition from South African labour history, an emphasis on general unionism that goes back to the formation of the Industrial and Commercial Workers' Union, the first national black union founded in the aftermath of World War I. However, the community unions seldom succeeded in consolidating an organisational presence in factories, and eventually withered under intense state repression.

Nonetheless, the community unions experienced rapid mobilisation through the early 1980s, and generated competition with shopfloor-based unions for the loyalties of black workers. Through the early 1980s black workers were experiencing the effects of a deepening social and political crisis, which can now be seen as the fundamental contradictions of the apartheid order. The crisis spawned a range of new social movements, including student, youth, and civics. The community unions were in step with these movements, and contributed to the growing opposition in the townships, especially from 1984. The community unions' increasing success forced FOSATU to re-evaluate its strategy of political nonalignment and its efforts to isolate a class-based politics from the broader national democratic struggle, a position that threatened to marginalise FOSATU from its own base.

The decisive break with political abstentionism was in November 1984 when FOSATU entered into joint action with student and civic organisations to participate in the first successful worker stayaway since 1976. This action was made possible by the overlapping membership of these organisations and the irresistible pressure from union members demanding action in the face of rising rents, transport costs, poor education, and the repressive local government system (LMG, 1985). Most importantly, FOSATU's involvement in the stayaway marked the emergence of social movement unionism: the federation was mobilising its considerable shop-floor power in pursuit of a political agenda. FOSATU's shift brought the shopfloor and national democratic traditions closer together, and facilitated efforts to promote unity among the emergent unions.

This unity was finally achieved by the creation of COSATU, which combined the industrial union emphasis of the shopfloor tradition with the political orientation — alliance with the ANC and SACP — central to the national democratic tradition. As this combination developed, those unions subscribing to Black Consciousness — notably CUSA — dropped out of the unity talks, and ultimately relinked themselves as NACTU. However, the largest and most powerful union in this grouping, the National Union of Mineworkers broke from CUSA to become the largest single affiliate in the new COSATU. In one of their first acts, the new office bearers of COSATU travelled to Lusaka and endorsed the ANC's leadership of the liberation struggle.

This marked the informal beginning of what is now known as the Triple Alliance between the ANC, SACP, and COSATU. In the period immediately after its formation COSATU embarked on a number of joint campaigns with the United Democratic Front [UDF] — the umbrella formation of internal opposition groups allied to the Congress Alliance — formed in 1983. It is significant that in this movement towards unity with the national democratic tradition COSATU entered the alliance not as a subordinate partner as was SACTU — lending its mobilisation power to the ANC's campaigns — but as an equal partner with an independent power base, strategy, and leadership. In this movement COSATU displaced SACTU, and from that time the latter came to exist largely in name alone. SACTU ultimately disbanded and was absorbed into COSATU when the ANC was unbanned. By that time very few of its personnel remained (Southall, 1995).

The increasing internal insurrection in 1985 and 1986 provoked massive repression in June 1986, which ultimately led to the banning of the UDF and many of its allied organisations. With the ANC and SACP still in exile, and internal political organisations under ban and leaders in detention or under trial, COSATU emerged as the *de facto* leader of the internal democratic movement. This position gave COSATU considerable influence over the course of internal politics, which it used to lead a boycott of local and parliamentary elections and to promote successful stayaways over government efforts to reverse labour law reform (Baskin, 1991). However, even as COSATU was consolidating its leadership position within the democratic movement, negotiations were developing between the ANC and the apartheid state over what was to become a "negotiated revolution" (Sparks, 1994). The beginning of the transition to democracy, symbolised by the unbanning of the ANC and SACP and their return to above-ground politics in South Africa initiated as well the ANC's return to hegemonic prominence within the internal democratic movement.

PART THREE: THE REASSERTION OF ANC HEGEMONY WITHIN THE ALLIANCE

In the euphoria that arose after February 1990 with the unbanning of the liberation organisations and the return of exiled and imprisoned political leaders, COSATU members assumed that their organisation would play a central role in the transition to democracy. Immediately following the unbannings, when the *de facto* alliance between the ANC, SACP and COSATU was formalised as the Triple Alliance, COSATU members expected that the federation would continue to play the same equal and independent role in alliance with the ANC that it had enjoyed over the previous five years. Indeed, a 1991 nationwide survey of COSATU shopstewards found that 70% of the respondents thought that the federation would be the best vehicle to represent their interests in the multipartite negotiations for a democratic constitution, later known as the Convention for a Democratic South Africa [CODESA]. Only 21% of the shopstewards saw the ANC as best placed to represent them, and a mere 9% identified the SACP (Pityana and Orkin, 1992, 58).

On the basis of these survey results, released confidentially to COSATU's Central Executive Committee in 1991, the CEC resolved to attend CODESA in its own right or not at all (Pityana and Orkin, 1992, 61). However, when COSATU applied for membership it was refused. Instead, the National Party government blocked its application (and presumably the ANC did not oppose the NP); COSATU's interests were to be represented indirectly, via its allies, the ANC and SACP. COSATU participated in a joint political committee consisting of six members each from the federation, the SACP and the ANC where COSATU would be briefed on developments at CODESA. Furthermore, COSATU would be indirectly represented with two union leaders on the ANC's CODESA delegation and two on the SACP's, but these would be directly accountable to their party's caucus, and only indirectly accountable to COSATU (Webster and Keet, 1992). CODESA thus became a parliament-in-formation responsible for drafting the interim constitution and deciding on transitional arrangements, including the elections, the re-incorporation of the "homelands," and the integration of all armed formations. It was comprised of political parties representing political society: no civil society formations – including COSATU – obtained direct representation.

This is the moment when the ANC formally established its hegemony within the Alliance, and COSATU (as well as other allied civil society formations) were reduced to a secondary role, influencing ANC policy through lobbying and pressure, rather than wielding a share of direct power over decisions. From this point political parties – not the civil society organisations that were the backbone of the 1980s insurrection against apartheid – were to be at the centre of the transition. In spite of this shift in hegemony, a second survey on the eve of the 1994 elections revealed that COSATU's rank-and-file members continued to believe that the federation should represent them directly (Ginsburg and Webster, 1995).

An important symbol of this shift was the disbanding of the UDF, the organisation that gave direct support and coordination to hundreds of civil society organisations in the 1980s. Without the UDF these groups lost resources; more importantly they were deprived of the voice in national political affairs the UDF historically provided. The transition created enormous and historic opportunities for mobility: many activists entered the ANC, the state bureaucracy, the corporate sector or withdrew from activism altogether. Though such individuals continued to make contributions in these new spheres, their departure tended to deprive civil society of left intellectual leadership at the moment when it was most needed. This trend can also be discerned amongst non-political organisations in civil society, such as NGOs, that faced a fiscal crisis with the withdrawal in foreign funding that accompanied normalisation in South Africa. These dynamics were sharply felt in the alternative media, and led to the closure of alternative newspapers and magazines and publishers, such as *Work in Progress, Learn and Teach* and Ravan Press (Shand, 1996).

However, COSATU never played a fully subordinate role during this period. At times it mobilised its constituency in support of the Alliance's negotiating position in CODESA. The most important example of this supportive role was the "return to mass action" in mid-1992, after CODESA deadlocked. The Alliance, led by COSATU and the SACP embarked on a series of general strikes and marches, that reached its climax in a bloody confrontation at Bisho in the Ciskei homeland in the Eastern Cape. The campaign brought the country to the brink of civil war, which propelled both ANC and NP to seek a pact that broke the deadlock in CODESA, leading the country to the 1994 elections and the relatively peaceful transfer of power. This campaign fits in comfortably to the political science analysis of mobilisation as functional to elite pacting, and it also encouraged Cronin to criticise what he called the "tap" theory of mobilisation, that reduces civil society and mass action to a mere resource for political elites.

The increasing centrality of political parties was reinforced once agreement was reached in CODESA on an election date which was to be 27 April 1994. This immediately set in motion two parallel processes in the Triple Alliance: the development of an electoral programme and the construction of a political machine. In both of these spheres, COSATU played an important role building and influencing the ANC — but in a subordinate position.

PART FOUR: THE ELECTORAL CAMPAIGN

The ANC's electoral campaign came to focus around one major initiative: the Reconstruction and Development Programme (RDP). The RDP originated in a attempt by the National Union of Metalworkers of South Africa [NUMSA] to produce an *accord* that would tie COSATU's electoral support for the ANC to the latter's commitment to a working class programme (von Holdt, 1991). The accord was given three separate meanings by COSATU. Firstly, it was understood as a framework for an independent, labour-driven campaign. It was also seen as the core pillar of the ANC's election manifesto to be implemented after the elections. Finally, it was viewed as a social contract, which would require reciprocal sacrifices by the ANC and the unions: the former committing itself to the programme, the latter to the cooperation needed to effect the new policies. While these different meanings were undoubtedly compatible, they contained ambivalences that laid the basis for contestation over the programme's meaning.

The ANC adopted the reconstruction accord, now re-titled as the RDP, in 1993 for very particular reasons of its own. The 1992 breakdown in CODESA was resolved through the Record of Understanding, a pact between the ANC and NP which included the controversial "sunset clauses" guaranteeing that the apartheid state bureaucracy would be kept relatively intact. The compromise at the core of the Record of Understanding — which was reached following the return to mass action that began with a tragic massacre at Boipatong Township south of Johannesburg and concluded with the Bisho massacre in September — was a bitter pill for the ANC's constituency to swallow. The RDP provided an opportunity for the ANC to boost its credibility within the movement by endorsing a participatory programme of economic and social transformation. The adoption of the RDP, Gotz argues, was an electoral gambit, rather than an item of faith, adopted in haste without thorough consideration of COSATU's and the SACP's vision of radical change, and it laid the basis for the recasting of the document's meaning in a direction more attuned to the ANC's complicated electoral needs. In particular, its macroeconomic orientation was re-defined away from the unions' commitment to "growth through redistribution" to a direction more attractive to domestic and international capital, with commitments to fiscal discipline and macroeconomic balance.

The redrafted RDP was sharply criticised on both procedural and substantive grounds at a special COSATU congress held in August 1993. The redraft was presented for adoption without being debated within COSATU structures, and its content had been changed to include a statement that "coherent, strict, and effective monetary and fiscal policies will be a cornerstone of our RDP" (Etkind and Harvey, 1993). This formulation provoked considerable debate at the Congress over what was seen as the thin end of the neoliberal wedge. However, COSATU adopted the programme without suggesting an alternative to this call for fiscal discipline at the heart of the RDP. The RDP soon became the paradigm within which all development policies were to be discussed, an extended wish list in which the homeless, the landless, workers, and international bankers could take equal comfort. In other words, it became all things to all people (African National Congress, 1994).

At the same special congress, COSATU constructed the other leg of its electoral strategy in support of the ANC. Twenty COSATU leaders were released to stand as parliamentary candidates on the ANC's list, including some of the organisation's most senior office bearers and strategists. A larger number of leaders were similarly released to stand on provincial lists (and later on local government electoral lists). The guiding idea was that such individuals would strengthen the capacity of the ANC and at the same time shape its direction towards labour's goals.

It proved difficult to fulfill both of these aims. Many ex-COSATU leaders gained influence, especially those who became cabinet ministers and chairpersons of Parliamentary committees, but COSATU as an organisation did not. Indeed, it suffered what has come to be known as a "brain drain" in which many of its leading figures, especially at regional and local levels, left the organisation (Buhlungu, 1994a,b). An estimated 80 key leaders left the organisation at the time of the national elections; a much larger number of lower-level leaders left in late 1995 after the local government elections. In the National

Union of Mineworkers itself more than 100 shopstewards went into local government structures. However, once in government these individuals found themselves detached from any accountability to their old federation while being isolated from the centre of power in their home, the ANC. Within the ANC and the SACP labour leaders seldom hold the same seniority and credibility as those who earned their status during imprisonment on Robben Island or through leadership in exile, especially in the ANC's armed wing, *Umkhonto we Sizwe.* Furthermore, these ex-unionists lack a COSATU caucus in parliament, and as ANC members they are subject to party discipline; indeed, a clause in the interim constitution compels MPs to resign their seats if they leave or are expelled from their party. This gives party leaders extensive power over dissident members.

The 1994 elections cemented the ANC's hegemony within the Triple Alliance. By virtue of its overwhelming electoral victory, the ANC became the majority party in a legitimate Government of National Unity. As described above, the party leadership − principally the ministers and the president himself − now enjoyed considerable leverage over its MPs (including the ex-COSATU unionists in Parliament), not to mention the organisation's extra-parliamentary structures. Furthermore, it could now summon the vast resources of the state bureaucracy in pursuit of its policy goals. The transition from movement to Government had been initiated, if not completed. In practical terms, this meant that policy developments such as the RDP, that had once been the object of bargaining within the Alliance, now became government policies to be developed within state structures, including a bureaucracy whose composition was largely unchanged as a result of the "sunset clauses."

From 1994 to 1996 the RDP became the ostensibly guiding document of the Government of National Unity, located in an RDP Office within the President's Office, under the immediate authority of Minister Without Portfolio, Jay Naidoo − ex-General Secretary of COSATU. Within months the Alliance's election document was redrafted into an official government White Paper (Parliament of the Republic of South Africa, 1994). However, the principles and programmatic objectives of the original RDP were re-conceptualised as a long-term strategic vision to realign all government effort around clearly stated economic targets, leaving little room for labour-, or indeed civil society-driven change (Gotz, in press).

Furthermore, the macroeconomic shift noted above became even more pronounced in the White Paper which significantly strengthened the emphasis on fiscal discipline that first appeared in the draft presented to the 1993 COSATU special congress. It developed a more robust commitment to an export-led growth strategy while loosening the RDP's original emphasis on a basic needs strategy stressing the need to reduce state expenditure, privatisation, and promoting private sector expansion. For example, the RDP placed ultimate responsibility on the government "for ensuring that housing is provided to all", and that housing be affordable "to even the poorest South Africans" (African National Congress, 1974, 23). Instead the White Paper envisions a market-based approach to housing through "innovative financial institutions and instruments which promote domestic savings and extend financial services to those who do not have adequate access to these services" (Parliament, 1994, 25). But whereas the RDP articulated a vision of housing and community banks and mechanisms to make the financial sector responsive to popular needs (and maintained government as the provider of last resort), the White Paper drops any explicit suggestions on these lines, while a high interest rate regime puts housing finance beyond the means of most South Africans (Parliament, 1994; Adelzadeh and Padayachee, 1994). As two commentators remarked, the RDP had become

> an essentially neo-liberal . . . strategy which . . . may well generate some level of economic growth. Should this happen, the existing mainly white and Indian bourgeoisie will be consolidated and strengthened, the black bourgeoisie will grow rapidly, a black middle class and some members of the black urban working class will become incorporated into the magic insiders; but for the remaining 60% to 70% of our society this growth path . . . will deliver little or nothing for many years to come (Adelzadeh and Padayachee, 1994).

In March 1996 the RDP Office was unceremoniously closed down and its activities were "relocated" under the Department of Finance and ultimately under Deputy President Thabo Mbeki. Although the Government explained this change as an attempt to improve the implementation of the RDP in previously reluctant line ministries by locating it under the authority of the Deputy President, most commentators saw the move as a break with the RDP in all but name and a conclusive shift towards a neoliberal macroeconomic strategy.

ECONOMIC POLICY AND TRIPARTITE INSTITUTIONS

If one leg of the labour movement's participation in the transition was electoral, the other was economic. Not only did labour claim the right to participate in the political process of transition, but it also sought to intervene in the process of restructuring the economy. In the late 1980s COSATU began to analyse the nature of the economic crisis facing South Africa, and at a deeper level, to begin exploring economic alternatives, fearing that a political transition would simply entrench a non-racial crisis-ridden capitalism. The public reason given for research into the economy was that COSATU was under attack for its support for sanctions and needed to examine "the impact of enforced isolation on the South African economy" (Joffe et al., 1995, xi). The federation commissioned union-linked university-based economists and other social scientists to conduct research under the rubric of the Economic Trends Research Group (Gelb, 1990).

In 1990 this research effort shifted, and the broad agenda of the Economic Trends Group was replaced by the Industrial Strategy Project, commissioned by COSATU to "develop an industrial policy that could address the poor performance of South African manufacturin." (Joffe *et al.*, 1995, xi). As laudable as such a research effort was, the federation faced three problems that in time came to plague its efforts to contest neoliberalism. Firstly, an industrial strategy focused on the manufacturing sector – a relatively small and declining percentage of South Africa's GNP – is not the same as an industrialisation strategy (Bell, 1996). Secondly, and more importantly, an industrial strategy is not an economic policy; the ISP's brief did not include fiscal and monetary policy, the core of neoliberalism's intervention into economic policy, and the federation did not commission any similar research project into such matters. And finally, the ISP report never became COSATU policy, which raises the complex question of the relationship between university-based research work and trade union organisation and how commissioned research efforts translate into organisational policy. In this sense COSATU's own efforts left it ill equipped to engage with the economic debate at the heart of the transition. Indeed, two years into the transition, the Department of Trade and Industry had not yet developed any proposals towards an industrial policy. Thus in one of the main areas where COSATU had made an intervention, it has not yet yielded a coherent policy intervention.[3]

The biggest challenge to neoliberalism came not from the research effort, but from the struggles by workers to resist the unilateral restructuring of the economy. These struggles were exemplified by a three-day stayaway in November 1991 to protest the apartheid government's IMF-inspired unilateral introduction of Value Added Tax. One of labour's core demands was for the creation of a National Economic Forum in which the unions could extend the transition's negotiation process to include economic restructuring. This institution parallelled CODESA, but it was composed of civil society formations: business associations and trade union federations. As a result, it allowed the labour movement to have a direct purchase on policy decisions, something it had lost in CODESA. In this realm, COSATU was not subordinate to the ANC, but had potential to act with autonomy.

In the perspective of Steven Friedman and Mark Shaw, who have conducted the fullest research on the unions' participation in the NEF, the unions were able to make gains through participation. However, these were not as significant as the unions had originally hoped, and they came with costs (Friedman and Shaw, in press). The unions had proposed rather bold initiatives for industrial restructuring as well as a social plan to deal with the attendant social costs. The concrete gains made were less far-reaching: "agreement on a revised offer to GATT; overturning a government decision to raise the petrol price; [and] agreement on parameters for a public works programme and disbursement of money to organisations applying to run programmes" (Friedman and Shaw, in press).

However, participation imposed costs on COSATU and revealed many weaknesses in the organisation. Many of its top negotiators and policy makers became tied down in a bureaucratised process that led them to neglect their basic union work. In addition, union negotiators were unable to report-back on a regular basis about developments in the NEF, and positions taken in the Forum could not effectively reflect a mandate from the organisation. This weakness was revealed in a 1994 survey of COSATU members in which 80% knew nothing about the NEF and had never been present when there was a report-back on the Forum (Ginsburg and Webster, 1995, 67-68).[4]

Researchers at the COSATU-linked research unit NALEDI made an even stronger criticism about the lack of participation at the NEF:

> Elements of the movement's leadership agreed to positions that were not only unknown to the broader leadership, but were, and in many instances continue to be, opposed by them. Hence the continued demands by some members and officials not to 'sign' or 'join' the GATT (Lloyd and Rix, 1995).

Thus, not only were the members out of touch with developments in the NEF, but so were the federation's leaders, such that agreements could be reached at the NEF that did not reflect the positions of many in the federation. They point out that social democratic institutions such as the NEF should emerge only after substantial debate within the movement, "albeit often only at leadership level". This, argues Chris Lloyd and Steven Rix, has not been the case; instead, COSATU "has plunged into this institution without the guidance of such debate", allowing a small leadership clique to make decisions "on the part of a broad movement whose thinking is in the opposite direction" (Lloyd and Rix, 1995, 14).

Finally, participation in the Forum revealed a glaring policy weakness in the Federation, in particular that it did not possess detailed economic plans — the point made above with reference to the Industrial Strategy Project — but this point can also be extended to its lack of a social policy, and indeed the absence of a social plan. The absence of an economic framework was most obvious in "the NEF's macro-economic policy work group, which was meant to review current policy and, by implication, consider COSATU's proposed alternatives"; however this group "failed dismally" (Friedman and Shaw, in press). According to Friedman and Shaw, COSATU entered the NEF,

> with an inadequate strategy and lacked the capacity to engage in the technical issues discussed . . . so ensuring that they would be out-bargained. The unions had not devoted to the negotiators the resources needed to win gains, and (paradoxically) had allowed union negotiators'

time and effort to be tied up in forums at the cost of a severe rupture with their constituency.

In the Forum the unions were able "to propose, but not to dispose", and as the 1994 elections came near, the imperative became blocking and delaying policy until an ANC-led government could come to power. In other words, a very promising opening to influence policy revealed similar weaknesses to the decisions to release COSATU leaders to stand for the ANC in the 1994 elections: in the NEF, as in both CODESA and the elections, COSATU embarked on an "exodus without a map". And in both cases, potentially independent interventions ended in a supportive role for the ANC.

NEDLAC

With the transition to democracy, one of the first Acts of the new Parliament was legislation merging the NEF with the National Manpower Commission to create NEDLAC.[5] NEDLAC is a statutory body composed of representatives of labour, capital, and the state, who sit in three chambers: Labour Market, Trade and Industry, Public Finance and Monetary Policy. A fourth — Development — chamber was created to include the broad range of organisations from civil society usually excluded from corporatist institutions: community and development organisations with a "mass base" and "definable national interests" which are independent of the state and not contesting parliamentary power (Webster, 1995b, 25-26). NEDLAC's central objective is to reach consensus and conclude agreements on social and economic policies before they go to parliament. Although parliament is sovereign and NEDLAC is an advisory body, a potential consensus between the social partners would be difficult for parliamentarians to disregard.

The NEDLAC framework was first put to test in February 1995 when a new labour relations bill was tabled in the council, based on a negotiating document devised by a legal drafting team appointed by Minister of Labour, Tito Mboweni. The bill proposed far-reaching changes to the industrial relations system, introducing for the first time enterprise-level co-determinist institutions called workplace forums, as well as extending union organising and representational rights while greatly strengthening the right to strike and legalising picketing. Indeed, the right to strike was subsequently entrenched in the new constitution following the 27 April 1996 general strike. At the core of the new system is a proposed statutory Commission for Conciliation and Mediation and Arbitration designed to shift work relations from adversarialism to a more participatory and co-operative style.

The bill thus laid the foundations for a new labour regime based on co-decision-making. It thereby extended unions' powers beyond wage-determination and distributional issues to production matters, making important inroads into managerial prerogatives. These rights go beyond the workplace, providing labour with access to sectoral and national economic policy-making through transformed sectoral negotiation chambers — called Bargaining Councils — and, ultimately, to NEDLAC. Taken together, these innovations provide labour with gains virtually unthinkable in any contemporary industrial democracy, leave alone in a country undertaking a transition to democracy.

Employers and unions deadlocked within the first month of discussions on the negotiating document, and labour embarked on a campaign of mass action over the next two-and-a-half months to support its demands, particularly for centralised bargaining and outlawing scab labour. In July, NEDLAC announced a breakthrough that enabled the social partners to reach consensus. The agreement was produced after 149 hours of formal meetings between employers, labour, and government, and in late-night "conversation groups".

The bill was passed by parliament in September 1995, marking the first fundamental break with the industrial relations system established in the 1920s. The new system gives labour an institutional voice over economic and social policy and the potential to shift the balance of power in debates over the emerging labour regime. The opportunity was thus opened for labour to craft policies over wages, employment standards, industrial policy, competition, privatisation, and trade in the interests of working people.[6]

Furthermore, the process through which this consensus was reached is remarkable in itself: tripartite arrangements drew the major stakeholders together into a compromise agreement in which all parties had an interest. Although tripartism is time-consuming and elusive and arrives at agreements not completely satisfying to all participants, they can improve the quality of decisions, build political bases of support for the proposed reforms, and help consolidate democratic institutions (Webster, 1995a).

The most recent issue to come before NEDLAC is a debate on economic policy that poses sharply contrasting positions between labour, capital and the state, each of which has presented economic programmes. Capital, in the form of a report from the South Africa Foundation, advocates a standard neoliberal solution: economic deregulation, dramatic reductions in the deficit, trade liberalisation in the form of lower tariffs, rapid privatisation, lower corporate taxes, and increased labour market flexibility to be achieved through dual labour market policies (South Africa Foundation, 1996).

By contrast, COSATU has developed an alternative plan, "Social Equity and Job Creation", inspired by left-Keynesian thinking that has become the common position in the labour caucus in NEDLAC, composed of COSATU, NACTU, and FEDSAL (Labour Caucus, 1996). The plan attacks neoliberalism and proposes instead a public and private investment policy geared towards job creation and growth. Central to the strategy is an active industrial policy to develop the manufacturing sector along with social adjustment measures to provide for the social costs of restructuring the economy. Importantly, the programme proposes a redistributive fiscal policy based on a strongly progressive tax system that will redirect spending towards social services for the poor. The programme also articulates a vision of regional reconstruction and development tied to support for a third world debt write-off and closer trade union solidarity. Finally, it incorporates demands for worker participation, both at the shop floor in the form of union-based Workplace Forums and at the sectoral and national levels.

The Government of National Unity proposed its own economic development document, which ambiguously straddled the neoliberal macroeconomic programmme of the South African Foundation's approach and the redistributive and equity orientations of labour's document (Inter-governmental Forum, 1996). However, this document was withdrawn because of opposition within the ANC and its allies, both to the process whereby the document was written and tabled and to its content. In June, after considerable internal disagreement within the Tripartite Alliance, Finance Minister Trevor Manuel finally released a macro-economic strategy, "Growth, Employment and Redistribution" [GEAR] (Department of Finance, 1996).

GEAR puts forward ambitious targets. It aims to achieve a "fast-growing economy which creates sufficient jobs for all work-seekers". It also envisions redistribution of income, the provision of sound services to all, and the achievement of 6% growth and the creation of 400,000 jobs per annum by the year 2000 (Department of Finance, 1996, 1). The controversial aspect of the plan is the means identified to achieve these goals. Its integrated strategy highlights fiscal deficit reduction, gradual relaxation of exchange controls, reduction in tariffs, tax reductions to encourage private sector (and especially foreign direct) investment, and restructuring of state assets (privatisation).

The document provoked strong criticism from COSATU as well as among leading figures in the South African Communist Party — though it was ultimately formally endorsed by the ANC's National Working Committee, on which COSATU and SACP representatives sit. However, COSATU General Secretary Sam Shilowa publicly criticised GEAR — tellingly at a seminar marking the 75th anniversary of the SACP — describing the strategy as an "unworkable and unwinnable" plan that "poses serious difficulties for the working class and the country as a whole". Most significantly, Shilowa identified the distance the ANC has moved right-ward from the original RDP by indicating that GEAR could never have emerged from the ANC before the 1994 elections (*Sunday Times*, 1996; *Sunday Independent*, 1996).

COSATU commissioned the National Institute on Economic Policy [NIEP] and NALEDI to conduct an analysis of GEAR. The conclusions cast doubt on the likelihood of the plan meeting its stated goals, and asserted that even if it meets its targets it will exacerbate existing inequality rather than promote redistribution (COSATU, 1996; NIEP, 1996). These conclusions informed

Shilowa's criticisms of GEAR, as well as later comments by COSATU's Assistant General Secretary, Zwelinzima Vavi. Their positions were approved by COSATU's Executive (*Business Report*, 1996).

When GEAR was released the government asserted that the policy was non-negotiable, a position that has been reiterated by numerous ministers and spokespersons. This stance has been sharply criticised by COSATU. Vavi recently commented, "There is no way that government will succeed in simply pushing its framework down our throats. It is just not possible . . ." The government has offered to discuss details of the plan, but has attempted explicitly to raise the framework itself above popular debate. COSATU rejected this position. According to Vavi,

> It is the entire framework which we wish to discuss. We are not simply seeking the amendment of minor details here and there, but a complete reassessment of their view of the role of the state in stimulating reconstruction and development (*Business Report*, 1996).

It will not be easy to bridge government and labour's positions since they come from different economic paradigms and represent different conceptions of labour regimes. In the words of the Minister of Labour, Tito Mboweni, the gap between them is as wide as the distance between the Cape and Cairo. Each of the programmes advocates rapid growth but differ fundamentally on how this is to come about and who is to bear the costs and share the benefits. The business plan and GEAR suggest that growth will come through unleashing the market: deregulating labour and driving down wage costs and labour standards. Labour's project, by contrast advocates growth through redistribution, the policy orientation that guided COSATU's original vision of a reconstruction accord with the ANC, but which eventually dropped out of the RDP. But the labour document is much less clear about how business and government will be brought around to contribute to growth.

NEDLAC's institutionalised role in policy making provides some of the preconditions for a social pact between the social partners. Such a pact was proposed by the Labour Market Commission appointed by the Department of Labour to investigate the development of a comprehensive labour market policy in South Africa (Department of Labour, 1996). However, GEAR puts less emphasis on a pact, speaking more vaguely of the "need to move towards a national social agreement" (Department of Finance, 1996, 20).

A pact, however, would discipline all parties: if labour is given increased influence over investment policy and process this will provide the possibility that the benefits of growth will improve living standards for workers and the poor. On the other hand, business, too, will gain advantages from a pact through providing labour with a strong stake in economic growth. This would contribute to industrial relations and wage stability, and thereby encourage investor confidence by providing business with increased certainty over key cost variables. Finally, government would be forced to develop macro-economic policies with respect to the interests of both capital and labour; at a minimum this requires a commitment to redistributive economic and social policies that perforce imply some relaxation of the government's cautious fiscal approach. This could be the core of a class compromise that could bring about an economic shift similar to that produced in the political transition: a turn away from the current neoliberal policy towards a programme much more oriented to the needs of labour and the poor.

It is not clear that any of the parties mentioned above will be committed to a pact. Indeed, in recent months all three have downgraded NEDLAC to some extent. Each party has at crucial policy junctures preferred a bilateral to a tripartite process. When faced with government plans for privatisation, labour by-passed NEDLAC and negotiated directly with its ally, the ANC. When the government was faced with resistance from labour over tariff reform, it, too, threatened to bypass NEDLAC, and its non-negotiable stance over GEAR follows the same pattern. Finally, business's "Growth for All" plan was developed not by its NEDLAC voice, Business South Africa, but by the South Africa Foundation, a mouthpiece for the so-called "Brenthurst Group", the ten top companies in South Africa.

If all the parties do not in some equal manner bear the costs and benefits of growth, then there will likely be a return to sharp conflict that could well prevent the consolidation of democracy in South Africa. For labour in particular, NEDLAC provides the best opportunity to shape economic and social policy. To date, however, the signs are not promising that labour will be able to realise opportunities afforded by NEDLAC, and it may well be that this extremely valuable opening is lost. In particular, the problems of capacity and accountability exposed by Friedman and Shaw and by Lloyd and Rix have not been adequately addressed by labour.

CONCLUSION

If labour has embarked on an exodus from apartheid to democracy, it lacks a clear understanding of its destination and the route to reach it. It faces difficult dilemmas. If it continues within the Alliance, but cannot develop policies of its own it may become a marginal actor within a context increasingly dominated by neoliberal economic and social policies. If it divorces itself from the Alliance it risks a confrontation in which it will be presented as a special interest concerned with a labour elite hostile to the "national interest". It here risks becoming irrelevant or, more ominously, the target of repression in a context where the ANC remains the hegemonic political force. Furthermore, divorce and opposition opens up the possibility that the governing party's policies will fail, and a less labour-friendly government will come to power. This may seem to be a remote prospect at present, but it is not unthinkable, and the withdrawal of the National Party from the Government of National Unity in May makes a right-of-centre political realignment a possibility in the future.

Finally, divorce would be opposed by COSATU's own constituency: the 1994 survey of COSATU members cited above revealed that 76% would vote for the ANC in the next elections, *even if the government fails to deliver!* Only 14% suggested that COSATU form its own political party. The members' views do not contradict the members' assertion that COSATU would best represent their interests in the transition; rather, they see COSATU as best representing them *within* the Alliance, where it can have a share in Alliance — and implicitly governmental — decision-making (Ginsburg and Webster, 1995, 74).

Between marginalisation and divorce lies a third option: the active contesting for hegemony within the Triple Alliance. This requires labour and the SACP to use their power of persuasion and ultimately COSATU's disruptive power in the economy to move the ANC away from neoliberalism. The third option involves a significant shift in COSATU's approach to the Alliance as well as to the new institutions established in the transition, and depends on the organisation's ability to revitalise itself and to increase capacity. These tasks are formidable. If they can be accomplished, the labour movement may ensure that civil society organisations have direct power over policy making in the state. In their absence, the transition is less likely to yield a meaningful reconstruction of society and the economy, without which the consolidation of democracy is unlikely.

ENDNOTES

1   Cited in Webster (1996).
2   Migrants were included under the Act through reforms during the early 1980s, while the latter groups were included only after the transition to democracy in the 1990s.
3   This result occurred despite the fact that many ex-ISP researchers went into senior positions in the Department. On the other hand, Alec Erwin, one of the ISP's strongest supporters in COSATU is now minister of trade and industry, and has indicated that the development of an industrial policy is a high priority for his ministry. The one area of ISP work that has connected with COSATU affiliates' organising activities is the section on "Human Resources, Corporate Governance and Public Policy."
4   The results are derived from a probability sample based on the area sampling method and conducted among 643 ordinary COSATU members in four of the federation's regions. The survey was conducted in March-April 1994.
5   The National Manpower Commission was established in the early 1980s as part of the labour reforms initiated by the Wiehahn Commission of inquiry. It was a tripartite body appointed by the minister of labour, with the function of monitoring the new labour system and advising the government on manpower issues. It was immediately boycotted by the emerging black unions until the transition to democracy, when they sought — unsuccessfully — to enter and transform it (see Schreiner, 1991).

6   This agreement did not win acceptance everywhere; in particular there was strong criticism from within COSATU, most prominently from the Wits Local, which condemned the consensus as a "miserable compromise" (von Holdt, 1995).

REFERENCES

ADELZADEH, A. and V. PADAYACHEE. (1994). "The RDP White Paper: Reconstruction of a Development Vision?", *Transformation*, 25.

ADLER, G. and E. WEBSTER. (1995) "Challenging Transition Theory: The Labour Movement, Radical Reform, and Transition in South Africa", *Politics and Society*, 23:1.

AFRICAN NATIONAL CONGRESS. (1994) *The Reconstruction and Development Programme: A Policy Framework* (Johannesburg, Umanyano Publications).

BASKIN, J. (1991) *Striking Back: A History of COSATU* (Johannesburg, Ravan).

BELL, T. (1996) "Improving Manufacturing Performance in South Africa: A Contrary View", *Transformation*, 28.

BUHLUNGU, S. (1994b) "The Big Brain Drain: Union Officials in the 1990s", *South African Labour Bulletin*, 18:3.

— (1994a) "COSATU and the Elections", *South African Labour Bulletin*, 18:2.

Business Report (26 August, 1996) "Cosatu Edges Closer to ANC Clash".

CONSTITUTIONAL ASSEMBLY (1996) "Constitution of the Republic of South Africa Bill" (Cape Town).

COSATU (1996) "Critical Assessment of Government's Proposed Growth Framework and Policy Scenarios".

CRONIN, J. (1992) "The Boat, the Tap and the Leipzig Way", *The African Communist*, 130.

DEPARTMENT OF FINANCE (1996) *Growth, Employment and Redistribution: A Macro-Economic Strategy* (Pretoria, Government Printer).

DEPARTMENT OF LABOUR (1996) *Restructuring the South African Labour Market: Report of a Commission to Investigate the Development of a Comprehensive Labour Market Policy* (Pretoria, Government Printer).

— (1995) *Annual Report* (Pretoria, Government Printer).

ETKIND, H. and S. HARVEY (1993) "The Workers Cease Fire", *South African Labour Bulletin*, 17:5.

FINE, A and E. WEBSTER (1989) "Transcending Traditions: Trade Unions and Political Unity", in Glenn Moss and Ingrid Obery, (eds) *South African Review* (Johannesburg, (Ravan Press).

FOSTER, J. (1982) "The Workers' Struggle — Where Does FOSATU Stand?" Address by Joe Foster to the 1982 FOSATU Congress (Johannesburg, FOSATU).

FRIEDMAN, S. (1987) *Building Tomorrow Today: African Workers in Trade Unions, 1970-1984* (Johannesburg, Ravan Press).

FRIEDMAN, S. and M. SHAW (Forthcoming) "Power in Partnership? Trade Unions, Forums, and the Transition", in G. Adler and E. Webster, (eds) *Consolidating Democracy in a Liberalizing World: Trade Unions and Transition in South Africa* (London, Macmillan).

GELB, S. (ed) (1990) *South Africa's Economic Crisis* (Cape Town, David Philip).

GINSBURG, D. and E. WEBSTER *et al.* (1995) *Taking Democracy Seriously: Worker Expectations and Parliamentary Democracy in South Africa* (Durban, Indicator Press).

GOTZ, G. (Forthcoming) "Shoot Anything That Flies: Claim Anything That Falls: Labour and the Changing Definition of the Reconstruction and Development Programme", in G. Adler and E. Webster (eds) *Consolidating Democracy in a Liberalizing World: Trade Unions and Transition in South Africa* (London, Macmillan).

HARVEY, S. (1996) "Labour Market Killing Fields", *South African Labour Bulletin*, 20:2.

INTER-GOVERNMENTAL FORUM (1996) "National Growth and Development Strategy" (Pretoria).

JOFFE, A. D. KAPLAN, R. KAPLINSKY, and D. LEWIS (1995) *Improving Manufacturing Performance in South Africa: Report of the Industrial Strategy Project* (Cape Town, University of Cape Town Press).

LABOUR CAUCUS [COSATU, FEDSAL, NACTU] (1996) "Social Equity and Job Creation: The Key to a Stable Future" (Johannesburg).

LAMBERT, ROB (1988) "Political unionism in South Africa: The South African Congress of Trade Unions, 1955-1965" (Ph.D. Dissertation, Department of Sociology, University of the Witwatersrand).

LLOYD, C. and S. RIX (1995) "Unions and Democratic Institutions", Discussion paper, National Labour and Economic Development Institute.

LMG [Labour Monitoring Group] (1985) "The November 1984 Stayaway", *South African Labour Bulletin*, 10:6.

MACUN, I. (Forthcoming) "Growth, Structure and Power in the South African Union Movement", in G. Adler and E. Webster, (eds) *Consolidating Democracy in a Liberalizing World: Trade Unions and Transition in South Africa* (London, Macmillan).

NIEP (1996) "From the RDP to GEAR: The Gradual Embracing of Neoliberalism in Economic Policy" (Unpublished paper).

PARLIAMENT OF THE REPUBLIC OF SOUTH AFRICA (1994) "White Paper on Reconstruction and Development", *Government Gazette*, 23 November.

PITYANA, S.M. and M. ORKIN (1992) *Beyond the Factory Floor: A Survey of COSATU Shopstewards* (Johannesburg, Ravan Press).

SAUL, J. (1996) "Liberal Democracy vs. Popular Democracy in Sub-Saharan Africa", in C. Daddieh and K. Mengisteab (eds) (Forthcoming) *Democratization and Nation-Building in Sub-Saharan Africa*.

SCHREINER, G. (1991) "Fossils From the Past: Restructuring the National Manpower Commission", *South African Labour Bulletin*, 16:1.

SHAND, N. (1996) "The Internal Dynamics of 'Small' Media Non-Governmental Organisations in South Africa" (MA Thesis, Department of Sociology, University of the Witwatersrand).

SOUTH AFRICA FOUNDATION (1996) "Growth for All: An Economic Strategy for South Africa" (Johannesburg).

SOUTHALL, R. (1995) *Imperialism or Solidarity?* (Cape Town, University of Cape Town Press).

SPARKS, A. (1994) *Tomorrow is Another Country: The Inside Story of South Africa's Negotiated Revolution* (Sandton, Struik).

Sunday Independent (1996) "Shilowa Ends Weeks of Restraint and Damns Government's Economic Plan".

Sunday Times (1996) "Shilowa's Bombshell: COSATU Rejects Macro-Economic Framework".

VON HOLDT, K. (1995) "The LRA Agreement: 'Worker Victory' or 'Miserable Compromise'?" *South African Labour Bulletin*, 19:4.

— (1991) "Towards Transforming SA Industry: A 'Reconstruction Accord' Between Unions and the ANC?", *South African Labour Bulletin*, 15:6.

WEBSTER, E. (1996) "Inside and Outside the State: Economic Reform, Trade Unions and the Consolidation of Democracy in South Africa" (University of the Witwatersrand, Sociology of Work Unit, Unpublished paper).

— (1995a) "The True Challenge to Tripartite Deals is Yet To Come." *Business Day*, 20 July 1995.

— (1995b) "NEDLAC — Corporatism of a Special Type?" *South African Labour Bulletin*, 19:2.

— (1986) "A New Frontier of Control? Case Studies in the Changing Form of Job Control in South African Industrial Relations", *Industrial Relations Journal of South Africa*, 6:1.

— (1985) *Cast in a Racial Mould: Labour Process and Trade Unionism in the Foundries* (Johannesburg, Ravan Press).

WEBSTER, E. and D. Keet. (1992) "National Economic Forum: Parallel to CODESA?", *South African Labour Bulletin*, 16:3.

Chapter Eight

The State and the Union Movement in Zimbabwe: Co-optation, Conflict and Accommodation

Lloyd M. Sachikonye

INTRODUCTION

The relationship between the Zimbabwean state and labour unions has undergone several phases in the first 19 years of independence. Initially, there was a honeymoon period, between 1980 and 1985, during which the co-optation of the labour movement was attempted and partially achieved. This was followed by a second phase — lasting between 1986 and 1993 — in which serious ideological disagreements and shift in economic policy strained the relationship considerably. From 1994 to 1997 sharp differences over the economic structural adjustment programme (ESAP) were tempered with labour's attempts at dialogue with the state, and a search for an institutional framework in which the policy conflicts and divergent interests could be accommodated. This search for accommodation occurred simultaneously with an emergent trend in recourse to constitutional challenges to specific state measures by unions. Increasingly, labour unions have challenged specific provisions and related legislation which impair their rights both at the work-place and in the wider community and political arena. These constitutional challenges have gained momentum under economic liberalisation; and they have taken both the form of national campaigns and demonstrations as well as legal presentations against the state in its highest courts.

This chapter attempts to develop a framework to explain the conflict, ambivalence and fragile pact which have characterized the relationship between the state and labour unions. It is a framework that is intended to illuminate the imperative for the current search for accommodation of their mutual interests by the two parties. Of course, our analytical framework needs to take into account the role of capital in the determination and implementation of labour legislation, and broadly its influence in the shaping of labour relations. We draw a great deal on the concept of labour regime (as broadly defined in the Introduction to the book) in seeking to account for the changes in relations between the state and labour unions specifically, and the shifting developments in post-independence Zimbabwe more generally.

THE FIRST PHASE, 1980-85: THE TRANSITION TO A POST-COLONIAL LABOUR REGIME

The first few years of independence were characterized by a transition from the colonial labour regime. The transition was partial rather than complete because there was continuity in certain aspects of that regime following independence. As we have explored in some detail elsewhere, there were many authoritarian aspects to the colonial labour regime [Sachikonye, 1986]. These ranged from repression of union rights, especially the right to organize along industrial union lines to denial of collective bargaining rights, and the right to strike in most sectors. Apart from a wholesale denial of political rights to black workers under the white minority system, racial segregation profoundly affected both union organization, and influenced managerial practices and culture in industrial relations at work-places. Black workers and unionists experienced no protection under colonial labour legislation, principally the Industrial Conciliation Act of 1934. They were later conferred only minimal safeguards under an amendment to the Act in 1959. In the absence of a strong collective bargaining structure, the wage conditions were generally poor for most black workers. At independence, this authoritarian labour regime was soon challenged not so much by the ruling party which had acceded to power as by thousands of workers.

In this section, we seek to explore the various aspects of the colonial labour regime that became objects of challenge, and the new elements of the post-colonial labour regime which emerged. However, it is necessary to begin by providing the broad context in which the process of regime transition occurred. First, the structural features of the labour movement need to be spelt out briefly. The movement has its basis in a formal sector working-class of about 1.5 million, which constitutes slightly more than 10 per cent of Zimbabwe's population of 12 million. The relatively small size of the working-class is an index of the limited level of industrialization in Zimbabwe. More profound perhaps than the size of the working class is the partial character of the proletarianisation process itself. The migrant labour system upon which commercial agriculture and mining, and to some extent manufacturing, drew during the greater part of the colonial period did not substantially change with independence. The oscillation of migrant workers between capitalist industry and the peasant sector contributed to the partial formation of their worker consciousness and therefore its ambiguity and ambivalence. Urban poverty partially ameliorated by the retention of close family links with poorer subsistence peasant farming limited the potential of a permanent organizational effort [Wood, 1987, 50].

A multiplicity of craft-based unions and of rival national centers at independence were but symptoms of the structural weaknesses of unions, and more broadly, of the labour movement. These related to organizational constraints. For example, one estimate put the total African union membership at 80 000 grouped into 25 unions at independence. Thus only about 8 per cent of the total work-force at independence was unionized. The low level of unionization was largely due to the authoritarian framework which inhibited the formation of large industrial unions by restricting membership mobilisation by union organizers.

At independence, there consequently existed a gaping vacuum in the labour relations structure. Absent were strong mechanisms to channel the interests and demands of workers, and to mediate the conflicts between capital and labour at both industrial and work-place levels. The colonial labour legislation had now become anachronistic in this new context. It was therefore scarcely surprising that soon after independence, there was a massive upsurge in the form of strikes to challenge the vestiges of the colonial labour regime. For instance, it was estimated that in the first three months of 1980, about 250,000 production days were lost through strikes. About 180 strikes were reported in the press as having been organized between March 1980 and March 1981 [Sachikonye, 1986, 268-272]. The number of both reported and unreported strikes was most likely higher still with 173 stoppages reported in the Mashonaland region alone [Raftopoulos, 1994, 1]. Cumulatively, these stoppages represented the largest strike wave since the 1948 general strike. The economic effects of the strikes were considerable. The impact on the economy was immediately felt with the strikes in April 1980 wiping out the trade surplus as exports declined by 10 per cent [The Herald, 14 May 1980].

This was the broad context in which new elements of a labour regime needed to be introduced. These related to relations between capital and the state, and the overall legal framework of labour relations. These relations were deeply influenced by state interventionism once the institutional vacuum that existed was identified as the main contributory factor to the industrial unrest mentioned above. While a weak union movement had been the goal or object of the colonial regime, it had become a serious liability to the new state at independence. The recourse to state corporatism was therefore a response to the spontaneous industrial conflict of the first few years of independence, as however, it was also partly a response to the lack of clout of the existing unions to restrain militancy amongst workers. The accent was to be on facilitating the growth of large industrial unions and the creation of a national labour center amenable to the new government.

The specific form which state intervention took during this phase was to sponsor the creation of the Zimbabwe Congress of Trade Unions [ZCTU] in 1981, and to pass a series of legislative measures pertaining to minimum wages and other employment conditions. These developments were primarily a response to the crisis created by the widespread resistance by labour to the colonial labour regime. The reconstruction of the labour movement and introduction of a legal framework for the conduct of labour relations were essentially aimed at containing the industrial conflict centred on worker's struggles for improved working conditions now that independence had been achieved. The unwritten pact which eventually defused the capital-labour conflict in 1980-82 specifically entailed state intervention [through statutory minimum wages]; the regulation of unfair labour practices and retrenchments [through statutory provisions on lay-off procedures]; and the promotion of work-place communication between workers and management [through worker's committees]. Indeed, the conflict over working conditions was not confined to capital and labour because the state was embroiled too as public sector workers also organized strikes during this period. Thus the state itself also sought a pact with labour.

Between 1980 and 1985, state corporatist arrangements were premised on a pact involving capital, the newly-created labour centre [ZCTU] and the state but not necessarily with individual unions on labour issues. This pact principally related to the question of the repression of the strikes. Clearly, it was a pact in which the labour movement was the weaker partner. Although they were primarily intended to contain industrial conflict, the definition and implementation of statutory minimum wages and related legislation were largely the preserve of the state. So was the drawing up of a rather paternalistic Labour Relations Act of 1985 which retained some of the authoritarian aspects of the Industrial Conciliation Act which it was supposed to supersede. Amongst those authoritarian aspects were the provisions proscribing strike action in most sectors of the economy. Redefined as "essential services", these were sectors in which the workers's basic right to withdraw labour, as one strategy to enforce their negotiating position, was still curbed considerably.

There existed a congruence of perspectives between the labour movement leadership and the state on the diagnosis of the labour relations crisis of 1980-82. The weak influence of the movement's leadership was confirmed in the admission by the then ZCTU Secretary General, Albert Mugabe, that the widespread strikes of 1980-82 had been organized spontaneously outside its ambit. Echoing basic agreement with the position of the state and capital, he argued that:

> strikes do more harm than good. We do not need to retard economic progress by arranging strikes . . . There are some bad eggs in the union movement . . . We will watch them closely and discourage striking as much as we can [Albert Mugabe as quoted in *The Herald*, 16 October 1981].

Increasingly, the ZCTU was seen as the principal vehicle for the de-radicalization of the working-class struggles whose channel of expression was plant-based industrial action. By its own admission, there were limits to the extent to which the centre could exert leverage on individual unions in the resolution of spontaneous plant-based strikes.

Nevertheless, in addition to its preponderant role in the determination of labour relations generally, the state sought to co-opt the labour center much more formally. For instance, there emerged a thinly disguised view within the ruling ZANU-PF party that the labour movement should be grafted onto its structures as one of its mass organizations alongside its youth and women's leagues. Similar co-optation strategies as then applied in Tanzania, Mozambique and Angola were cited as precedents. The rationale for co-optation was spelt out by a Minister of State for Political Affairs who argued that:

> because of our class position as a party and government, we expect the trade unions to operate within the parameters of our socialist objectives. Because of Zimbabwe's history of settler colonialism, most working people have very little technical, scientific and managerial skills and their ideological consciousness is still too low [Maurice Nyagumbo as quoted in The Herald, 17 July 1984].

Thus the state defined its role as one paternalist ideological guidance to what was perceived as a weak and fragmented labour movement.

Internal maladministration within the ZCTU in 1994 provided a 'propitious' opportunity to the state to intervene in the running of the affairs of the labour centre. Like in Nigeria a decade earlier in the mid-1970s, it appointed 'administrators' to run the national centre in the run-up to a labour congress where fresh elections would be held. Meanwhile, fissions within the labour movement became more pronounced. Struggles for leadership became intense between the incumbent leadership which professed allegiance to the ZANU-PF party and government, and a fraction which advocated autonomy for the labour movement. Furthermore, difficult economic conditions provided a basis for the questioning of state paternalism. A recession in 1982-84 had a severe squeeze on workers' incomes, and a state-imposed wage freeze compounded the slump in living standards.

It has been observed that state corporatism is associated with a particular stage of capitalism, especially when a transition to democracy is occurring [Coleman, 1985, 108-9]. Pluralism is still fragile during this stage; the system may break down into social conflict and the bourgeoisie still lack the organizational cohesion and political strength to restore order. The state is therefore compelled to intervene. In such a context, state corporatism provides the bourgeoisie with a political framework within which it can rely on the force of law to contain the demands of its class opponents . In the Zimbabwean case, state paternalism in the handling of labour relations soon after independence was a pronounced trend. Nevertheless, certain features of state corporatist arrangements were apparent in its resolution of the industrial conflict which was an expression of labour's resistance to the colonial labour regime whose various facets had become untenable in the new political context. What were viewed as obnoxious aspects of labour legislation such as the Master and Servants Act and the above-mentioned Industrial Conciliation Act had come under sustained challenge from labour. Furthermore, the low-wage structure which had buttressed that labour regime also came under pressure through strikes; autocracy and despotism at the work-place became objects of revulsion and challenge.

In sum, the modification of the colonial labour regime was accomplished through the design of new labour legislation which partially met the expectations of labour in the new political context. The Labour Relations Act [1985] spelt out what it termed "fundamental rights of workers" and "unfair labour practices". It contained provisions against racism and sexism in recruitment of labour, and provided safeguards against arbitrary dismissal. The minimum wage provisions went some way to provide basic income protection to the lowest-paid strata in the colonial labour regime. Nevertheless, it was a framework which invested preponderant authority, power and discretion in the state. Before long, both capital and labour would, however, challenge this framework but for different reasons. In the short-term, however, the regulatory framework and incomes policy had succeeded in defusing industrial conflict through the pacification of the work-force. But this was more of an interlude than a permanent arrangement or solution, as we shall see in the next section.

In sum, the period 1980 to 1985 thus witnessed the laying of the foundations of the post-colonial labour regime. As we observed above, these foundations rested on a shaky basis. The pact that had been concluded by the state and a labour movement leadership which did not have strong roots within the unions lacked legitimacy. Moreover, the pact did not incorporate a structure for a collective bargaining system. Unilateral wage determination by the state pre-empted such a collective bargaining framework. Against the state paternalism and authoritarian approach must be set initial determined efforts to expand the infrastructure and delivery of social services, principally health and education. Together with prescribed minimum wages, these social wage goods represented real gains in the first few years of independence. This redistributive element was a new feature in the emerging labour regime. The broad accumulation strategy was basically capitalist but with a specific theoretical emphasis on growth and equity. In reality, both objectives turned out difficult to reconcile and achieve, thereby sowing seeds for a crisis and conflict in the latter part of the 1980s. Notable though for their low profile in economic policy-making during this period were the international financial institutions (IFIs) [the WB and the IMF]. They were kept at arms length; domestic stabilization measures did not incorporate IFI conditionalities. Although it operated within clear structural constraints, the state still possessed some leverage in economic and social policy making. However, this would soon change during the next phase that we now turn to.

THE PHASE OF CONFLICT BETWEEN THE STATE AND THE LABOUR MOVEMENT

The years between 1986 and 1993 experienced major changes in economic and social policy, and in the content of the labour regime. Changes in accumulation strategy were mirrored in shifts in the labour regime. This period witnessed the adoption of economic liberalization measures from 1989 under pressure from the IFIs whose influence had grown. The growth of this influence was related to the pressing need of the Zimbabwe state to borrow for both balance of payments support and investment. The accumulation strategy of growth with equity was abandoned. This represented a volte-face in ZANU-PF's largely theoretical commitment to socialism, and a retreat from social redistribution measures [the broad provision of free education and health services for the lowest-income groups, and funding for rural resettlement]. Anyhow, the flirtation with socialist ideology had sat uneasily with the preservation of capitalist structures in the economy and the domestication [if not repression] of labour militancy. The adoption of a neo-liberal Investment Code in 1989 which envisaged the de-regulation of labour conditions, principally job security and income protection presaged the implementation of an economic structural adjustment programme [ESAP] in 1990.

Typically, Zimbabwe's ESAP contained the orthodox elements and conditions of adjustment programmes elsewhere in Africa. It prescribed measures relating to:
* budget deficit reduction;
* fiscal and monetary reform;
* trade liberalization;
* public enterprise reform (including privatization); and
* deregulation of investment, labour and price controls [Zimbabwe Government, 1991].

The case for ESAP itself was premised on the need to raise the annual growth rate to 5 per cent between 1990 and 1995. This would partly be achieved by creating more attractive conditions for foreign investment. Low production costs were to be achieved by de-regulating labour controls that had been incorporated into post-independence legislation such as the LRA. On the whole, however, the envisaged restructuring entailing fiscal and monetary reform and trade liberalization would have a direct impact on the labour regime, as we will see below.

In the meantime, there are two sets of issues that need to be addressed schematically. These are first the convergence of interests between the domestic and international bourgeoisie on the issue of economic liberalization, and secondly, the selective incorporation of organized interests and the exclusion of the labour movement in the design of ESAP. The shift to economic liberalization was not simply the result of a diktat from the IFIs, i.e. the WB and the IMF because by the late 1980s, certain fractions within the ruling elite (concentrated in the ZANU-PF party and government) had come out strongly against the lip-service to socialism and redistribution policies. These fractions of the petit-bourgeoisie were in the process of transforming themselves into a bourgeoisie proper through utilization of opportunities made possible by access to state resources. Their acquisitive tendencies contributed to a retreat from implementation of a Leadership Code which had been envisaged to restrain those tendencies amongst ZANU-PF leaders. The lengths to which their emergent bourgeoisie (which included some cabinet ministers) went to exploit accumulation opportunities provided through the state was exemplified in their profiteering in a racket known as the "Willogate scandal" of 1988. This stratum of the bourgeoisie was not opposed to economic liberalization. Organized business interests in manufacturing, mining and agriculture also generally welcomed the shift to liberalization in the expectation that access to foreign exchange, imported inputs, export openings and investment would be facilitated to their benefit. It was their representative associations such as the Confederation of Zimbabwe Industries (CZI) which were consulted in the design of ESAP. Thus this version of limited corporatism was confined to the state and private sector interests to the exclusion of the ZCTU. The subsequent critique from the ZCTU harped incessantly on this exclusion from the design of ESAP. This was the broad political and class context in which the shift to neo-liberal economic policy was organized.

But what was the specific impact of developments between 1986 and 1993 on the labour regime? This period witnessed the unravelling of state corporatist arrangements, such as they were at this stage. First, individual unions asserted their disgruntlement with the performance of the ZCTU leadership, that had acquiesced to co-optation, by voting it out of office in 1985. But this represented more than simply a change in leadership. The assertion of labour movement autonomy placed relations with the state on a different level. Increasingly questioned critically were the state's economic and labour policies. The unilateral setting of minimum wages by the state came under fire. There was growing pressure from both individual unions and employer organizations for autonomy in wage determination. Strikes in such sectors as agro-industry and public service during this period exposed the limitations of unilateral minimum wage setting. Collective bargaining was sought to replace statutory guide-lines on minimum wages which were now yielding diminishing returns.

The shift to explicit neo-liberal economic measures under ESAP in 1990 had a significant impact on the labour regime. For instance, the new accumulation under ESAP envisaged a substantial retrenchment of workers as a consequence of restructuring in both the private and public sectors. An estimated 26,000 jobs in the private sector (representing nearly 2,5 per cent of the sectoral work-force) and 20,000 in the private sector (representing nearly 2,5 per cent of the labour force) were to be axed. The rationale of these retrenchments in a context of high unemployment of about 40 per cent was inevitably a source of friction between the labour movement on the one hand and both the state and capital on the other. Under ESAP, mass retrenchments also occurred in such sectors as textiles and clothing, engineering and steel, and in services. At the same time, the much-vaunted capacity of ESAP measures to create a significant number of new jobs (envisaged at about 100,000 formal sector jobs a year) failed to materialize.

One of the more immediate and visible aspects of the new labour regime was therefore the substantial reduction of labour costs through lay-offs, and the tightening of managerial supervision systems geared towards increased productivity. The vulnerability of workers was exposed in these lay-offs which no longer required cumbersome procedures to implement. Amendments to the LRA removed safeguards against arbitrary "hiring and firing". Statutory minimum wages were phased out in most sectors in 1989. Most unions proved quite skilful in wage negotiations with their employers in both the private and parastatal sectors in 1989-91. Under this emergent labour regime, unions extracted considerable concessions from management through collective bargaining. Hitherto, state intervention in wage-setting had tended to depress wage scales with the exception of a few sectors such as agriculture and domestic service where union bargaining capacity was still low.

During this phase, these were notable developments concerning work-place bargaining power (WBP) of workers. The institutionalization of the collective bargaining system strengthened the role of industrial unions and employers' associations in their bipartite national employment councils (NECs). Bilateral pacts negotiated in these NECs became the basis of displinary codes and wage settlements in the relevant industrial sectors. These industrial-level pacts reflected the negotiating capacity of each of the parties, and the economic performance of particular sectors. It was a new framework in which state paternalism or state-driven corporatist arrangements were no longer relevant nor workable.

Nevertheless, this new labour regime was not established without obstruction or contestation from the state. For example, a bone of contention over collective bargaining concerned state opposition to high wage awards ostensibly because they fuelled inflation. In 1990-91, wage awards ranged between 19 and 30 per cent in the private sector prompting the state to prescribe staggered payment of the increases. In turn, the labour movement criticized what it viewed as the state's "double standards" on collective bargaining. Although the state was rhetorically committed to the de-regulation of labour conditions, including wage-bargaining, it still sought to regulate the process in practice. Indeed, through the LRA provisions, the state still wielded considerable powers over collective bargaining. For instance, the Minister of Labour still retained powers to veto wage increases "in the interests of the economy or the consumers" [Dhlakama and Sachikonye, 1991]. More significantly, as evidence of state inconsistency over the institutionalization of the collective bargaining system, public service workers (constituting nearly 20 per cent of the formal sector labour-force) were excluded from this collective bargaining system. Their working conditions were prescribed under a Public Service Act which denied workers' associations the right to bargain legally binding agreements with their state employers. This state of affairs triggered a number of prolonged strikes involving public service workers, health workers, teachers, tax assessors, aviation workers amongst others in 1990, 1994 and 1996. The strikes in August and November 1996 were the longest and most acrimonious, and eventually forced the state to commit itself to negotiating a pact under which a collective bargaining structure would be set up. This would be accomplished through a Harmonization Labour Act that would prescribe a uniform set of rights for both private and public sector workers. Set for 1999, this will introduce an important component into the labour regime.

In the Introduction to this volume, we observed the significance of the reproduction of the labour power as a major element of the labour regime in a particular society. Under ESAP, there occurred a severe contraction of social services thereby diminishing access to them especially by low-income strata. At the same time, following the withdrawal of subsidies on basic commodities such as food and services like public transportation, prices and inflation sky-rocketed. Social consumption issues therefore became a major bone of contention between the state and the labour movement. For example, the first two years of ESAP experienced an inflationary spiral that climbed to 46 per cent in 1992, and this had a direct impact on prices. In the following years, inflation decreased but only gradually; at the beginning of 1996, it was still above 22 per cent before climbing to 55 per cent in early 1999. Union attempts at consumer boycott through "bread demonstrations" and other forms of protest were, however, unsuccessful in stemming the general tide of price increases under ESAP. Responding to pressures being felt by the membership of industrial unions, the ZCTU was compelled to articulate a regular criticism of the soaring prices of basic commodities.

We should not lose sight of the political dimensions of the labour regime under ESAP. Differences over production politics (the collective bargaining issue) and over social consumption politics (the de-regulation of prices) spilled over into the wider political arena. The political differences between the state and the ZCTU leadership also sharpened over the issues of democracy and human rights. In asserting its autonomy and its desire for a broad-based democracy, the movement lambasted the orchestrated growing constituency within the ruling ZANU-PF party for a one-party state in the late 1980s. A leading force in the campaign against the one-party state, the ZCTU also lampooned the growing authoritarian and corrupt tendencies of the state. Following his condemnation of the detention of University of Zimbabwe student protesters, the ZCTU Secretary-General, Morgan Tsvangirai, was detained for a month in 1989. The ZCTU further asserted its autonomy on political issues by refusing to endorse ZANU-PF in the 1990 general election. The critique of ZANU-PF's political orientation was made in a broader context of the upsurge against authoritarian one-party states elsewhere in Africa. The Zambian experience in which the labour movement directly challenged the Kaunda regime unseating it from power was not lost on the minds of both the ZANU-PF and the ZCTU leadership. Suspicion increased within ZANU-PF that the ZCTU intended to combine its economic and political critique to provide a basis for an opposition movement. Some analysts saw some scope for the labour movement to venture afield and organize a political wing "which will advance the interests of workers" [Makamure, 1992]. However, for its part, the ZCTU initially stopped short of transforming itself into an opposition movement at that stage, preferring instead to build grassroots structures at regional level, promoting women's issues and strengthening cooperation with other mass organizations and professional associations such as representing students, academics and public servants. Nevertheless, ZANU-PF viewed the ZCTU as a potential opposition movement and treated it as such. For instance, from 1992 President Mugabe boycotted its May Day rallies in a symbolic gesture.

Feeling piqued by the ZCTU, the state now actively sought means of weakening both the national centre and industrial unions. Amendments were made in 1992 to the LRA to reverse the "one industry, one union policy; collective bargaining was to be decentralized in a bid to weaken the NECs. Furthermore, provisions were made so cumbersome making it "practically and legally impossible to carry out a lawful strike" [Tsvangirai, 1992]. In response, the labour movement organized nation-wide demonstrations against both the LRA amendments and the austerity ESAP measures. These were in turn heavily suppressed by the state as Tengende recounts in the next chapter. By 1993, the relations between the state and the ZCTU had reached a nadir. The implementation of ESAP liberalization measures was in full swing. The state co-optation strategy had collapsed. Yet in spite of the difficult economic conditions, labour's work-place bargaining power was gradually being consolidated even if its market-place bargaining power had been eroded considerably in the first few years of ESAP.

In sum, during this phase, the international context of the state's accumulation strategy had changed; it was now characterized by direct intervention by the IFIs in economic and social policy-making. The autonomy of the state in these spheres diminished as the price for considerable borrowings from these IFIs.

Meanwhile, the hardships stemming from the new neo-liberal economic and social measures drew the ire of an increasingly autonomous and assertive labour movement. The labour regime was conditioned by this wider context; de-regulation measures included provisions for the creation of export processing zones [EPZs] which would provide extremely favourable conditions to capital. Nevertheless, labour did not respond passively to this authoritarian labour regime . In the next section, we explore why both the state and labour began to reconsider their strategies.

TOWARDS AN ACCOMMODATION BETWEEN THE STATE AND LABOUR?

The phase beginning in 1994 to 1997 is one in which the limits of the adjustment strategy under ESAP was exposed and in which a review became necessary. The five-year programme [or ESAP 1] came to close at the end of 1995. The restructuring in both the private and public sectors had achieved mixed results but generally had fallen well below the targets set at the outset of the programme. Meanwhile, the wider political context was one in which ZANU-PF consolidated a *de facto* one-party state in what had practically become a dominant party system following the poor electoral showing of opposition parties in the 1990 and 1995 elections. However, the organizational capacity of civil society organizations grew during this period. For instance, the lobbying capacity of business organizations and labour expanded.

In this section, we examine the challenges presented by labour to the restructuring in the public service sector, and then assess the debate on the next stage of ESAP and the tentative attempts by both the state and labour together with capital to develop an institutional framework for cooperation. A major aspect of public sector restructuring has been retrenchment of nearly a quarter of workers in the public service, as we observed above. Another has been the attempt at cost-cutting through selective award of performance-related bonuses in place of previous pay-out of the 13th cheque to all public service workers. Following the suspension of the bonus in 1995, public service workers challenged the government's decision in both the High Court and Supreme Court. This unilateral decision on the bonus by the government's Public Service Commission (PSC) in September 1995 was regarded as a major blow by public service workers whose salaries and wages had generally lagged behind those of their counterparts in both the private and parastatal sectors. The decision by the PSC to suspend the bonus payment for 1995 was ostensibly for the reason that the government would experience a shortfall of Z$598 million [*The Sunday Mail*, 10 Sept. 1995]. The shortfall arose from salary adjustments following a job evaluation exercise that awarded 20 per cent to most grades in the public service. In effect, the position of the PSC was that it could not afford to pay public service workers the bonus in addition to the recommended increments. More far-reaching was its announcement that even if the bonus payment was resumed in 1996, it would no longer be universal but "based on the performance of the individual employee" *[Ibid.]*.

The Zimbabwe Teachers' Association [ZIMTA], representing an estimated 55,000 teachers and the Public Service Association (PSA) representing workers in various departments, challenged the PSC decision in the High Court and won their case. The presiding judge argued that:

> I find myself in agreement with the view that the state is legally obliged to pay a bonus where it has contracted to do so. The view that accepts the contractual liability of the state is more enlightened and in line with needs and exigencies of a modern state. The state should not be seen to be in the practice of deceiving its servants by promising its servants one thing and reneging on such promises at will with impunity (Justice Chidyausiku as quoted in *The Herald*, 25 January 1996).

Furthermore, the legal and moral authority of the PSC itself was questioned. Its members were appointed and not elected. They represented nobody nor were they accountable to anybody. In spite of this landmark judgement, the PSC took its case to the Supreme Court where it became a full-blown constitutional case. On that occasion, the Supreme Court ruled in favour of the PSC.

The significance of this case was that it symbolized the readiness of workers' institutions to use available legal and institutional channels to defend the interests of their members. In recent years, it has been a notable trend within the labour movement to utilize existing legal and constitutional means to reverse what it considered unjust measures or decisions by employers and the state. This reflects an increasing awareness of their rights but just as importantly a notable readiness to challenge institutions which trample on those rights. A major episode of such a challenge was the 1996 strike by public service workers on both the bonus issue, the size of wage awards and denial of collective bargaining rights. The nation-wide strike was the longest and costliest since independence and succeeded in forcing the state to award the universal bonus payment in 1996 as well as make an undertaking to extend collective bargaining rights through a Harmonization Labour Bill to be tabled in 2001. To that extent, labour struggles have clearly been instrumental in seeking significant changes to the labour regime.

The significance of these struggles thus relates to an emerging constitutionalism in the approach of the movement, which potentially could be useful in the negotiation of corporatist arrangements. The struggles have included specific campaigns against the Law and Order Maintenance Act [LOMA] and the defeat of attempted de-registration of the ZCTU by the Ministry of Labour over its controversial levy in 1992. The challenge against LOMA — which had previously been used by the colonial regime against the nationalist movement — was taken to the Supreme Court by the ZCTU also in 1992 in the wake of the arrest of six unionists who had participated in a peaceful demonstration against ESAP.

Dismissing the charges against the six unionists, a judge argued that:

> under section 6 of LOMA, the power of the regulating authority was uncontrolled and the holding of a public procession was criminalised [*The Worker*, February 1994].

The securing of the unimpeded right to demonstrate was a significant gain not only to the labour movement, but also to other social forces including students, professional associations and political groups soon took advantage of the space created by the landmark Supreme Court ruling. The contestation waged by the labour movement has therefore not only contributed to the modification of the labour regime but also to the broadening of the democratic space in society.

Let us turn our attention to the scope of the second phase of ESAP which became a major issue of debate beginning in 1995. There were several positions on what the content and focus of ESAP should be.

The first was that the restructuring of the public sector should be achieved through a substantial privatization programme and a significant reduction of the budget deficit. Tight fiscal and monetary measures together with trade liberalization should continue to be sustained. This was the position held by the IFIs, principally the WB and the IMF. A second position held by labour and business interests was that the content of ESAP should be a subject of consultation and negotiation in the light of the adverse experiences under ESAP. Those experiences had included the near-collapse of certain sub-sectors such as textiles. The position of the government was more ambiguous; it resisted wholesale privatization and moved slowly on the reduction of its budget deficit. It sought to exert political control over the adjustment process but dependence on funding from the IFIs limited its options.

This was the broad context in which the tripartite parties — labour, business and the state — began to explore common grounds of interest. The labour movement now broadly accepted in principle the case for adjustment to improve the performance of the economy. As the Secretary-General of the ZCTU put it:

> over the past five years, we have realized that criticizing ESAP is not the best we can do. The government is committed to the programme, and we do not see it getting out . . . [Tsvangirai, 1995].

However, the ZCTU has gone further to draw its own alternative framework for the envisaged second phase. Tactically, it intended its alternative to be drawn upon by the state and the IFIs in this second phase of adjustment in the post-1995 period. The labour movement sought not to be marginalized again in the design of economic reform, hence its proactive approach. However, the ZCTU intervention was critical in connection with the current public enterprise reforms particularly the envisaged privatisation of most parastatals.

The approach within the ZCTU, at least up to 1997, appeared to be that the ZANU-PF government would reciprocate to its pro-active articulation of its proposals on the economy and labour relations. Unlike in the past, initial signs in 1996 pointed to a willingness by the government to discuss germane issues relating to the proposals. Some of the issues discussed between them have included the legal protection of workers in the EPZs which were set up. The ZCTU succeeded in convincing the government that the LRA should apply in the EPZs as well.For its part the state is consulting both the ZCTU and the Employers' Confederation of Zimbabwe [EMCOZ] on the Harmonization Labour Bill, a process which commenced in 1993. In addition, the ZCTU also sits on tripartite institutions including the National Social Security Authority [NSSA]. Clearly, it is still too early to judge whether these initiatives represent a genuine basis for corporatism. Nevertheless, the expressed sentiments of the labour movement leadership appear to reflect a desire for a corporatist pact:

> it is important that we change our attitudes towards each other, in a way that allows national interests to subordinate our narrow interests. Government needs to look beyond the next election. Business needs to look beyond the next balance sheet. Labour needs to look forward beyond the next collective bargaining round. I firmly believe we can all of us look, as social partners, beyond ESAP . . . [Sibanda, 1996].

In a major policy initiative, the ZCTU went on to propose a national consultative body to be called the Zimbabwe Economic Development and Labour Council [ZEDLAC]. The proposed council would provide a forum to the tripartite partners or "stakeholders" to engage jointly in formulating, implementing and monitoring development strategies [Ibid.].

In the final analysis, the terms of corporatist arrangements reflect the balance of the particular social forces at a particular conjuncture. It would be somewhat premature at this stage that the state is now seriously committed to bargained corporatism in which the labour movement is treated as an equal tripartite partner.

Politically, ZANU- PF remains in a formidable position in a dominant-party system. However, their cooperation in economic matters is crucial: increased investment, employment creation, wage moderation and inflation containment will require the negotiation of a compromise between the state, labour and business organizations.

At the same time, the chances of negotiating such a corporatist pact can be undermined by the substantial intervention of the IFIs in policy-making. This raises the general issue of whether corporatist pacts can be successfully negotiated in IFI-driven adjustment processes. As we observed in previous sections, the room for manoeuvre of the state is substantially constrained; the restructuring process weakens some sectors of the economy and undercuts the bargaining of some unions. In the Zimbabwean context, the conditions for a feasible form of corporatism still remain to be determined in a fragile economic environment. The realization of the need for a corporatist arrangement by the tripartite parties is an important milestone in this regard.

POST-SCRIPT: THE LABOUR MOVEMENT WADES INTO POLITICS (1998-2000)

Although developments in the mid-1990s pointed to a possible rapprochement between the state and the labour movement, economic and political factors in the late 1990s militated against it. For one thing, the economic conditions themselves worsened considerably from the end of 1997. The initial projections of sustained growth under ESAP proved elusive. By 1999, the average growth for the 1990s was below one per cent. Retrenchments soared and real incomes shrank while living standards collapsed. In the manufacturing sector, there were genuine fears of de-industrialisation. Meanwhile industrial conflict centred around wage issues surged with more than 230 separate strikes reported during that year alone. The economic reform programme itself ground to halt as lending and investment dried up. It was a deepening economic crisis which was accentuated by profligate state spending on appeasement of war veterans who campaigned for a pay-back of their role in the independence struggle. There followed an immediate run on the Zimbabwe dollar. A costly military intervention in the conflict in the Democratic Republic of the Congo proved to be a very heavy burden on the economy. It was also a largely unpopular excursion. In sum, the context had changed considerably by the end of the 1990s. The hegemony of the Zanu-PF government and related institutions were therefore undermined considerably. Efforts to conduct negotiations for a social contract in 1997 and 1998 were half-hearted and inconclusive. The discourse around economic issues became increasingly politicised. Governance became a central issue which embraced not only the handling of the economy but constitutional reform and democracy.

The labour movement took advantage of this deepening crisis in governance to develop into a focal point of initiatives to the Zanu-PF hegemony hitherto virtually unchallenged. The first phase of the initiatives involved the constitutional reform process. There was a concerted attempt on the part of civil society to make the process as inclusive and transparent as possible. The labour movement — through its leadership — was the lynch-pin of the civil society alliance grouped under the National Constitutional Assembly (NCA). The major area of contestation was over conduct of the reform process and the content of the new constitution. Under the leadership of Morgan Tsvangirai, the NCA was successful in 2000 in campaigning against a constitutional draft drawn up by a government-appointed Constitutional Commission.

Meanwhile pressure had grown within the labour movement and more generally in civil society on the ZCTU to form a political party to contest the

2000 election. Their assessment was that Zanu-PF would lose substantial support to the new party in those elections. That loss would be attributable to the government's poor handling of the economy, growing corruption within the ruling elite, and major shortfalls in accountability and transparency in state institutions. Union structures played a strategic role in the consultations with workers on the nature and programme of the envisaged party. Through the 'labour forums', the foundations of the new party were laid in 1999. The major landmarks in this process were the National Working Peoples' Convention held in early 1999, and the founding of the Movement for Democratic Change (MDC) in September 1999. The significance of the founding of the MDC lay in that it was the first political organisation in the post-independence period founded on a working-class base. It soon widened its base to include middle-class and business supporters which had become disgruntled with the Mugabe government. The youth and students were another important constituency of the new party. The cities and towns would be the main centres for mobilisation into the new party, and the rural areas would be difficult to penetrate without inital and crucial bridgeheads of support. The 2000 election results broadly confirmed the immense strength of the newly-founded party in cities and towns, sweeping almost all of them. With the exception of Matabeleland and Manicaland, the rural constituencies proved difficult to rally behind the MDC especially in the context of the intimidation and violence which characterised the election campaign. On the whole, however, the MDC win of 46 per cent of the total vote (compared with Zanu-PF's 48 per cent) was impressive given the Zanu-PF monopoly of public funding and of the public media. This translated into 57 directly-elected seats for the MDC and 62 for Zanu-PF.

Clearly however, the ZCTU will now need to re-define its role in the post-election period. It would need to fill up the vacant leadership positions at the national centre and in some individual unions following the trek into political positions in the MDC. New overtures from the state — relating to the issue of a possible social contract — will need to be responded to. It would therefore have to decide on long-standing invitations for its participation in the National Economic Consultative Forum (NECF) and the Tripartite Negotiating Forum (TNF). There may well be a need for a review of its previous position, and a decision on whether the political engagement (pursued by the MDC) through parliament did not require a counterpart in economic and social policy forums. In such forums, there is now a potentially greater chance that the ZCTU would negotiate from a stronger position than before. This would be due to its proven political weight as reflected through the MDC.

REFERENCES

B. BECKMAN and A. JEGA (1995) "Scholars and Democratic Politics in Nigeria" *Review of African Political Economy*, 22 (64).

M. BUROWAY (1985) *The Politics of Production* (London, Verso).
L.G. Dhlakama and L.M. Sachikonye (1991) *Collective Bargaining in Zimbabwe* (Geneva, ILO).
W.D. COLEMAN (1985) 'State Corporatism as a Sectoral Phenomenon: The Case of the Quebec Construction Industry' in A. Lawson *Organized Interests and the State* (London, Sage).
B. RAFTOPOULOS (1994) 'The State and the Labour Movement in Zimbabwe' (mimeo).
B. RAFTOPOULOS and I. PHIMISTER (1997) *Keep on Knocking: A History of the Labour Movement in Zimbabwe* (Harare, Baobab).
L. M. SACHIKONYE (1986) 'State, Capital and Unions' in I. Mandza (ed.) *Zimbabwe: The Political Economy of Transition* (Dakar, Codesria).
— (1992) 'The New Labour Regime in Zimbabwe' *SAPEM*, 5 (7).
— (1995) 'Industrial Restructuring and Labour Relating Under Adjustment in Zimbabwe' in P. Gibbon (ed.) (1995) *Structural Adjustment and the Working Poor in Zimbabwe* (Uppsala, NAI).
— (1997) 'Trade Unions, Economic and Political Development in Zimbabwe since Independence' in B. Raftopoulos and I. Phimister (eds.) *Keep on Knocking: A History of the Labour Movement in Zimbabwe* (Harare, Baobab).
G. SIBANDA (1996) Address by the ZCTU President on the Launching of the "Beyond Esap" Final Report, 15 March 1996, Harare.
M. TSVANGIRAI (1992) 'The Labour Relations Amendment Bill, 1992' in Friedrick Naumam Stiftung (1992) *ESAP, Industrial Relations and Employment Creation* (Harare).
— (1995) 'Interview with Morgan Tsvangirai', *SAPEM*.
B. WOOD (1987) 'Roots of Trade Union Weakness in Post-Independence Zimbabwe',
South African Labour Bulletin, 12 (6-7).
The Worker Newspaper (February, 1994) (Harare).

CHAPTER NINE

Economic Liberalization and Public Sector Workers in Zimbabwe

NORBERT TENGENDE

We were told in 1990 to tighten our own belts and that things would get tougher. But we have gone further than tightening our belts: we have lost our jobs, our rights to health and dignity . . . To the government, we don't look at your balance sheets or your bank accounts to see whether we are going the right way. Look at your people. Look at the jobless, hungry and demoralized people of Zimbabwe . . . and then judge the failure or success of your ESAP . . . We are moving in the wrong direction.
Zimbabwe Congress of Trade Unisons (ZCTU) May Day Speech, 1993.

INTRODUCTION

This chapter examines the shifts in the labour regime in the public sector in Zimbabwe during the era of economic liberalization between 1990 and 1996. This era witnessed the first phase of Zimbabwe's economic structural adjustment programme [ESAP]. As has been observed in Sachikonye's chapter, a major feature of ESAP was the de-regulation of labour laws which previously provided employment security and safeguards against peremptory dismissals. The specific focus of this chapter is on how the de-regulation measures affected workers in Zimbabwe's relatively large public sector. In particular, management strategies and union responses in this changed economic environment are explored to identify new elements in the labour regime.

The first section provides an overview of the impact of ESAP on the public sector in relation to the original objectives of the programme. The amendments to the labour legislation are then explored; they constituted the basis of significant shifts in the labour regime. The response to these amendments included legal and constitutional challenges by organized labour. The chapter reviews the pattern and outcome of opposition by organized labour to this new labour regime. Particular attention is paid to changing management strategies which took advantage of the new conditions of de-regulation of measures and structures which had been previously "labour-friendly". This is accomplished through an examination of two case-studies of railway-workers and posts and telecommunication workers.

ECONOMIC LIBERALIZATION AND THE PUBLIC SECTOR

Like in most SAPs, one of the principal objectives of Zimbabwe's reform programme was to reduce spiralling public expenditure, especially the government's budget deficit. The main strategy was to reduce levels of staffing in public sector institutions. These institutions included government ministries and parastatals. Thus substantial retrenchments amounting to 25 per cent of total staff were envisaged for the government ministries beginning in 1991. There retrenchments were to be administered during the five-year ESAP period and the parastatal sector was included in the general "down-sizing" of staff [Zimbabwe Government, 1991]. Ostensibly to limit the losses of parastatals and their burden on public finances, a number of measures were envisaged. These included a substantial retrenchment of workers at the National Railways of Zimbabwe (NRZ), Zimbabwe Iron and Steel Corporation (ZISCO) and at the Agricultural Finance Corporation (AFC) [IMF, 1993]. In this new approach, efficiency was to be enhanced through increased autonomy, restructuring, closure of unviable enterprises, and increased private-sector participation. Furthermore, management performance contracts were to be specified for parastatal corporations including NRZ and the Post and Telecommunication Corporation (PTC) which will be examined in this chapter.

From independence, the public sector had been one of the few sectors to experience phenomenal job expansion. However, under adjustment, most parastatals have retrenched staff as originally envisaged. This retrenchment was an intrinsic aspect of their restructuring process. Employment security — which had previously cushioned parastatal workers — was removed. By the end of ESAP's first phase in 1995, an estimated 28 000 workers had been made redundant in the public service and the parastatal sectors.

Nonetheless, this public sector, as a whole, still provides a substantial proportion of formal sector employment in Zimbabwe accounting for nearly 25 per cent of employment in the formal sector. However, different categories of public sector workers have been governed under different labour legislation. There are two such categories of labour laws. These are namely the Labour Relations Act (LRA) of 1985, and the Zimbabwe Constitution which created a Public Service Commission responsible for regulating employment conditions of public service employees. Instructively, the LRA covers employees in the private sector and that segment of the public sector constituted by parastatals (including the NRZ and PTC covered in this chapter) and local government institutions. That portion of the public sector which forms the public services has its employees governed by the constitution, and has a different system of resolving diputes from that utilized in the private and parastatal sectors. Thus there exists a two-tiered labour law regime in contemporary Zimbabwe [Sachikonye, 1996; Madhuku and Sibanda, 1997]. However, there was a tripartite agreement to introduce a new Harmonized Labour Act later in 1999 to cover both sectors. In the remainder of the chapter, we confine our focus to the LRA which governs labour relations in the parastatal sector.

The Labour Relations Amendment Act and the Response of Labour

As elsewhere in Africa, the de-regulation of existing labour legislation (and safeguards contained in it) is a prominent element in economic liberalisation. The Zimbabwean experience of de-regulation between 1990 and 1996 was a heavily contested affair. It was strenuously contested because the tampering of the existing legislation was viewed by labour unions as undermining their post-independence gains. Protest against amendments to the LRA was strong because they were seen as constituting a threat to the structure of the labour regime which unions believed was weighted towards workers' interests. The tussle over the new amendments amply demonstrated that labour law was a contested zone between the state and unions. The authoritarian tendencies of the state were displayed in the ensuing stalemate over the extent to which the labour regime would be modified by the new legal amendments. A centerpiece of the agenda of the state was to weaken the industrial unions and national centre which had increasingly grown in power and influence. The fomenting of fragmentation of unions through an amendment to promote union pluralism was a major element of this agenda while the decentralisation of collective bargaining in different sectors was another. However, as we will observe, this agenda met with stiff resistance from both the national centre (the ZCTU) and individual unions as our illustrative case-studies show. Unions actively mobilised against the unilateral change of labour regime conditions by the state. While they met with setbacks at the national level (the passing of the Amendment Act), they scored some notable successes at the industrial sector. The labour regime has therefore remained a contested zone under economic liberalization.

We observed that a principal objective of ESAP was a de-regulation of labour controls to liberalize the labour market so as to reduce costs. The government's Investment Code promulgated in 1989 to create a more investment-friendly atmosphere was a harbinger to the liberalization of the labour legislation through the LRA Amendment Act passed in 1992. We trace the different stages in the design of the Amendment Bill, and the subsequent response to it by organized labour.

Originally, the main changes recommended to the existing LRA were wide-ranging. They were:
(a) Legislating one labour law for the country;
(b) Speeding up the dispute settlement machinery;

(c) Changing the balance of free collective bargaining between employers and labour and ministerial intervention with a shift to bipartite arrangements;

(d) Streamlining the designated "essential services" to bring them into line with international labour standards; and

(e) Reviewing the procedures for collective job action [ZCTU, 1992a].

Meanwhile, there were several areas of consensus established through prior tripartite discussions. These related to agreements to restore collective bargaining, and set up the Incomes and Prices Board to establish the parameters within which the parties could operate, so departing from legislated minimum and maximum wages. A Labour Relations Board and a Labour Relations Tribunal were to be established to mediate in disputes. There was, however, no consensus on the issue of restoration of managerial right to dismiss workers. Organized labour through ZCTU raised some objections proposing instead that workers should only be suspended during which time they would be entitled to at least 50 per cent of their salaries.

Principally, the ZCTU objected to the following provisions contained in the LRA Amendment Bill:

(a) Continued concentration of immense powers in the minister of labour and his officials;

(b) Placing of works councils agreements above employment councils with the overall result of "fragmenting" and "destabilizing" industrial relations in Zimbabwe.

The thrust of the provisions of the Amendment Bill was to undermine the trade unions by reducing their role in collective bargaining while extending it to workers committees and undermining the financial viability of the labour centre *[Ibid]*. The ZCTU argued for the re-definition of "essential services" in the Act by limiting it to services relating to the generation, supply or distribution of electricity; any fire brigade or fire services; any medical hospital or ambulance services [ZCTU, 1992a] while continuing to further press for a restoration of the right of workers to strike because "the law has made it impossible for employees to engage in collective job action". Except for those employed in "essential services", all other employees should have the right to strike provided that they would have given seven days of such intention and the reasons to the party against whom the strike was to be taken

The ZCTU therefore sought to mobilize its membership against the Amendment Bill with calls to its affiliates "to work flat out to mobilize workers to chart a way to render the Act inoperative" [The Worker, 1992]. Frustrated with the attitude of the Ministry of Labour and its refusal to enter into a dialogue over the Bill, its General Council resolved to organize nation-wide demonstrations against both the Bill and ESAP reforms.

Preparations for the demonstrations began with a well-attended general meeting of workers addressed by the ZCTU leadership. It transpired that police had refused the ZCTU permission to hold a demonstration. Under pressure from the floor, it was agreed to press on with the planned demonstrations. Significantly, speakers from the floor took turns to denounce the insensitivity of the government and especially President Mugabe towards the workers' plight. The demonstrations were planned to take place on a Saturday to minimize disruption to production. However, during the two days preceding that Saturday, the official media was mobilized against the ZCTU, for example, radio programmes were interrupted to carry out propaganda against the centre and the planned demonstrations. Extensive coverage was given to comments of the Minister of Home Affairs, in charge of police, who apposed the demonstrations.

On the day of the demonstrations, the police turned out in full force in all major centres throughout the country. In some towns, like Gweru, the army presence on the street intimidated anyone who might have tried to venture out to demonstrate. In the suburbs, police patrols broke up gatherings of more than five people. However, in Chinhoyi, Gweru and Harare, processions managed to take off. In Harare, six demonstrators were arrested; while in Gweru, an estimated 40 people were also arrested.

The official media portrayed the 'failure' of most demonstrations to take off as a reflection of the organizational weakness of the ZCTU. Yet no mention was made of the heavy presence of police and their harassment of people in the streets. Bolstered by the crushing of the demonstrations, the Labour Minister then sought to open dialogue with the ZCTU over the Amendment Bill. However, the supposed dialogue turned out to be an occasion to "educate" the ZCTU on the Bill rather than examine its contents substantively with a view to incorporating the ZCTU's concerns. The ZCTU therefore refused to proceed with the meeting.

As the Amendment Bill sailed through Parliament, and the labour ministry showed no further interest in dialogue with the ZCTU, the labour centre was forced to petition the President to delay its gazetting before the tripartite partners had an opportunity to convey their concerns. In the same petition, the ZCTU argued the need to create "a national consensus on the way forward" instead of the current imposition of ESAP which did not have the necessary consensus between the concerned social partners. Hence the ZCTU proposed a national economic summit to chart the best possible way forward. Not surprisingly, the government did not entertain the idea of a national convention. In September 1992, the Bill became law.

Although the unionists failed to stop the Bill from becoming law, their struggle against it led to an historic victory against the Law and Order Maintenance Act [LOMA]. The six unionists arrested in Harare had been charged with participating in an illegal demonstration under section 6 [Chapter 65] of the Act. This section granted powers to the police to veto planned demonstrations and public meetings. The police could prevent a planned demonstration by simply refusing to signal concurrence. Hitherto, this provision had been used against opposition parties and university students. However, the six unionists appealed to the Supreme Court for a ruling on the constitutionality of the provisions. In February 1994, the Supreme Court ruled that Section 6 of the LOMA [Chapter 65] was unconstitutional and unreasonable in a democratic society. The Minister of Home Affairs and the Attorney-General themselves declined to contest the unconstitutionality of these provisions.

There were further union legal challenges in labour-related issues mounted by unions against the government in 1994, 1995 and 1996. These challenges took the form of legal contestation against specific government institutions over salary and wage conditions. As we will explore more fully in the next section, unions in the railways and telecommunications industries took their cases against management to the High and Supreme Courts in 1992 and 1994 respectively. In 1995 it was the turn of the public service workers' associations to challenge the Public Service Commission's refusal to award a bonus or 13th cheque. The bonus issue went up to the Supreme Court in early 1996 where an earlier favourable judgement for workers was subsequently overturned. Increasingly, however, unions found the legal process a useful weapon to direct at management in the public sector. The significance of these legal and constitutional struggles by unions have been examined in relation to public service workers' associations in Sachikonye's chapter in this volume. In the next two sections, we examine changing management strategies under the modified labour regime in two parastatal corporations and the responses of unions and workers in the context of adjustment.

CASE-STUDY 1: MANAGEMENT STRATEGIES AND UNION RESPONSES AT NRZ

As Valenzuela (1989) points out, containment strategies pursued by regimes in response to labour organizations vary. The regime might choose "syndical harshness" as part of a containment strategy toward a labour organization. This is effected through the creation of organizational obstacles against it, limiting the capacity of unions and reducing channels for "the expression of collectively formulated worker grievances" [Valenzuela, 1989]. The regime might also curb strike action and circumscribe a substantive labour input into the collective bargaining process. Furthermore, the regime would seek to pre-empt a popular movement coalescing around the demands of the unions.

In the 1987-1990 period, the ZCTU had already begun moving out of the state's embrace. However, in this context of general dissatisfaction and perceived potentialities for its destabilization, the organizational crippling of the ZCTU was imperative from the viewpoint of the government. The government pursued this strategy by abandoning the 'one industry, one union' principle which it had supported in the 1980s. Its intention was now to fan divisions and splits within unions. The experiences of the Zimbabwe Amalgamated Railways Union [ZARU] under the new dispensation amply demonstrated the changed government strategies in key parastatals like the NRZ and the PTC which have strong unions. The 1992 strike by railway workers illuminates much about the state-union relations in the adjustment era, and so will be traced here in some detail.

A plan to break the strength of ZARU was launched in earnest in 1991 even before the enactment of the LRA Amendment Act. The NRZ general manager, artisans and enginemen employed by the corporation met with the Registrar of Trade Unions [who is also the Chief Labour Relations Officer [CLRO] at the Ministry of Labour offices in May 1991. At the meeting, the three parties concurred to do away with the 'one industry, one union policy' in the railways where the policy had lumped together skilled and unskilled workers under one union. They preferred the old system of craft-based unions in the railways. The argument for this was that it had become difficult to meet the rising salaries needed to retain skilled manpower while simultaneously with representatives of unskilled workers who cried foul. The Labour Minister supported this view and confirmed that there was consensus in government to abandon the 'one industry, one union' policy.

Meanwhile, the CLRO promised "to fight all legal hurdles" until artisans and enginemen unions were registered independently of ZARU. The CLRO was actually now spearheading the break-up of ZARU. Artisans were urged to speed up the formation of their union and assured that there would be no hurdles with registration. Since the LRA was still in effect, this meant that the CLRO, by encouraging the formation of a splinter union, was actually breaching Section B (f) of this Act which he was entrusted to administer with the full backing of the Labour Minister.

The NRZ General Manager, with the collusion of the CLRO, was determined to see the formation of splinter unions by the artisans and enginemen. In January 1992, when they held a joint meeting with the latter, ZARU was not invited to this meeting nor informed of the proceedings. During the same month, artisans went on strike demanding a 13.5 per cent wage increase, and the resolution of their outstanding grievances. ZARU then petitioned the state Vice-President requesting his intervention against the machinations of the Labour Minister and NRZ management. There was no response.

Artisans had always resented being represented by ZARU because they felt that it was dominated by clerks and other office workers who had no appreciation of their interests, including job requirements. ZARU itself had always boasted of its support from 'madhara enjanji' [the unskilled and semi-skilled men who man the track lines]. The agreement to dissolve the craft-based unions and merge them into ZARU to accommodate the government demand for 'one industry, one union' had been taken in good faith and obedience to a government that was believed to be in favour of workers [Keet, 1992]. However, ZARU subsequently failed to genuinely accommodate the special interests of the various categories of workers including artisans. Instead of a simple hierarchical structure to represent all workers, there should have been representative organs created to allow for the accommodation of "the different origins, needs and aspirations of its components" [Keet, 1992]. Artisans and enginemen were heirs to the elitist craft traditions of the pre-independence era. This was clearly shown by their imitation of the language and work habits of white workers in colonial times.

Earlier, in July 1989, artisans disregarded ZARU and organized a strike demanding an extra 20 per cent increase on top of the 5 to 16 per cent increase won by the union. They were joined by enginemen who sought an additional 15 per cent increase in allowances for themselves. Although the workers had been threatened with dismissal if they did not resume work, they subsequently won a 13 per cent wage increase. In addition, they also received a 2 per cent "across the board" increase. Although the 2 per cent increase was clearly aimed at appeasing other workers, the division amongst the workers had already been sown. In July 1990, enginemen were awarded an additional Z$3 000 described as an annual critical allowance [*The Herald*, 25 July 1990]. In reaction, ZARU pressed for a change to the job classification system. In October 1990, ZARU succeeded in securing an agreement with management to change job categories. Previously, artisans and clerks had belonged to the same grades, Grade 4 to 6. While artisans were classified in Grades 4a or 6a, clerks were in the 'B' categories. This meant that artisans earned slightly more than clerks. The new agreement between ZARU and management meant that artisans and clerks were now at par in terms of pay. Artisans were angered by this arrangement charging that clerks had only secondary education while artisans had an additional four years of apprenticeship. Moreover, artisans were on call for 24 hours a day. By 1990, only a third of artisans were still members of ZARU.

Artisans then decided to form the Railways Association of Mechanical and Technical Staff (later the Railways Artisans Union) and in September 1990, enginemen broke away from ZARU charging that it had negotiated with management on their conditions of service without consulting them. They formed the Railways Association of Enginemen which held its first congress in April 1991. The artisans and enginemen's strike in January 1992 appeared to have had the blessing of the NRZ management and the Labour Ministry.

The striking artisans were awarded a 7 per cent wage increase which was called 'special skills allowance' but ZARU was not formally informed of this development. Workers Grades 7-12 — the semi-skilled and non-skilled grades — were up in arms against the award charging that it was discriminatory and divisive. On 14 January, about 2000 workers gathered outside the railways headquarters demanding that the general manager explain to them how the increase had been awarded to only one category and not to all. The general manager refused to address the workers saying that he was not prepared to address a public rally [Interview with ZARU President, 1994]. The workers came back the following day with banners, some of which read "unskilled plus = NRZ". The striking 6000 workers continued to demand to be addressed by the general manager who refused to do so until 17 January. No agreement was reached at that meeting.

ZARU then decided to take up the matter of the increases to the High Court for a ruling arguing that the NRZ had failed to negotiate with a properly constituted trade union as per provisions of Section 8 (c) of the LRA. The NRZ had also failed to comply with a collective bargaining agreement and decisions made by the Employment Council as per section 8 (d).

Meanwhile, a Principal Labour Relations Officer, issued "a disposal order" to ZARU which instructed workers to return to work that same day. However, the delivery of the 'disposal order' was one and a half hours late and thus invalid. Meanwhile, the High Court issued a Court temporal 'Interdict' ordering NRZ not to pay the 7 per cent increase, and to show why the increase should not be permanently stopped from being paid. After receipt of this ruling, ZARU instructed all workers to return to work.

However, the general manager proceeded to lock out the workers and announce that they were all dismissed under Section 123 of the LRA. Those who needed their jobs back would have to re-apply for engagement as temporary workers on monthly contracts. This was challenged by the High Court which ordered NRZ to re-instate all the dismissed workers. Much to the chagrin of NRZ management and the Ministry of Labour, within five days, ZARU had won all its petitions against management actions in the High Court.

However, the minister had still another card to play against ZARU. The union itself was suspended the day after the ministerial approval of the dismissals. Union members were barred from membership for four months under the LRA. The reason behind the suspension was obvious. Without funds from members' subscriptions, ZARU could not engage lawyers to contest the dismissals and the suspension. The suspension of ZARU was partly aimed at giving management breathing space to deal with various industrial issues without the participation of the union. Meanwhile, the High Court ordered that the interdicted payment of 7 per cent allowance for artisans and enginemen be paid. However, it reserved its judgement on the suspension of ZARU.

External support was conveyed to ZARU. The International Confederation of Free Trade Unions [ICFTU] appealed to President Mugabe on behalf of the union stating that "the dispute of ZARU with the state-owned railway is in pursuance of a legitimate ZARU wage claim in conformity with the internationally-recognized labour practices". The International Transport Federation also called on President Mugabe to intervene. Furthermore, the ZCTU had tried to mediate during the whole dispute but this was rejected by both the Labour Ministry and NRZ management.

The final phase of the dispute was between the end of January and early March. On 29 January, the strike ended with all the workers reinstated. The ZARU suspension was lifted unconditionally on 3 March. NRZ had sustained considerable losses during the strike. The plan by the NRZ management and the ministry had been to break ZARU because it was seen as too strong. ZARU was one of the best organised and financed unions with a truly national presence in Zimbabwe. The railways themselves were the largest parastatal employer. Developments in the parastatal sector formed an important part of the background to these confrontations; if the budget deficit was to be tackled, then previously subsidized parastatals had to be turned into viable profit-making enterprises. This entailed structural changes in the management of parastatals such as the NRZ as the momentum toward privatisation increased. A powerful railway union was likely to resist some of the envisaged changes. ZARU had already declared its opposition to the privatisation of the railways. Hence the onslaught on the union by management with state backing.

CASE-STUDY 2: MANAGEMENT STRATEGIES AND UNION RESPONSE AT PTC

The strategy of creating splinter unions to weaken the established one was pursued in other industries and parastatals. In the PTC, one of the largest parastatals targetted for privatization, management engineered a split in the Zimbabwe Posts and Telecommunications Workers Unions [ZPTWU]. To weaken the position of the ZPTWU, management initiated the formation of a splinter 'Posts and Telecommunications Progressive Workers Unions' led by some disgruntled former leaders of the ZPTWU. The reasons given for the attempted split by the splinter union was that the ZPTWU "had failed to represent workers' interests and (that) its existence had been characterized by frequent clashes with management" [*Daily Gazette*, 2 November 1992]. The new union promised to engage in open dialogue with management and the resolution of workers' grievances. However, this splinter union failed to attract members from the existing union.

Referring to such engineered splits in established unions, the Labour Minister stated that:

> much as we would want to discourage workers from forming splinter unions, the government is encouraging democracy to prevail in the labour movement as well as in the political arena [Keet, 1992].

Thus the state had appropriated the labour movements' demand for pluralization as a strategy of weakening the movement. Well-timed pluralization in conditions of a weak civil society can be an effective instrument in disrupting centres of organized opposition. As we observed above, the official media had been mobilized to portray the ZCTU as resistant to pluralization since it continued to uphold the 'one industry, one union policy'. This implied that the ZCTU was against the constitutional provision of freedom of association despite that this had all along been its mobilizing slogan against the Emergency Powers Act and LOMA. The ZCTU proposals on the Amendment Act did not oppose the intended pluralization. However, the disinformation campaign on the ZCTU resulted in one positive development: the speed up of the publication of the ZCTU's own monthly newspaper called the *Worker*.

Let us revert our attention to developments at the PTC. In early 1994, it witnessed a major and successful strike by workers. Here we will review the context and outcome of the strike. The ZPTWU had been engaged since 1992 in negotiations for 12,5 per cent wage increase back-dated to July of the same year. As part of its strategy to split the strong union, the management sought to discredit it in the eyes of its membership by dragging its feet on the issue of the increase. Negotiations became deadlocked with the union rejecting the low increase offered by management.

The ZPTWU then took the dispute to the Labour Relations Tribunal for arbitration. The Tribunal ordered the PTC management to pay the 12,5 per cent increase back-dated to July 1992 sought by the union. The back-dated increase would cost the PTC upwards of Z$33 million against a record profit of Z$85 million in 1993. This was the context in which workers demanded their "fair share" and a just living wage [Interview with ZPTWU Secretary-General, March 1994]. Workers were aggrieved that management had awarded itself large salary increases and perks of up to 65 per cent in the some cases. For example, the Post-Master General's salary shot up to Z$ 209 000 per annum and yet the lowest-paid worker received Z$7 466 per annum.

Management refused to implement the Tribunal's ruling and instead appealed to the Supreme Court. In the meantime, efforts were made to dismiss the union's secretary-general, and to cripple it financially by reducing check-off subscriptions to a paltry 50 cents. The union could therefore no longer afford to pay for its rented accommodation from the dues of Z$3 000.

On 14 February, the ZPTWU leadership notified management of their intention to strike. Management continued with its intransigence over the issue. The strike began on 16 February with 8 500 workers immediately taking part. The nation-wide posts and telecommunications services came to a halt. It was a resounding demonstration of the collective power of labour. The labour minister, like before, resorted to the draconian provisions of the LRA to deal with the strike. He issued a 'show cause order' to the union directing that workers report to work on 17 February and that the PTC would be allowed to dismiss the workers if the order was not obeyed.

The Labour Ministry then issued a disposal order to authorize the dismissal of all striking workers. However, they were invited to re-apply on new terms; one condition was that each striker should state their role in the strike. The re-application forms required workers to identify the strike ring-leaders, those who urged workers not to return to work, and those who had shut the gates at workplaces. Meanwhile, the union leaders urged workers to return to work on 18 February. However, on 21 February, union leaders advised workers who had returned to work to show solidarity with their fired colleagues by returning to work. All re-joined this strike again on the issue of the terms of their re-empoyment. The union leadership was then arrested by the police for questioning on allegations of engaging in an illegal strike and contravention of LOMA.

Throughout the strike, the police played "a cat and mouse game" with the union leaders and the strikers. However, unionists were a step ahead of both the police and management most of the time. To prevent those workers who had returned from being forced to work by the police, they were switched around. Technicians and other workshop staff gathered at the post offices while office staff were stationed at the workshops. The management could not get any work done by the available staff at various points. Striking workers were instructed not to gather in groups, and urged to return home to avoid attracting police who were likely to invoke LOMA on public gatherings to arrest the strikers.

After their arrest, union leaders were released to meet with the Minister of Information, Posts and Telecommunications. Following the meeting, management was ordered to pay the 12.5 per cent increase sought by workers, and to withdraw its appeal to the Supreme Court. Incriminating re-application forms were withdrawn and workers ordered to return to work immediately.

The workers' union won. Workers had scored a resounding victory against an intransigent management. *Moto* magazine described the union leadership as "mature militants" who had displayed "astute bargaining skills and smart organization" [*Moto*, April 1994]. The strike was significant in several ways. It directly challenged the provisions of the LRA under which the PTC was defined as a "essential service", and strike action as "illegal". The strike was "illegal" because the union had not given the required 14-day notification of its intention to strike to the labour ministry. The strike was therefore a major test of will of both the union and government resolve in dealing with it. Many observers, before this strike, had begun "writing off" unions with the passage of the LRA Amendment Act and the various changes brought to industry by the de-regulation of controls. A widespread view had been that workers were now virtually at the mercy of employers especially in a context of prevalent retrenchment. The effect of the PTC strike reverberated throughout the economy.

While it lasted, it effectively isolated the country in terms of communications with the outside world.

The strike was an immense morale booster for the labour movement and it instilled confidence in other unions. It forced a realization on most employers that they could not deal with unions with impunity. Business concerns realized that organized labour could still frustrate their interests. Hence, the strike came at an opportune movement in the life of the labour movement.

CONCLUSION

Under ESAP, the Zimbabwe government yielded to pressure from domestic and international capital to de-regulate labour conditions so as to become "investor-friendly". The ensuing economic restructuring took its toll on workers. The liberalization of labour laws represented a tactical move on the part of the state aimed at throwing unions into disarray. Liberal concessions by the state can be used as a pre-emptive manoeuvre against potential sources of resistance. However, it is up to the organizations in civil society to counteract the effect of such moves by fashioning new strategies to maintain their organizational unity. The ZCTU, including its affiliates, had to re-define their strategies in the changed circumstances. No longer could unions and the national centre continue to play the "mediatory brokers' role" between the workers, employers and the state. The inauguration of ESAP had seen a shift from a strategy of "paternalistic incorporation"of unions by the state towards their fragmentation and marginalization.

The severance of links between the state and unions — which had actually been a major factor in union paralysis — meant that unions were in a better position to mobilize workers in their own right. The mobilization of workers in the railways, posts and telecommunications testified to this new trend. The severance also created opportunities to forge fresh links with workers on the shop-floor, to develop dynamic relations with workers' committees, and to build industrial unions rather than have them legislated into existence. Unions now had the opportunity to change the public perception of their role from 'brokers' to that of genuine defenders of the rights of workers, and other popularly-based organizations in civil society.

The sharp deterioration in working conditions, especially wages, created conditions for growing impatience and frustration among public sector workers. While unions were prepared to make the new framework of collective bargaining to work, management continued to pursue its bureaucratic and authoritarian strategies. The unions were prepared to go further and pursue the struggle for their rights and better wages in the highest courts. In addition, they could resort to the strike weapon to force parastatal management to abide by court rulings. As the strikes by railway and telecommunications workers demonstrated, ESAP had not succeeded in paralyzing unions.

REFERENCES

S. HAGGARD (1985) "The Policies of Adjustment: Lessons from the IMF's Extended Facility", *International Organization*, 39 (3).

J. HERBST (1990)"The Structural Adjustment of Politics in Africa" *World Development*, 18 (7).

E. HUTCHFUL (1991) "Structural Adjustment and Political Regimes in Africa. A Framework for Analysis", Paper presented to a Conference on *The Politics of Adjustment* (Dakar, Codesria).

R. GULHATI (1990) "Who Makes Economic Policy in Africa and How", *World Development*, 18 (8).

D. KEET (1992) "Zimbabwe Trade Unions: From Corporatist Brokers Towards an Independent Labour Movement", *South African Labour Bulletin*, 16 (4).

IMF (1993) "Zimbabwe: Staff Report on the First Review of Arrangements Under the Enhanced Structural Adjustment Facility and the Extended Fund Facility" (Washington).

L.M. SACHIKONYE (1996) "Collective Bargaining in Zimbabwe's Public Sector. An Overview" Paper presented to the ARLAC-ILO Workshop on *Collective Bargaining in the Public Service Sector*.

A. SAWYER (1990) *The Political Adjustment of Structural Adjustment Programmes* (Accra, Ghana Universities Press)

A. VALENZUELA (1989) "Labour Movement in Transitions to Democracy: A Framework of Analysis" *Comparative Politics*, 21 (4).

C. S. WHITAKER (1991) 'Doctrines of Development and Precepts of the State: The World Bank and Fifth Iteration of the African Case", in R.L. Sklar and C. S. Whitaker, *African Politics and Problems in Development* (London, Boulder).

ZCTU (1992 a) "ZCTU Proposals on the Labour Amendment Bill".

— (24 June, 1992 b) "The ZCTU Appeal to the President".

ZIMBABWE GOVERNMENT (1991) *Zimbabwe: A Framework for Economic Reform, 1991-95* (Harare).

Newspapers and Magazines
Daily Gazette
The Herald
The Worker

Select Bibliography

ADELZADEH, A. AND V. PADAYACHEE (1994) "The RDP White Paper: Reconstruction of a Development Vision?", *Transformation*, 25.

ADLER, G. AND E. WEBSTER (1995) "Challenging Transition Theory: The Labour Movement, Radical Reform and Transition in South Africa", *Politics and Society*, XXIII, 1.

AKWETEY, E. (1994) "Trade Unions and Democratization: A Comparative Study of Zambia and Ghana" (Ph.D. Thesis, Stockholm University).

ANANABA, W. (1969) *The Trade Union Movement in Nigeria* (Benin, Ethiope Publishing Corporation).

ANDRAE, G. AND B. BECKMAN (1991) 'Textile Unions and Industrial Crisis in Nigeria' in I. Brandell (ed) *Workers in Third World Industrialisation* (London, MacMillan).

— (1992) "Labour Regimes and Adjustment in the Textile Industry", Paper to a Workshop on the *State, Structural Adjustment and Changing Social and Political Relations*, organised by the Nordic Africa Institute, Uppsala, May 1992.

— (1996) "Bargaining for Survival: Unionised Workers in the Nigerian Textile Industry", Discussion Paper 78 (Geneva, UNRISD).

— (1998) *Union Power in the Nigerian Textile Industry: Labour Regime and Adjustment* (Uppsala, Nordic Africa Institute; Somerset, New Jersey; Transaction Publishers, Kano; Centre for Research and Documentation).

AREMU, I. (1991) 'The Social Relevance of Trade Unionism: The Case Study of the National Union of Textile and Garment Workers in Nigeria (MA Research Paper, The Hague, ISS).

ARRIGHI, G. (1983) "The Labour Movement in 20th Century Western Europe" in I Wallerstein (ed.) *Labour in the World Social Structure* (Beverly Hills and London, Sage).

BANGURA, Y. (1992) 'Authoritarian Rule and Democracy in Africa: A Theoretical Discourse' in P. Gibbon *et.al.* (eds.) *Authoritarianism, Democracy and Adjustment* (Uppsala, Nordic Africa Institute).

BANGURA, Y. AND B. BECKMAN (1991) 'African Workers and Structural Adjustment with a Nigerian Case Study, in D. Ghai *et. al.* (eds) *The IMF and the South: The Social Impact of Crisis and Adjustment* (London, Zed Press).

BASKIN, J. (1991) *Striking Back: A History of COSATU* (London and New York, Verso).

BECKMAN, B. (1992) 'Empowerment or Repression? The World Bank and the Politics of Adjustment' in P. Gibbon, Y. Bangura and A. Ofstad (eds). *Authoritarianism, Democracy and Adjustment* (Uppsala, Nordic Africa Institute).

— (1993) "The Liberation of Civil Society: Neo-Liberal Ideology and Political Theory", *Review of African Political Economy*, 58.

— (1995) 'Interest Groups and the Construction of Democratic Space' in J. Ibrahim (ed.) *Expanding Democratic Space in Nigeria* (Dakar, Codesria).

179

— (1996) 'The Politics of Labour and Adjustment: The Experience of the Nigeria Labour Congress' in T. Mkandawire and A. Olukoshi (eds). *Between Authoritarianism and Oppression: The Politics of Structural Adjustment in Africa* (Dakar, Codesria).

BECKMAN, B. AND A. JEGA (1995) "Scholars and Democratic Politics in Nigeria", *Review of African Political Economy*, 64.

BEININ, J. (1989) "Labour, Capital and the State in Nasserist Egypt, 1952-1961), *International Journal of Middle East Studies*, Vol.21.

BEININ, J. AND Z. LOCKMAN (1988) *Workers on the Nile* (London, Tauris).

BIAUCHI, R. (1986) "The Corporatization of the Egyptian Labour Movement", *The Middle East Journal*, Vol.40.

— (1989) *Unruly Corporatism: Associational Life in Twentieth Century Egypt* (New York, Oxford University Press).

BRANDELL, I. (1991) *Workers in Third World Industrialization* (London, MacMillan).

BRATTON, M. (1994) 'Economic Crisis and Political Realignment in Zambia', in J. A. Widner (ed). *Economic Change and Political Liberalization in Sub-Saharan Africa* (Baltimore, John Hopkins).

BRATTON, M. AND N. VAN DE WALLE (1992) "Popular Protest and Reform in Africa", *Comparative Politics*, 24 (4).

BUROWAY, M. (1979) *Manufacturing Consent: Changes in the Labour Process under Monopoly Capitalism* (Chicago and London, University of Chicago Press).

— (1985) *The Politics of Production* (London, Verso).

CALLAGHY, T.M. (1989) 'Lost Between State and Market: The Politics of Economic Adjustment in Ghana, Zambia and Nigeria' in J. Nelson (ed). *Economic Crisis and Policy Choice: The Politics of Structural Adjustment in the Third World* (Princeton, Princeton University Press).

CAWSON, A. (1986) *Corporatism and Political Theory* (Oxford, Basil Blackwell).

COHEN, R. (1971) 'Nigeria's Central Trade Union Organizations: A Study Guide', *Journal of Modern African Studies*, 9 (3).

— (1974) *Labour and Politics in Nigeria, 1945-71* (London, Heinemann).

— (1991) "Resistance and Hidden Forms of Consciousness among African Workers' in R. Cohen (ed). *Contested Domains: Debates in International Labour Studies* (London, Zed Books).

COLEMAN, W.D. (1985) 'State Corporatism as a Sectoral Phenomenon' in A. Cawson (ed). *Organised Interests and the State* (London, Sage).

DANSEREAU, S. (1995) "Unions in Southern Africa: Structural Adjustment and Reorganisation", *South African Labour Bulletin*, No.14.

DAVIES, I. (1966) *African Trade Unions* (Harmondsworth, Penguin).

DHLAKAMA, L. G. AND L.M. SACHIKONYE (1991) *Collective Bargaining in Zimbabwe: Procedures and Prospects* (Geneva, ILO).

DUNLOP, J.T. (1958) *Industrial Relations Systems* (New York, Holt).

EL-NAGGAR, S. (1996) "Development, The Liberal Way", *Al Ahram Weekly*, 11 April 1996.

EL-SHAFEI, O. (1995) "Workers, Trade Unions and the State in Egypt, 1984-89", *Cairo Papers in Social Science*, 18 (2).

FASHOYIN, T. (1980) *Industrial Relations in Nigeria* (London, Longman).

— (1990) "Nigerian Labour and the Military: Towards Exclusion?", *Labour, Capital and Society*, 23 (1).

GHAI, D. (ed). (1991) *The IMF and the South: The Social Impact of Crisis and Adjustment* (London, Zed Books).

GHAI, D. AND C. HEWITT DE ALCANTARA (1991) 'The Crisis of the 1980s in Africa, Latin America and the Carribean: An Overview' in D. Ghai (ed). *The IMF and the South: The Social Impact of Crisis and Adjustment* (London, Zed Press).

GINSBURG, D. AND E. WEBSTER, *et. al.* (1995) *Taking Democracy Seriously: Worker Expectations and Parliamentary Democracy in South Africa* (Durban, Indicator Press).

HARVEY, S. (1996) "Labour Market Killing Fields", *South African Labour Bulletin*, 20 (2).

HASHIM, Y. (1987) 'State Intervention in Trade Unions: A Nigerian Case Study' (MA Research Paper, The Hague, ISS).

— (1994) 'The State and Trade Unions in Africa: A Study in Macro-Corporatism' (Ph.D. Thesis, The Hague, ISS).

HAVNEVIK, K. (ed). (1987) *The IMF and the World Bank in Africa: Conditionality, Impact and Alternatives* (Uppsala, Nordic Africa Institute).

HINNEBUSCH, R. (1993) "Class, State and the Reversal of Egypt's Agrarian Reform", *Middle East Report*, September-October, 1993.

HUTCHFUL, E. (1989) 'From Revolution to Monetarism: The Economics and Politics of Structural Adjustment in Africa' in B.K. Campbell and J. Loxley (eds). *Structural Adjustment in Africa* (London, MacMillan).

HYMAN, R. (1989) *The Political Economy of Industrial Relations* (London, MacMillan).

KEET, D. (1992) "Zimbabwe Trade Unions: From Corporatist Brokers Towards an Independent Labour Movement", *South African Labour Bulletin*, 16 (4).

LAMBERT, R. (1988) 'Political Unionism in South Africa: The South African Congress of Trade Unions, 1955–1965' (Ph.D. Thesis, University of Witwatersrand).

LEHMBRUSH, G. AND P.C. SCHMITTER (eds). (1982) *Patterns of Corporatist Policy-Making* (London, Sage).

LLOYD, C. AND S. RIX (1995) "Unions and Democratic Institutions", *Discussion Paper* (NALEDI, Johannesburg).

LOXLEY, J. (1994) "Rural Labour Markets in a Mineral Economy" in V. Jamal (ed). *Structural Adjustment and Rural Labour Markets* (New York, St. Martins Press).

LUBECK, P. (1986) *Islam and Urban Labour in Northern Nigeria: The Making of a Moslem Working Class* (Cambridge, CUP).

MADHUKU, L. AND A. SIBANDA (1997) 'Developments in Public Sector Labour Relations' in E. Kalula and L. Madhuku (eds). *Public Sector Labour Relations in Southern Africa: Developments and Trends* (Cape Town, FES and Institute of Development and Labour Law).

MALLOY, J.M. (1977) *Authoritarianism and Corporatism in Latin America* (Pittsburgh, Pittsburgh University Press).

MEEBELO, H.S. (1986) *African Proletarians and Colonial Capitalism* (Lusaka, Kenneth Kaunda Foundation).

MUNCH, R. (1988) *The New International Labour Studies: An Introduction* (London, Zed Books).

NDIAYE, I. A. (1992) 'Crise économique prolongée et formes de réponses des travailleurs: Etude de la résistance due travailleur Senegalais' (Ph.D. Thesis, University of Cheikh Ana Diop).

NDIAYE, I. A. AND B. TIDJANI (1995) 'Mouvements ouries et crise economique. Les syndicats Sénégalais face á 'adjustment structural', *Monograph Series, 3/95* (Dakar, Codesria).

NYANGORO, J. E. (1987) 'On the Concept of "Corporatism" and the Africa State", *Studies in Comparative International Development*, 22 (1).

— (1989) "The State of Politics in Africa: The Corporatist Factor", *Studies in Comparative International Development*, 22 (1).

OLUKOSHI, A. O. (ed.) (1984) *Structural Adjustment in West Africa* (Lagos, Pumark and NIIA).

ONIMODE, B. (1992) *Imperialism and Underdevelopment in Nigeria* (London, Zed Books).

OTOBO, D. (1986) *Foreign Interests and Nigerian Trade Unions* (Ibadan, Heinemann).

PEACE, A. (1975) 'The Lagos Proletariat: Labour Aristocratcs or Populist Militants?, in R. Sandbrook and R. Cohen (eds). *The Development of an African Working Class* (Toronto, Longman).

PITYANA, S.M. and M. Ordin (1992) *Beyond the Factory Floor: A Survey of COSATU Shopstewards* (Johannesburg, Ravan Press).

POSUSNEY, M. (1991) 'Workers Against the State: Actors, Issues and Outcomes in Egyptian Labour-State Relations, 1952–1987' (Ph.D. Dissertation, University of Pennsylvania).

PRIPSTEIN, M. (1995) "Egypt's New Labour Law Removes Worker Provisions", *Middle East Report*, 52-53.

RAFTOPOULOS, B. and I. Phimister (1997) *Keep on Knocking: A History of Zimbabwe's Labour Movement* (Harare, Baobab).

RUESCHEMEYER, D., E. H. Stephens and J. D. Stphens (1992) *Capitalist Development and Democracy* (Cambridge, Polity Press).

SACHIKONYE, L.M. (1986) 'State, Capital and Unions' in I. Mandaza (ed.). *Zimbabwe: The Political Economy of Transition* (Dakar, Codesria).

— (1981) 'State and Unions in Nigeria: The Restructuring of the Nigerian Labour Congress' (MSC Thesis, Ahmadu Bello University).

— (1992) "The New Labour Regime Under SAP", *Southern Africa Political and Economic Monthly*, 5 (7).

— (1993) 'Structural Adjustment, State and Organised Labour in Zimbabwe' in P. Gibbon (ed.) *Social Change and Economic Reform* (Uppsala, Nordic African Institute).

— (ed.) (1995a) *Democracy, Civil Society and the State: Social Movements in Southern Africa* (Harare, Sapes Books).

— (1995b) 'Industrial Restructuring and Labour Relations under Adjustment in Zimbabwe, in P. Gibbon (ed.) *Structural Adjustment and the Working Poor in Zimbabwe* (Uppsala, Nordic Africa Institute).

— (1997) 'Unions, Economic and Political Developments' in B. Raftopoulos and I. Phimister (eds.) *Keep on Knocking* (Harare, Baobab).

SANDBROOK, R. (1985) *The Politics of Africa's Stagnation* (Cambridge, CUP).

SAUL, J. (1996) "Liberal Democracy vs. Popular Democracy in Sub-Saharan Africa", *Review of African Political Economy*, Nos. 72 and 73.

SCHMITTER, P.C. (1974) "Still the Century of Corporatism?", *Review of Politics*, No.36.

— (1979) 'Introduction' in P. C. Schmitter and G. Lehmbruch (eds.) *Trends Towards Corporatist Intermediation* (London, Sage).

SCHMITTER, P.C. AND G. LEMBRUCH (eds.) (1979) *Trends Towards Corporatist Intermediation* (London, Sage).

SHIVJI, I. (1986) *State and Constitutionalism in Africa* (Harare, Sapes).

SOUTHALL, R. (1995) *Imperialism or Solidarity?* (Cape Town, University of Cape Town Press).

STREEK, W. (1982) 'Organisational Consequences of Neo-Corporatist Cooperation in West German Labour Unions' in G. Lehmbruch and P. C. Schmitter (eds.) *Patterns of Corporatist Policy-Making* (London, Sage).

TENGENDE, N. (1994) 'Workers, Students and the Struggles for Democracy: State-Civil Society Relations in Zimbabwe' (Ph.D. Thesis, Roskilde University).

TSVANGIRAI, M. (1992) 'The Labour Relations Amendment Bill, 1992' in Friedrich-Naumann-Stiftung, *ESAP, Industrial Relations and Employment Creation* (Harare).

VALENZUELA, A. (1989) "Labour Movements in Transitions to Democracy: A Framework of Analysis", *Comparative Politics*, 21 (4).

VAN HEAR, N. (1988) 'Nigerian Labour in the 1980s' in R. Southall (ed.) *Trade Unions and the New Industrialization of the Third World* (London, Zed Books).

VON HOLDT, K. (1991) "Towards Transforming SA Industry: A `Reconstruction Accord' Between Unions and the ANC?", *South African Labour Bulletin*, 15 (6).

WADE, R. (1990) *Governing the Market: Economic Theory and the Role of Government in East Asian Industrialization* (Princeton, Princeton University Press).

WATERMAN, P. (1983) 'Aristocrats and Plebians in African Trade Unions? Lagos Port and Dock Worker Organization and Struggle' (Ph.D Thesis, Nijmegen).

— (1982) 'Division and Unity Amongst Nigerian Workers', *Research Report Series II* (The Hague, ISS).

WEBSTER, E. (1985) *Cast in a Racial Mould: Labour Process and Trade Unionism in the Foundries* (Johannesburg, Ravan Press).

— (1995) "NEDLAC — Corporatism of a Special Type?", *South African Labour Bulletin*, 19 (2).

— (1986) "A New Frontier of Control? Case Studies in the Changing Form of Job Control in South Africa Industrial Relations", *Industrial Relations Journal of South Africa*, 6 (1).

WHITE, G. (1994) "Civil Society, Democratization and Development (I): Clearing the Analytical Ground", *Democratization*, Vol. 13.

WOLPE, H. (1988) *Race, Class and the Apartheid State* (London, James Currey).

WOOD, B. (1987) "Roots of Trade Unions Weakness in Post-Independence Zimbabwe", *South African Labour Bulletin*, 12 (6-7).

ZIMBABWE CONGRESS OF TRADE UNIONS (ZCTU) (1992) *ZCTU Proposals on the Labour Amendment Bill 1992* (Harare).

ZIMBABWE CONGRESS OF TRADE UNIONS (ZCTU) (1996) *Beyond ESAP: A Framework for Long-Term Development in Zimbabwe* (Harare, ZCTU).

ZIMBABWE GOVERNMENT (1991) *Zimbabwe: A Framework for Economic Reform, 1991-95* (Harare).

Index

Name Index

Subject Index

www.ingramcontent.com/pod-product-compliance
Lightning Source LLC
Chambersburg PA
CBHW021905020426
42334CB00013B/491